# Barter and the Future of Money

# Barter and the Future of Money

## *The Currency Crisis*

Terry L. Neal
and
Gary K. Eisler

MasterMedia Limited New York, New York

Library of Congress Cataloging-in-Publications Data

Neal, Terry L. and Eisler, Gary K.
Barter and the future of money: the currency crisis

p. cm.
ISBN 1-57101-061-0 : $24.95



MASTERMEDIA and colophon
are registered trademarks of MasterMedia Limited.

Design by Cranston Communications, Inc.
Manufactured in the United States of America

# Dedications

*To Maureen Neal, my life partner for 35 years,*
*mother to our eight children, grandmother of 13*
*and a pillar of strength and support to all.*
*She is the wonderful woman who brings*
*the beauty to my life. Thanks to her, I consider*
*myself one of the luckiest men alive.*
—Terry L. Neal

*To the memory of Bonnie Eisler, who lost*
*her eight-and-a-half-year struggle with*
*breast cancer during the writing of this book.*
*My wife and companion for 28 years, mother of our*
*three children and grandmother of one,*
*she lived out her days with dignity and courage.*
*She inspired those of us who loved her*
*to reach beyond our grasp—we all miss her.*
—Gary K. Eisler

# Acknowledgments

Many individuals contributed to the writing of this book, and for that support the authors are honored to here express appreciation to: Paul Suplizio, chief executive officer of the International Reciprocal Trade Association, for his personal friendship and assistance in the writing of this book, as well as his enormous value to the barter industry in general; Dale Weight, president of Willamette University in Salem, Oregon, Ph.D. in economics and past official with the Federal Reserve, for his advice and counsel in explaining some difficult concepts in this book; to Kevin Andersen, CPA, MBA, partner in Andersen, Andersen & Strong, who helped the writers present barter and taxes; to Robert Meyer, editor and publisher of *Barter News* magazine, for being a continuing source of information; to Michael T. Baer, CTB, president of ITEX Corporation, for his support and encouragement; to Lee Morgan, CTB, whose continual assistance is greatly appreciated; to Susan Stautberg, MasterMedia publisher, whose patience and encouragement helped bring this book to completion; to Dr. S.L. Meinberg, author, who encouraged us in this project; and to Kate Larue for her attention to detail in reading the manuscript. Our thanks to all, and may our efforts measure up to the invaluable contributions so freely given.

# Table of Contents

# Appendices

# Introduction

Is there really "a currency crisis," and if so, how in the world does barter play any part in resolving the situation? Currency is in crisis because of massive foreign counterfeiting assaults on the U.S. dollar; because of new copier and computer technologies that make it easy to create fake money; because of the flow of U.S. cash out of the country and into hiding under foreign mattresses; because government's attempt to protect the currency—the first new U.S. money in half a century—is seriously flawed.

The emergence of new ways to exchange value, not exactly money but serving the same purpose, also contributes to the currency crisis. These include smart cards, E-cash and trade dollars. It is our conclusion that government, thus far, is not in step with the development of these new value-delivery systems.

We observe trends in banking that will affect the future of money. And we see new tools—the personal computer and the Internet—and recognize that their impact is quickly transforming commerce. These things are not just happening; there is one particular creative genius who is producing the tools that are commercial catalysts. The software of Bill Gates has opened undreamed of possibilities for everyone. And he's not done yet.

The modern commercial barter industry is truly a child of these technological and economic developments. Barter opens new opportunities for the creation and exchange of wealth. Unfortunately, it is a system that is still struggling to achieve the respect and understanding it deserves. The currency crisis has also created enormous opportunities, especially for a commodity-based, electronic currency such as may be offered by the modern barter industry.

What does it all mean? How do these events, conditions, trends and personalities interact to create a new economic reality? Perhaps most important, where is it all headed?

We are unaware of any other book that offers a synthesis of all this into a big picture, but to us it all fits together. We therefore present our own interpretation of the situation, because without the vision this book offers, we are all flailing about in a dark place.

Everyone has, spends or wants money. It is to society what blood is to the body. Yet those who have money should wonder about its health. How well are the institutions entrusted with creating and protecting our money doing their jobs? By that we mean the U.S. Congress, Treasury and Mint, the Secret Service and FBI, Federal Reserve and the nation's banking system.

Those who spend money will be interested to know how it is changing, what new forms of cash are coming and how to use them. And those who want money will get a new perspective on the forces that have and will change the way it is earned. Between the people who have, want and spend money, that's just about everybody who could benefit from reading this material.

But this book is also written for specific people—such as the 400,000 business owners and professionals currently trading through a commercial barter exchange. To them, this book offers an overview of how barter works. More important, it also offers understanding of how barter fits into the current situation of economic flux.

For professionals in the barter industry, this book offers the vision of barter's future in the electronic age. The authors hope that these readers will be inspired and encouraged to press on because of the new understanding they will gain about the service they are offering. Barter professionals should take pride in their role in shaping the future.

Also of interest to the barter industry—as well as to attorneys and accountants—are the documents in the appendix of the book. This appendix contains for the first time in book form the reference materials that form the legal and accounting framework for the entire barter industry. As such, they ought to be part of the primary sources library of every professional person whose clients are or may become part of the growing barter economy.

Although we deal with important issues, the authors nonetheless sometimes have their tongues planted firmly in their cheeks—and will rely on the intelligence of the readers to figure out when. We want the reader to have as much fun reading this material as we did writing it.

Many books are written so that the reader can start practically anywhere. This is not one of them. Each chapter builds on the ones before. Chapters can be read out of sequence, but many concepts in them will not make sense. The only chapter the reader could possibly live without is Chapter 6, "Is Anything Sacred?", which provides information that supports previously made points and is included mainly because the anecdotes fascinated us and make wonderful tales to tell.

Readers who are tempted to pass over too much of the material in this book, however, are reminded of the multiple choice test that follows immediately upon completion.

Happy reading!

—Terry L. Neal
—Gary K. Eisler

SECTION

# ALL ABOUT MONEY

ONE

# 1

# The Origin of Money

*"Unprovided with original learning,*
*unformed in the habits of thinking,*
*unskilled in the arts of composition,*
*I resolved—to write a book."*
Edward Gibbon

A fellow somehow traded himself into ownership of a warehouse full of sardines. These sardines were canned and boxed and packed in cartons and resting on pallets, ready to go. But the guy had no cash customers for his sardines. Clever trader that he was, he came up with a way to get some value out of them nonetheless.

### *Tradin' Sardines*

He wrote claim checks, receipts or due bills against the sardines and used these pieces of paper as a form of payment. If he was putting a deal together that wasn't coming out right, he would toss in a few skids of sardines, as evidenced by the due bills.

The people who got the receipts didn't necessarily want the sardines either, but they in turn used the due bills the way the first guy did—as a form of currency to buy what they wanted. Before long, these receipts had passed through dozens of hands. Eventually, though, someone actually wanted the sardines and went to the warehouse to claim them.

The holder of the due bill presented his receipt and immediately pulled a box off the stack, opened it up and took out a can. By this time, his mouth was really watering for the taste of good sardines. When he finally rolled back the tin covering, however, what he got instead was the nauseating smell of rotten fish. Indignant, he took his receipt back to the person who had transferred it to him. No luck, nor was there to be any satisfaction until he had gone back through transaction after transaction to find the original guy who had issued those first receipts.

"Hey!" our unhappy sardine lover said, waving the due bill in the trader's face. "Those sardines I traded for are rotten."

The trader looked him in the eye and explained: "I'm sorry you're disappointed, but those aren't eatin' sardines ... those are tradin' sardines."

This anecdote is part of the folklore of the barter industry. Whenever someone acquires goods not for their own sake but as a medium of exchange—gemstones or raw land, for example—we say they're "tradin' sardines."

The sardines receipts would be a medium of exchange to this day if one guy had not wanted to actually claim what his due bill promised to deliver. When people learned that all that was backing up their due bills was cans of stinky fish, they lost faith in that currency and stopped trading in it.

We begin with this fish story because we believe it illustrates a basic truth about all money. There are two things that make a currency tick: number one, what's behind it; and number two, how people feel about it. And number two is more important than number one.

### *Mysterious Origins*

The very origins of money remain clouded in mystery and controversy. How did it come to be? The commonly held position is that money arose as a system to replace barter. While barter is a straightforward way to do business, it is problematic in its purest form. How many fish should my ax be worth, and how to divide my ax into smaller denominations in exchange for a small fish? But did the cumbersome nature of early barter lead directly to currency or did the whole process come about for some other, more subtle reason?

Glyn Davies, the Welsh author of *A History of Money From Ancient Times to the Present Day*, takes the position that economic factors were not the most important in the development of money. He wrote: "Archeological, literary and linguistic evidence of the ancient world and the tangible evidence of actual types of primitive money … demonstrate that barter was not the main factor in the origins and earliest development of money."

Instead of money for commerce, Davies theorizes that an organized money form developed out of a need for some form of compensation for the victims of crimes of violence. He suggests that payment with a currency seemed preferable to "an eye for an eye, and a tooth for a tooth." (Would you call this blood money?)

He goes on to say that the verb *to pay* stems from the Latin *pacare*, which means to pacify, appease or make peace with, by means of the appropriate unit of value customarily accepted by both sides. He also theorizes that money came about to pay for a wife. The head of the family had to be compensated, Davies speculates, for the loss of services performed by the daughter.

"Thus, the use of money evolved out of deeply rooted customs—the clumsiness of barter provided an economic impulse but that was not the primary factor," wrote Davies. If he is right about money arising from impulses far removed from the mere desire to do business, then perhaps there are other motives fueling the development of money, motives that are crucial to understanding its future.

Davies defines money as "anything that is widely used for making payments, and accounting for debts and credits." Tradition and current definition tell us that money is a unit of accounting, a common measure of value, a medium of exchange, a means of making payment, a standard for deferred payments, and a store of value.

In a larger sense, though, money has an even greater function.

### *Money Is Power*

We contend that regardless of the initial motive for its development, money is an instrument of national prestige and power; the nation with the most highly respected and efficient monetary system will likely be the dominant force of its day.

This was true from the most ancient times. "Coins were by far the best propaganda weapon available for advertising Greek, Roman or any other civilization before mechanical printing was invented," Davies maintains. One example might be the coin issued by Philip of

Macedonia, on which he celebrates his chariot race triumph in the Olympic games of B.C. 356.

But prestige is merely the fragrance of power. Money was and continues to be a weapon of national domination. In coinage as in other matters, the Greek city-states strived desperately for predominance, as did their arch-rivals, the Persian emperors.

When Philip's son, Alexander the Great, succeeded in vanquishing the Persians, he quickly put an end to one aspect of that rivalry by eliminating Persian currency and establishing uniformity over much of the known world with Greek money. In so doing, he followed the example set a century earlier among the Greek city-states. Athens, in B.C. 456, forced the city Aegina to take Athenian "owls" as their currency and to stop minting their own "turtle" coins. A few years later, in B.C. 449, Athens issued an edict ordering all foreign coins to be handed in to the Athenian mint and forced all her allies to adopt the Athens standard of weights, measures and money.

In the many wars of the 20th century, it was common practice for conquerors to displace the currency of the vanquished with their own. After goose-stepping into a country, the Nazis, to cite one example, shoved aside the local money and substituted the Reichsmark, then rigged the rate of exchange in their own favor. That, according to William L. Shirer in his *Rise and Fall of the Third Reich*, was how Germans were able to buy up factories and other assets in Austria and elsewhere.

From earliest times, then, money has been both symbol and method of control. With that in mind, it should surprise no one to learn in forthcoming chapters that—in the aftermath of the Cold War—there is more American cash in Russia than in any other country outside the United States, and that the people of that nation prefer it to their own currency.

It should also not surprise anyone to learn that U.S. currency is the target of economic terrorists and counterfeiters, simply because the dollar is also America's Achilles' heel. Yet as the predominant power of the day, America is also the source of newer, more efficient electronic money and a new, electronic marketplace.

### *The Revolution of Money*

The marriage of money and power found no more graphic expression than in ancient Britain. The early Brits used sword blades as coins—a practice Julius Caesar regarded as backward. Backward or not, they got the connection right. As a rule, the more highly evolved a nation's system of exchange, the more powerful that nation is likely to be.

The Mayan Indians of pre-Columbian Central America, for example, developed a high civilization with an elaborate system of barter as their means of commerce. Their cities often included vast market areas full of bright colors and wonderful smells, similar to the Indian markets of Guatemala and Mexico today. The lowland Mayans put together three- and four-way trades, so that the person with beeswax could trade for blankets and eventually wind up with pottery. The Mayans enjoyed this form of commerce because it was also a way for them to socialize.

The Quiche Mayans of the northern Yucatán Peninsula lost their independence when they were conquered by the invading warrior Toltecs of central Mexico. The Toltecs emphasized both human sacrifice and currency—cacao beans (chocolate), gold and jade. It's sad that the Mayans' highly social way of doing business was overwhelmed by a more aggressive one. But one of the reasons the Toltecs prevailed was that they were more efficient—they spent less time and energy conducting business and they had more time to produce goods and to fight. Use of currency was a causative factor in the Toltecs' potential for war.

There is a nostalgia for the gentler way of doing business, and it lives on in those who even to this day resist the forces of change. These spiritual heirs of the lowland Mayans—the Luddites—meet their nemesis in Bill Gates. We're getting ahead of ourselves, however, and that is the subject of a later chapter.

### *Commodity Currencies and Banking*

The Toltecs' chocolate was a commodity currency—a currency based on a substance that is so universally desired that it is accepted as payment by almost anyone. The ancient Greeks, for example, used iron nails as currency. The Romans used salt because it was always needed for preserving food and was widely desirable. In fact, they often paid their soldiers with sacks of salt, which is where the word *salary* comes from. Cattle, being easy to transport and in nearly universal demand, were also used by the Romans as a form of cash until the fourth century B.C. The word *pecuniary,* or pertaining to money, comes from *pecus,* the Latin word for cattle.

Davies writes that in his mother tongue, Welsh, the word *da* used as an adjective means "good," but used as a noun means both "cattle" and "goods." And in English, the words *capital, chattel* and *cattle* all have a common root.

Animals have continued to be a medium of exchange throughout the 20th century. The Kirghiz of the Russian Steppes, for example, used horses as their main monetary unit. Sheep were secondary, so sheep skins were used only for small transactions. And in parts of Africa, even today, wealth is measured by the size of one's herd of cattle. The problem with cattle as cash is that wealthy people find themselves spending too much time feeding and watering their money—which is why a dead commodity currency makes more sense than a living one.

Other commodities used as money at one time or another include amber, beads, drums, eggs, feathers, gongs, hoes, ivory, jade, kettles, leather, mats, oxen, pigs, quartz, rice, vodka, and yarns.

Banking is really more nearly an outgrowth of barter than it is of currency. In the Greek world the basic unit of weight was the drachma, which means "a handful of grain." Grain was the basis of trade in ancient Mesopotamia and Egypt. Unlike a commodity currency such as beads or feathers, here it was the actual commodity itself that was transferred.

Grain and other commodities were stored in royal palaces and temples for safekeeping. Because grain is so bulky, receipts for it came to be used for transfers not only to the original depositors but also to third parties. Eventually, private houses in Mesopotamia also became involved in these banking operations and laws regulating them were included in the Code of Hammurabi.

In Egypt, banking was the result of centralizing grain harvests in government warehouses. Written orders for the withdrawal of portions of grain became used as a way to pay debts to others, including the tax collector and the religious establishment as well as other traders.

When the Greeks under Alexander conquered Egypt and set up the Ptolemy dynasty (from B.C. 323 to B.C. 30), this warehouse banking became even more sophisticated. The scattered government granaries became a network of grain banks with a central bank in Alexandria where the main accounts from all the state banks were recorded. Payments were transferred from one account to another without grain changing hands.

This system bears many similarities to the modern barter exchange in which accounts are credited or debited for many goods and services, again, with no cash in the transaction. More on that later.

The Egyptians continued to use this system even after they introduced coins into their economy. Internal commerce could be conducted with receipts for grain, while precious metals were reserved for foreign purchases. This arrangement was a precursor to the way international commerce is conducted today, with paper money serving internal commerce and bullion being reserved for transactions between nations.

Banking that centers on currency rather than commodities arose because of the many coins in circulation. Money changers carried around a table on which they exchanged coins of different nations, taking a profit for the transaction. The word *bank* comes from the Italian *banca,* which means "bench" or "counter." These business tables often got set up around temples or other public buildings. It was evidently one of these early bankers whose table Christ overturned when he used a whip to drive the money changers from the Temple of Jerusalem.

From ancient times banking was an industry that appealed to enterprising souls in isolated places with few natural resources. In the second and third centuries B.C., the barren island of Delos off the Greek mainland became the ancestor of today's Bahamas, Caymans and other island banking centers. Delos had only two assets—a good harbor and the Temple of Apollo, around which trading and financial activities developed. Coinage was king in Athens, but on Delos financial transactions became very sophisticated. Coins were replaced by real credit receipts; accounts were set up and maintained for clients; on simple instructions of a debtor, a payment was made to a creditor.

Delos prospered and survived because it was not a threat to the major powers of the day. Carthage and Corinth, both banking centers, were destroyed by Rome. As a result, when Roman commerce needed to became more complex, it adopted from the model of Delos. Unfortunately, though, the Romans remained stubbornly attached to coins instead of progressing to a system of payments on account.

As a matter of fact, banking was practically forgotten with the fall of the Roman Empire and had to be reinvented many centuries later. Not until the Crusades was banking as an institution resurrected, and then only because the urgency of warfare demanded a system to transfer huge sums of money to pay for supplies, equipment, soldiers and ransom funds.

A piece from the Portland *Oregonian* shared this tidbit of interesting historical trivia:

### *First-Degree Writer's Cramp*

Any Roman who tried to multiply in his head CCLXV by XLIV had his work cut out for him. But imagine what the ancient Egyptians were up against with their system of symbols, described in a recent article from the *Journal of Economic Education*:

> The symbol for 100 was a coiled rope, for 1,000 a lotus blossom, for 10,000, a pointed finger, for 100,000 a tadpole, and for 1 million, a man stretching his arms to the heavens in astonishment.
>
> For the Egyptians, 3,456,789 would appear as three amazed men, four tadpoles, five pointed fingers, six lotus blossoms, seven coiled ropes, eight circles and nine vertical lines.

An economist analyzing the budget deficit would begin by drawing some 400,000 pictures of amazed men.

### *Money and Sex*

*Money, it turned out,*
*was exactly like sex,*
*you thought of nothing else*
*if you didn't have it*
*and thought of other things*
*if you did.*
—JAMES BALDWIN

Warfare is not the only impulse behind the development of money. Sexuality played a major role as well. Objects that can be invested with a high degree of emotional value because of their use as adornment or jewelry can have a dual life as currency. In the tropical Fiji Islands, it may be noted, the natives used whale teeth especially as bride money, serving the same purpose as an engagement ring in Western society. Whales' teeth are called *tambua,* meaning they had a religious significance—and from which we get the word *taboo.*

In North America the natives used *wampum,* or seashells, as currency not only because they are easily transportable, but also because they could be used as jewelry. The earliest countable metallic money or coins were the Chinese *cowrie* made of bronze or copper and named after the cowrie shell of the Indian Ocean. A pictograph of the cowrie was adopted into Chinese as the written symbol for money. In Western Africa the natives wear *manillas,* which are metallic objects that served as both jewelry and currency as recently as 1949. Davies describes them as an "ostentatious form of ornamentation, their value in that role being a prime reason for their acceptability as money." In many other cultures even to this day women wear gold coins as jewelry.

It is precisely because gold and silver make good jewelry that they have been universally acceptable as mediums of exchange.

### *All That Glitters*

The ancient Lydians (who once lived in the area occupied by modern Turkey), stamped small round pieces of metal into coins as early as B.C. 2500. Because their metals were so common, however, they were extremely easy to counterfeit. As a result, people did not have enough faith in these early coins to use them for large purchases.

Then the Lydians found that the rarer and prettier the metals used, the better the coins served as a medium of exchange. As early as B.C. 700 they minted coins of a pale yellow, gold and silver alloy called electrum. Concerned about counterfeiting, the Lydians stamped weight and intricate seals on their coins to make them harder to duplicate. Thus they endeavored to guarantee purity and value. Coins worked and their use spread from Lydia to both Greece and Persia.

As a means of exchange, the Romans began using raw chunks of copper. Each pound of such copper was called an *as*. In fact, the word *estimate* comes from *aes tumare*, which means "to value copper." Selling objects in exchange for pounds of copper was a form of commodity currency. Goods were exchanged for goods.

A major leap in money production came when government got into the picture by issuing currency—objects symbolic of goods rather than being the goods themselves. Rome began issuing copper coins in B.C. 338. To convey a sense of value, these often bore the image of an ox, a sheep or a hog. Similarly, some 3,000 years ago, the Chinese began stamping their coins with images of useful items, such as spades, hoes and knives.

In B.C. 269 the Romans also issued coins of silver, such as the denarius, equal to 10 asses, and the sestertius, or 2 1/2 asses. Then in B.C. 217 came Rome's first gold coins, the aurei, with values of 20, 40 and 60 sesterces. The talent, which was equal to 6,000 denarii, was also a unit of weight, varying from Rome to Greece to the Middle East, but generally being the equivalent of around 58 pounds.

The words *spend, expenditure* and *pound* all came from the Latin *expendere,* which means "to weigh." The currency of some countries still implies a unit of weight. Consider the British pound sterling and the Italian lira, which comes from the Latin word for pound. The peso of many Spanish-speaking countries is also a unit of weight. But the names are strictly symbolic. If the Italian lira indeed weighed a pound, it would take a three-quarter-ton pickup to haul around enough of them to equal one U.S. dollar.

One of the benefits of coins is that they can be counted out rather than weighed. Coins are also relatively easy to transport—certainly easier than a herd of cattle—and they can be stored without having to clean up after them. Coins can be minted in small or large denominations, so goods can be priced more precisely.

Coins were practically perfect as a medium of exchange ... except for one thing.

### *The Vulnerability of Money*

From the earliest times, nations at war have known that the best way to cripple an enemy is to strike at its currency. When the Spartans captured the Athenian silver mines at Laurion, they released the 20,000 slaves who kept the supply of precious metal flowing. With the mines closed, the Athenians faced a shortage of money and, in B.C. 406, issued bronze coins with a thin coating of silver.

The result was that the coin shortage became even worse. The good, pure silver coins disappeared from circulation because people hung onto them while spending the new ones to get rid of them. Aristophenes commented on this situation in his play *The Frogs*, produced in B.C. 405. He wrote, "The ancient coins are excellent ... yet we make no use of them, and prefer those bad copper pieces quite recently issued and so wretchedly struck." The Athenians took the bad coins out of circulation as soon as they could—in B.C. 393.

It wasn't long after the Roman government got into the currency business that it made a discovery. In B.C. 264, in the first of Rome's three wars against its main rival, Carthage, the Romans found they did not have enough copper to pay their war debts. Through experimentation, though, they learned they could reduce the *as* from one pound to two ounces of copper. By cutting the value of the currency by five sixths, they liquidated their war debt quickly.

By B.C. 202, the Roman government had reduced the metal content of the *as* coin to one ounce, and by B.C. 87 to half an ounce. Now, as then, the problem with government-issued currency is that too often it is debased in order to pay for what government could not otherwise afford—most often its wars. Many governments that came into being to protect people from one another, themselves became the thief.

Post-World War I Germany is a prime example of theft through inflation. To pay its war debts, the German government simply issued currency until it lost all value. The hard work and savings of the people evaporated and the Allies were left holding a bag of worthless paper money. In the five years following the war, the German mark had so depreciated that it took 726 million of them to buy what one mark formerly bought in 1918. By 1923, according to the *Wall Street Journal Guide to Money & Investing*, it was actually cheaper in Germany at that time to burn money than to use it to buy firewood.

### *Profit in Money*

Burning money instead of firewood is the exception. Because money is so useful, its perceived worth generally far exceeds its actual cost of production. This is certainly true of paper money, and was almost always true with coins.

"Coins commonly carried a substantial premium over the value of their metallic content, more than high enough to cover the cost of minting," writes Davies. "Kings could turn this premium into personal profit." And, of course, they did! This profit on the production of currency is called seigniorage, and amounts to hundreds of millions of dollars annually for the U.S. Treasury. (More about this later.)

Profits from the production of money opens it to abuse. In times past, currency was regularly recalled and replaced—in ancient capitals every six years, then every three years and eventually every other year. Existing coins were brought in to maximize profit as well as to prevent counterfeiting of earlier issues. New coins were struck with new images, yet they had to be made clearly distinguishable by authorities and be readily acceptable to the public.

Issuing money is historically such a lucrative business it is really no surprise that governments insist on a local monopoly. The profits from minting supplemented the revenue English monarchs raised from taxes. Such profit from reissuing currency may also explain why Britain redesigns its money so often—and may be one hidden reason for the new U.S. currency.

### *In God We Trust*

There has been a credibility problem ever since government got into the money business, which is why heads of state do everything possible to build confidence in their currency. The images of the ox, sheep and hog of early, more innocent times, gave way in time to profiles of the Roman emperor himself. Jesus Christ, when questioned about the justification for paying taxes, pointed to a denarius and asked whose portrait was on it. When the people said it was Julius Caesar's portrait, Christ instructed them to give to Caesar that which was Caesar's and to God that which is God's.

Certainly money has always belonged to Caesar. When Caesar died, the Roman treasury contained 700 million sesterces, and his own private treasury, 100 million. This looting of the public funds by the one in power has been endemic in societies even to our own day. It is a serious reason to question government's monopoly control over the money supply.

To gain credibility with the people, the Roman government stored its treasure in strongly built temples to the gods. Perhaps the rulers thought religious scruples would discourage thieves. More likely those managing the money simply wanted to imply that the gods were behind the currency.

As a matter of fact, the word *money* comes from the Latin word *moneta,* which was another name for the goddess Juno, wife of Jupiter, king of the Roman pantheon of gods. When the Romans established a mint at the temple of Juno Moneta, the word *moneta* became a generic term for a place where money is made.

Putting "In God We Trust" on the U.S. dollar may not be much more than America's way of saying "me too" to an old tradition.

# 2

# Paper Money

*"The most important thing I have learned is that we don't spend money as much as we consume it. Money is food.*
*We consume it and convert it into things—*
*the feelings, associations, symbols, and statutes we believe in.*
*To some, money is converted into power.*
*To others, money is converted into security.*
*To others, money is converted into getting by the best way they can.*
*To others, money is converted into self-esteem.*
*To others, money is converted into survival.*
*To others, money is converted into magic.*
*To others, sex.*
*To still others, beauty.*
*To many, money is converted into sin.*
*And to still others, money is converted into evil.*
*The fact is that money does not exist without people.*
*Money has no meaning without people.*
*Money is simply an idea we have agreed upon.*
*An idea which represents to every one of us*
*our net worth in the world."*

Michael E. Gerber

When Marco Polo returned to Venice after traveling to the throne of Kublai Khan, the great Mongol emperor of China, he told stories of wealth so fabulous his fellow Italians assumed he must have made them up.

### *A Great Discovery*

One of the most farfetched of these stories was about money made of paper, stamped with the emperor's seal—a red token in the middle of the note—and signed by his treasurer. Polo reported that the Chinese did not use gold or even silver in their transactions, but notes printed on a cotton paper about the size of the palm of a hand. This was totally incredible to his fellow Italians, who, like their Roman forebears, thought of money as coins and nothing else.

Polo actually saw this paper money being minted. He was amazed at the flimsiness of the paper it was printed on. Although the money wore out quickly, it could be returned to the government and traded in for new. But for every 100 bills the Chinese turned in, they received 97 in return. This three percent is the profit from making money—*seigniorage*. The lure of profit from seigniorage was so powerful that the Chinese government suppressed the notes issued by the banking guilds of Szechuan Province, and Kublai Khan himself prohibited use of Chinese metal coins—that bore images of spades and hoes—in order to give his paper money a better market share.

The Mongols did not introduce paper money; about the year 650, the Chinese Imperial Treasury issued the earliest paper cash. The Chinese learned to accept paper for their goods, and they were still accepting it a century after Khan, during the Ming dynasty, when the emperor issued the Kwan—currency the size of a piece of typing paper—which is the oldest surviving paper money. The Chinese paper money was originally guaranteed by metal reserves, but when these were exhausted, the emperor printed more notes nonetheless. As a result, the notes depreciated in value.

### *The Need for Paper Money*

Earlier forms of currency did not disappear with the introduction of paper money. Goods have continued to be used as a form of currency from ancient times until today. At the end of the 14th century in Europe, for example, when imported spices were rare and precious, people could buy a plow horse for a pound of saffron, or a sheep for a pound of ginger. Coins did not disappear, either, when paper money made its appearance.

But as the value of commerce increases, traders need more flexibility in making exchanges than giving either goods or coins. This is especially true in frontier areas. When government money is rare, private paper currency has often been the fuel for growth. Frontier New Zealand makes the point. When Scottish farmers arrived in 1848, there was no local bank, nor even a bank branch from elsewhere. On the opposite side of the world from Great Britain, these hardy adventurers had no way to issue currency that would represent the goods and services they created.

James Macandrew arrived in 1851 with some bank notes he had brought along. With the hope of starting a bank, he set up a store, then wrote to the local newspaper about the "effect which would be produced by the circulation of 5,000 or 10,000 pound notes, judiciously distributed among the honest and industrious tradesmen and agriculturalists of the colony. It would be to industry and labor what fuel is to the steam engine—setting all its wheels and parts in motion."

Unfortunately, because the would-be banker failed to do his paperwork properly, he could not get a charter from the colonial administrators. His bank was not able to circulate bank notes. By the next year the settlers were clamoring for money. Forty of them sent him a letter pleading for promissory notes, no matter how small the amount.

Stepping into the void, Macandrew issued his own paper money, and he backed it up with the goods being offered for sale at his store. Soon, the settlers were using Macandrew's scrip to pay their debts. Some of his competitors objected, but the local newspaper said it was of no concern to anyone except Macandrew and the people who could either use or refuse his money as they saw fit. In only 10 months, his private currency accounted for a third of all the money in the area. Macandrew's paper money worked because people trusted that it was backed by goods from his store, because they were on the other side of the world from the mother country and needed a medium of exchange, and because government had not stepped forward to satisfy the need.

Sweden introduced paper bank notes to Europe in 1661. Picking up on the idea, the British issued paper promissory notes to their soldiers from Massachusetts in 1690. The colonies also paid their fighting men with promissory notes. This early paper money promised an eventual payment of "hard currency," which, in those days, meant gold or silver. But precious metals were in short supply, and all commerce with the mother country had to be in hard currency.

The early settlers in New England saw that the Indians traded among each other for seashells, or wampum, and quickly figured out how to turn that to their own profit. They originally used the shells to buy beaver pelts, which could be sold to the mother country. But once the settlers generally developed confidence that the wampum would always be worth a pelt, they used the shells as currency among themselves. According to Peter Wayner, author of *Digital Cash,* the practice was so widespread that in 1641 the government of Massachusetts officially recognized wampum as currency.

The benefit of wampum was that, unlike beaver pelts, the shells would not rot. The disadvantage of wampum was that black shells were twice as valuable as white ones, and in short order counterfeiters were using small drops of dye to change colors. The "shell game" lasted until the beavers were killed off and the natives could no longer produce pelts. With nothing else of value behind the shells, they became worthless.

A year after Massachusetts recognized wampum as money, Virginia made tobacco leaves its currency. By 1727, its colonial government recognized paper currency backed by tobacco as legal tender that could be used to settle debts. The government set up tobacco warehouses that graded the quality of the tobacco and issued paper that could be redeemed for specific grades. Like the wampum that could be exchanged for beaver pelts, the tobacco was sold mostly to Europe in exchange for hard goods. Tobacco continued to be used as a currency until 1787, when the Constitution banned the states from having their own currency and reserved that right for the federal government.

England wanted the colonists to pay taxes to the mother country in gold. The colonists wanted to pay in paper money similar to that which England was circulating in America. The notes England was paying its soldiers had no value in England, and the colonies' scrip was considered worthless. To put an end to the problem, in 1751 the crown forbade New England from issuing any paper money and, in 1764, banned printing of money in the rest of the colonies as well. This heavy-handed suppression of domestic paper money helped bring about the Revolution. The colonials decided not to pay for the rebellion through taxation. They instead issued paper money and used it to pay the troops. It was an act of patriotism for a shopkeeper to accept paper currency.

### *Private Money*

Through the Coinage Act of 1792, the dollar became the basic unit of money in the United States. It was copied after the Spanish dollar then circulating widely in the fledgling nation.

The word *dollar* actually comes from the German name for a silver coin minted in a valley in Bohemia in the 16th century—Joachimsthaler. The coin was popular throughout Europe, and was called the *daalder* in Holland and the dollar in Britain. At least a dozen other countries besides the U.S. call their currency dollars—countries from the Bahamas to Zimbabwe.

Not long after independence, in 1791, the First Bank of the United States was chartered. Modeled after the Bank of England, it was able to enforce discipline among the many other banks by requiring them to redeem their paper currency for gold or silver—an action that spawned enemies by restricting the supply of money. Adding to the antagonism, the First Bank of the United States was a private bank that competed against the others for loans and deposits.

Eventually the First Bank of the United States became so unpopular that the Senate voted it out of existence in 1810. The immediate result was monetary chaos. Banks filled the void with private paper money called scrip, which was supposed to be backed by gold or silver, although all too frequently neither of these was actually available. When it came to working with bank notes, "buyer beware" was the watchword. Picture a gentleman from Philadelphia traveling to

Baltimore to make a purchase without knowing what his money was worth there or which local bank currencies he could trust.

Some banks acted with integrity and issued currency only in proportion to deposits. Others issued more — debasing the value of their money. When banks failed, the private money became worthless. Because of these troubles, bank-issued money sometimes had to be exchanged for a fraction of its face value, especially if the notes were issued by a bank in a distant state. The War of 1812 led to creation of the Second Bank of the United States in 1816. To build faith in the value of the bank's notes, each piece of currency had to be personally signed by both the president of the bank and the cashier. People were still suspicious of the power of a central bank, and it too went out of business.

There was not the same credibility problem with privately minted coins and, as a matter of fact, many of them were more highly regarded than those produced by the government. One of the first private coiners was John Higley, a blacksmith in Granby, Connecticut, who minted copper coins in 1737 and 1738. He let the market determine the value of his coins, according to Brian Summers, senior editor of *Readers Digest* in his paper "Private Coinage in America" (http://www.fame.org/ch05.htm). The coins said nothing about trusting in God—merely: "I am good copper/ Value me as you please." These coins were in general use until the U.S. Mint opened in 1792.

In 1783, I. Chalmers of Annapolis, Maryland, minted silver shillings that people of the day considered very good quality. Reporting on privately coined gold, Joseph Coffin wrote that between 1830 and 1861 many private gold coins were struck in various sections of the country. The first was in 1830 by Templeton Reid, an assayer at the gold mines of Lumpkin County, Georgia, the same county in which the Dahlonega Federal Mint was located. His coins were in denominations of $2.50, $5 and $10. Many were later melted because they were worth more as bullion than their face value.

Christopher Bechtler of Rutherfordton, North Carolina, his sons and nephew arrived in this country from the grand duchy of Baden in 1830. Getting into the money business, between 1831 and 1847 they produced gold coins in denominations of $1, $2.50 and $5—and they prospered despite competition from the federal mint established in 1837 in Charlotte.

Bechtler's coins were accepted and passed at face value in all of western North Carolina, South Carolina, western Tennessee, Kentucky and parts of Virginia. One person of that time said he was 16 years old before he ever saw a coin other than that produced by the Bechtlers. The coins filled a need and continued to circulate after the mint closed in 1847. The Bechtler coins had no national emblem nor official guarantee of purity, but were accepted by all. When owners turned them in to be reminted into federal currency, there was enough extra weight in them to pay the government the cost of reminting—seigniorage—which is the profit from making money.

Bechtler made his profit by keeping some of the gold people brought in to be minted into coins. He weighted it out in their presence. A visitor to his mint at the time said, "Christopher Bechtler's maxim was that honesty was the best policy, and the maxim appeared to govern his conduct." The visitor observed that Bechtler's "transactions were conducted with quite as much simplicity as those at a country grist mill, where the miller deducts the toll for the grist he has manufactured." Bechtler minted more than 3 million coins, which continued to have an important role in the War Between the States.

Today, new money comes into being as the commercial banks expand the money supply through the "fractional reserve system." They are empowered by government to lend out more than they have on deposit. In effect, they have made "new money" by extending credit to businesses and others, letting them borrow money that does not exist, to accommodate new value they have created by making new goods and services. There never is as much currency in existence as the sum total of all money that bank records would indicate, but to try to catch up, the Department of Treasury's Bureau of Engraving prints money; in 1993 alone the total was 10.6 billion currency notes. The government's fee for producing this new money—seigniorage—is the $400 million extra dollars it retained to pay its own bills.

Bechtler's was not the only private mint. As a matter of fact, these sprang up in a number of places, especially in the West, when there was not enough government money to handle the flow of commerce. But some other private mints, because they were less honest, were not as successful as Bechtler's. After gold was discovered in California in 1848, at least 15 mints sprang up between 1849 and 1855. The bullion content of some of these coins was less than their face value, so the coins were rejected by the marketplace and passed out of circulation.

Some private mints in the Gold Rush days held to principle and produced high-quality coins. The specie of Moffatt & Co., Kellogg & Co. and Wass, Molitor & Co. were widely accepted in the Old West. The *San Francisco Herald* (Jan. 8, 1852, as cited by Brian Summers) had especially high praise for the coins of Wass, Molitor & Co., because the company "had stepped forward in this emergency, and are now issuing a coin of the value of $5 to supply the necessities of trade."

Their coin was actually worth $5.04 because it was heavier than the U.S. $5 gold piece. "The high reputation for honor and integrity enjoyed by Wass and his associates in this enterprise is an additional guarantee that every representation made by them will be strictly complied with. The public will be glad to have a coin in which they can feel confidence, and which can't depreciate in their hands," the newspaper commented.

Another private Western mint of high reputation was the one in Denver, operated by Clark, Gruber & Co. Between 1860 and 1862 they minted coins to satisfy the demand for a circulating medium, something the central government had not accomplished. The Clark, Gruber coins either met or exceeded the gold bullion value of similar U.S. pieces, and in less than two years they issued $3 million in coins. They did such a good job the federal government bought them out for $27,000 and closed one of the last private mints.

The United States backed its currency with both gold and silver—a practice referred to as bimetallism. The U.S. mint valued one ounce of gold as worth 15 ounces of silver. But since the supply and demand of these metals varied, their market prices changed. If gold was in short supply, it became worth more than 15 ounces of silver. Like the ancient Greeks of Athens who held onto their silver coins when copper ones were introduced, Americans stopped circulating their gold when it became more valuable than silver.

In this young country, the value of the metals fluctuated against each other as new discoveries brought new sources of supply into production. The U.S. government shifted the relative weights of the coins to bring their market value into line. Wayner observes, "This realignment process often brought much debate as people would choose sides based upon their interests. The debtors would endorse whatever metal was growing cheaper, hoping that they would be able to pay off their debts with less work. The lenders would push for 'hard' money that was contracting so as to force people to pay off their debts with more metal."

### *The Civil War*

Once again, warfare was the impetus to vast changes in the monetary system. When the Civil War broke out in 1861, few people could have envisioned its huge costs. Abraham Lincoln was correct when he said that less than one-half day's expense for fighting could have purchased the freedom of all the slaves in Delaware. The *Wall Street Journal* reports (Feb. 13, 1996) that the Civil War cost the two sides a total of $6.6 billion in 1860 dollars, which was enough to buy the freedom of all the slaves at their 1860 market value, give each slave family 40 acres and a mule and $3.5 billion in reparations to former slaves in lieu of 100 years of back wages.

No sooner did blood begin to flow than the money followed, and there were runs on the banks as people brought in their paper money and demanded gold bullion. By the end of the first year of the Civil War, neither the banks nor the U.S. Treasury would honor redeemable paper currency. Paper dollars did, however, become the standard in the U.S. during the Civil War. To pay its war debts, the federal government first issued paper money in February 1862. Salmon P. Chase, Secretary of the Treasury, replaced the gold-backed money with notes that were theoretically redeemable at some unspecified time. This money was called "greenbacks" because the bills were printed in green ink to avoid confusion with the gold certificates also in circulation. The greenbacks quickly fell in value relative to gold coins and bullion still in circulation. The government issued new notes in June of 1862 and again in January 1863.

War made for drastic actions. Nevada was brought into the Union as a state during the Civil War because of its booming silver mines. By the time the war actually broke out, one report holds that as many as 10,000 brands of private paper money were circulating and perhaps a third of it was no good. The National Banking Act of 1864 established a uniform currency and in the process drove out of business the competing private money. The Act allowed holders of these notes to turn them in for legal U.S. currency. Thereafter, no one besides the U.S. government has been empowered to mint currency. While the war was underway, the value of paper money seesawed back and forth along with the fortunes of the Union. When the Union was losing, their paper money lost value. When it was winning, greenbacks were almost on par with gold.

In the Confederacy, people came to view their own paper money with suspicion. The South did not issue specie, according to Summers. Instead, people hoarded their Bechtler coins and many contracts and agreements during the war specified Bechtler gold as compensation rather than the Confederate states' paper money or the scant supply of federal coins still in use.

Following the war, in 1873, the U.S. temporarily stopped minting silver dollars, which had the effect of ending bimetallism. In 1879 the federal government began issuing paper money redeemable for gold. (The first U.S. silver dollars were minted in 1794, and almost 900 million of them have been minted since. Although the Treasury stopped routine production of silver dollars in 1935, it has occasionally produced limited editions, such as the rather famous Eisenhower silver dollar.)

In the late 1800's and on into the early 1900's, America was in an uproar about which metals should back the currency. The supply of gold was not increasing as fast as the economy, which meant money became harder to get and bought more goods and services than previously—classic deflation. This was good for lenders, because it meant their debts would be repaid with more valuable money, but it was bad for debtors—many of whom were farmers.

The bullion controversy divided the nation. The farmers of the prairie states wanted money backed by silver, which was abundantly streaming out of the Nevada mines. But the bankers of the East—like their forebears, the English overlords—wanted "hard money," which meant gold. Silver-tongued orator and politician William Jennings Bryan was a supporter of the prairie populists. While seeking the Presidential nomination of the Democratic party in 1896, he delivered his famous speech, in which he said: "We will answer their demands for a gold standard by saying to them: 'You shall not press down upon the brow of labor this crown of thorns, you shall not crucify mankind upon a cross of gold.' "

Bryan was defeated by William McKinley, and the Free Silver movement disappeared when the bimetallism problem righted itself as more gold discoveries brought the monetary expansion the populists wanted. But the struggle left its imprint on the American psyche.

### *The Wizard of Oz*

Was *The Wizard of Oz* a metaphor of its era? According to Hugh Rockoff of Rutgers University, that is the case. He maintains that the children's classic by L. Frank Baum was a Jonathan Swift-style literary treatment of the controversy of the day—one that would have been immediately recognized by people living then. He points out that the controversy about bimetallism was as heated a subject in their day as abortion issues are in ours. Everyone had an opinion, and everyone felt strongly about it.

Mr. Rockoff points out some recognizable symbols:

- **The Wizard of Oz.** Oz is the abbreviation for ounce—as in an ounce of gold or silver.
- **The Silver Slippers.** The movie has Dorothy wearing ruby slippers, but in the book they were silver. She had to fight the Wicked Witch of the West for control of them.

- **Dorothy.** She was swept away from the prairie states by a tornado. Dorothy represented the goodness and innocence of the American people. The evil forces are always trying to keep her and her silver slippers from returning home.
- **Toto.** Rockoff says the dog's name represents the teetotaling party, which stood for Free Silver and against free alcohol.
- **The Wicked Witch of the East.** Represents the Eastern bankers and their demand for gold.
- **The Wicked Witch of the West.** Represents McKinley because he dominated the West and subjugated its people by keeping America on the gold standard.
- **The Yellow Brick Road.** Gold is customarily stored in ingots or bricks.
- **The Cowardly Lion.** William Jennings Bryan, who roared about silver during the election of 1896 but after his defeat by William McKinley dropped the issue.

Curiouser, and curiouser, as Alice said in Wonderland.

### *Making Money*

It wasn't until 1963 that the U.S. government ceased issuing silver certificates that could actually be exchanged for silver. Today, what the Department of Treasury prints is called "federal reserve notes," and they are backed only by the full faith and credit of the government. This is a "fiat currency"; as the creation of the government, it has no intrinsic value and can't be redeemed for anything. Consequently, U.S. government money is now totally symbolic. The value of the currency has been abstracted from commodities, meaning that it is not redeemable for anything but another bill of the same denomination. The value of money is now strictly a function of the credibility of the American government, its military, and the greater economy.

As "legal tender," the currency circulated by the U.S. government must be accepted as payment of debt. Checks, credit cards and trade dollars are not legal tender, because the issuers are private organizations and not the government. That's why merchants can refuse to accept your check or credit card, but not your cash. Although, as a practical matter, it's difficult to rent a car, let alone travel, without a major credit card.

The dollar has now reached an exalted position of usefulness and has many sterling qualities. It is fungible, which means that if a person loses a $20 bill, any other $20 bill will replace it. It is anonymous, which means a person can spend it without having to show identification or give a signature. It's almost as if cash were just made to be spent. But we don't have to sell anyone on the desirability of money, do we really? Just how sought after the U.S. dollar has become is our next order of business.

# 3

# The Almighty Dollar

*"The chief value of money lies in the fact that one lives in a world in which it is overestimated."*
H.L. Mencken

The U.S. dollar has become the coin of the realm for much of the world. At the end of the 20th century, the dollar is more highly regarded, and more sought after, than perhaps at any time in its history. This has enormous value for the average American.

***The Value of a Dollar***

Consider these pieces of information:

- As many as half the residents of the former Soviet Union keep their savings in American currency—$45 billion of it in $100 bills.
- The people of Russia hold more U.S. dollars than rubles. There is more U.S. cash in Russia than in any other country except the United States.
- American cash accounts for one fifth of the world's currency supply.
- The dollar makes up 60 percent of the world foreign exchange reserves.
- Of the $390 billion of U.S. currency now in existence, as much as two thirds, or more than $250 billion, may be in circulation overseas.
- The proportion of U.S. cash held abroad more than doubled between 1980 and 1993.

### *The Coin of the Realm*

In Latin America, Africa, Asia and across the whole span of the former Soviet Union and its former Eastern European satellites, people who have anything of value also have a cache of U.S. money in the household, tucked away in a safe or under the mattress.

While staying in the home of friends in Vera Cruz, Mexico, author Terry had a powerful illustration of how important U.S. dollars appear to others. It was a weekend and he needed to change some U.S. currency into pesos. Ruben, the 14-year-old son of the folks he was staying with, asked the coauthor to wait briefly. Returning from some secret hiding place in his home, the young man began to count out $1,000 at the current exchange rate in pesos. Like so many others in the world, he had already learned that stockpiling American dollars was the thing to do.

His father, who was part of the ruling family of the area, explained the reality of life today: "Terry," he said, "If you speak English and have U.S. money, you can go anywhere and do anything in the world." The reality of this statement is almost overwhelming. The U.S. dollar has become the coin of the realm, as perhaps no other currency has since the dinarius of Roman times.

Why would the average Russian prefer dollars to rubles? Let's take the example of a typical Russian veteran of World War II who had served his country faithfully in the war, and then went on to work the rest of his days within the Communist system. If he had been frugal and had managed to amass a savings of 50,000 rubles when he retired in 1990, his nest egg would have been worth $87,500 U.S. dollars at the official exchange rate (one ruble in 1990 was worth $1.75).

Within six years, however, as the Soviet system crumbled and the ruble had to duke it out unprotected against stronger currencies, Soviet money plunged to its market value: 5,290 rubles to the dollar. That means that the Russian retiree saw a life savings evaporate: The 50,000 rubles in 1996 was worth $9.40—scarcely enough for a meal at McDonald's.

### *A Major Export*

Currency is quite possibly America's most important export, but it is much more than that. The real value to America is that the flow of currency does not come back into the U.S. economy. Because of this, we live better than we otherwise would. If all of the U.S. money were circulating here, there would be a surplus of cash in our economy and runaway inflation.

It works like this: Cash is printed here and pays for the goods and services purchased by the U.S. government. Instead of circulating in our own economy and driving up prices, however, that money is siphoned off and does not return. Because the U.S. Treasury pays no interest on the dollars held overseas that don't make their way into American interest-bearing accounts, it saves an estimated $15 billion per year, according to *Time* magazine. The *New Yorker* maintains that every bill in circulation is in effect an interest-free loan; an equivalent amount in government securities would cost the United States more than $25 billion in annual interest payments. And the rest of us benefit because our own dollars are relatively scarcer in our own economy.

The U.S. Treasury makes a profit on our money. Like the ancient Mongol emperors of China and the German coinmaker of the Old South, the U.S. government charges a few points for the value added by producing the currency. This seigniorage amounts to about $400 million per year. William Safire, columnist for the *New York Times,* adds: "The Treasury borrows ... money for nothing and lends it at about 6 percent—which means we make nearly $25 billion every year on the cash 'float,' mostly from abroad. No wonder Treasury and the Federal Reserve are so eager to protect the faith of dollar-holders in the dollar; cash *is* our cash cow."

It is a good export for U.S. banks, too. In effect, they "buy" cash from the Federal Reserve, pack it up, fly it abroad in the original U.S. government packaging and receive fees for such transactions. In 1994 alone, a small number of American banks shipped more than $20 billion in new $100 bills to about 50 Moscow banks, accepting in return other currencies or gold bullion.

Money is such a good business that the Feds produce loads of it. Somewhere in the world there exists for every single American the equivalent of about $1,400 in bills, which is a curiously large quantity. So much cash per person could lead to ruinous inflation, except for the exodus of money. The Federal Reserve may not have a solid grasp of how much cash is flowing abroad—but they have a good idea that two thirds of all U.S. currency has left the country.

Adding to the control issue, a *Wall Street Journal* article (June 3, 1996) contained the following: "The San Francisco Fed's Los Angeles branch is being investigated for doctoring numbers in the cash handling reports it compiles for Washington. Monthly discrepancies sometimes totaled tens of millions of dollars."

"Estimates of currency held abroad are subject to considerable error," Federal Reserve Chairman Alan Greenspan was quoted in *Time* magazine. "We are looking at this issue in considerable detail." But it is bound to continue. According to Theodore E. Allison, assistant to the Board of Governors of the Federal Reserve, "Issuing currency is about the best racket there is for a government."

### *Why the Dollar*

What makes one currency more valuable than another? Quite simply, it is the political, economic and military strength of the country. The U.S. dollar is sought after because our government, for the most part, has a history of respecting its value. Even if the dollar were devalued, it is not likely to be steamrolled, as regularly happens to the peso of Mexico. If money is a store of value, those who have crystallized their efforts into currency don't like to have all that work go up in smoke through hyperinflation or sudden devaluation. That's why a stable currency is a desired currency.

Political upheaval leads to money problems. Fascist dictators take the money and send it to Swiss bank accounts. Revolutionaries start social programs they can't pay for and wind up bankrupting the country their own way.

Most people in the world believe American democracy assures there will be no drastic swings to the left or to the right. Observes William Safire: "Despite all the grumping here about unresponsive government; and despite the tut-tutting abroad about American hegemonism and cultural decay—the eager acceptance of the new U.S. C-note proves that people everywhere have faith in the stability that flows from freedom in the United States of America."

America remains the largest economy in the world with technology and productivity that are among the best. The country's natural and human resources and her political and economic systems have given more prosperity to more people here than anywhere else on earth. All the activity of conducting much of the world's business in dollars helps keep the U.S. dollar in high demand.

### *Wealth Through Strength*

The virtually undiscussed true strength of our currency is our military. Our cash is the coin of the realm because we are perceived as the greatest power in the world. This is why an investment of 3 percent of GNP in our armed forces is a bargain by any standards. Because we are viewed as impregnable, people all around the world feel safe with their savings in U.S. money and with their assets in this country.

Which is why much of the world's gold supply is stored underground, 14 floors below the Federal Reserve Bank in New York. Foreign governments maintain as much as 10,000 tons of gold there, more than anywhere else in the world, and by far more than in Fort Knox. With gold considered the currency of last resort, government banks trust the Federal Reserve system to transfer it among themselves—from holding area to holding area—deep below the hustle of the city. It's there because governments believe we have the strength to protect it.

Seen in this light, Americans have been feasting for decades on the victories won in World War II. But the real banquet was served as a direct result of the defeat of Communism in the Cold War. We basically bankrupted the competition—ran them out of business. There now is no viable alternative to the economic system we have evolved; capitalism is the only game in town. The frosting on the cake was the Persian Gulf War. It showed how technologically superior U.S. armaments are to anything else on the market and, by extension, how safe the U.S. is from major threats.

Everyone wants to associate with a winner, and this is why, despite occasional perturbations and fluctuations, the German mark and the Japanese yen are not real threats to the U.S. dollar. There will be those who argue, as did Linda Himelstein of *Business Week* in 1995, that international fund managers who control as much as $2 trillion in assets will demand higher interest rates in the U.S. or they will take their money elsewhere, but we doubt it. Nor do we agree that the dollar will be eclipsed by stronger currencies, the way the British pound was displaced by the dollar.

A universal currency must grow from a strong economy and a strong military to protect that economy. The former Soviet Union once had a strong military but a weak economy. Germany and Japan have strong economies but weak militaries. At this particular point in time, the U.S. is the only country with both.

### *Looking Hard for Hard Money*

Even before the USSR collapsed, the U.S. dollar was well received everywhere in the world. Now, throughout Russia, China, Cuba and Eastern Europe, dollars are indispensable. Taxi drivers in Almaty, Kazakhstan, want to be paid in dollars, as do many restaurants in Kiev and Moscow. A major museum in St. Petersburg won't take rubles—only dollars. A Russian importer of IBM computers flashed his wad of American $50 bills to a *Time* magazine reporter and said: "What do I need rubles for? I want real money."

What is "real money"? In the island nation of Western Samoa, tala is real money, but that is the only place on earth where it is changeable. If you leave the country with tala in your pockets instead of dollars, the Samoans have trapped hard currency in their country and you have something you can't spend. The same is true of the Chinese yuan. Try to convert that off the mainland.

Financial managers may flirt with yen and Deutschmarks. At a grassroots level, though, people rely on dollars as their backup currency. It's the next best thing to gold, and a lot easier to carry. But, the reader may ask, if the U.S. dollar is in such an enviable position, how can there possibly be a crisis in currency? Do read on....

# 4

# Problems With Cash

*"The truth is rarely pure and never simple."*
Oscar Wilde

The very qualities that make paper money convenient also make it problematic. The convenience store, the Automatic Teller Machine, the Amish man going home from work on payday—all deal in cash; all are vulnerable to attack.

### *Cash Draws Thieves*

The Amish of Nappanee, Indiana—southeast of South Bend and near Chicago— have become targets for robbery precisely because of their preference for cash. Eschewing cars, electricity, telephones and other developments of the modern age, members of this religious sect go from place to place on foot, horse and wagon or bicycle. Because they won't fight back when attacked and they seldom take their problems to the police, the Amish are easy targets for thieves. The attacks usually occur on Thursday or Friday—payday at the recreational vehicle plants where many Amish work. Everyone knows that on those days the men head home with cash.

Eventually, law enforcement officials began receiving anonymous calls, each telling the same story: An Amish man on his way home from work was followed by a car with two or more people. The Amish man was then assaulted with a pipe or tire iron and robbed. There wasn't much the police could do; the Amish believe that the legal system is not the way to resolve disputes. Finally, one of the Amish, Earl Slabaugh, spoke up. A car filled with people, one of them waving a tire iron, chased him. He was afraid someone would get killed if he didn't report it to the police.

"I don't consider it a hate crime," commented Detective Sergeant Tom Brindle. "They weren't doing it because they were neo-Nazis or anything like that. They were just doing it because [the Amish] were easy prey. Amish men don't carry credit cards; they don't carry checkbooks. They always carry cash."

### *Other Problems*

Because cash is anonymous and untraceable, it is also the preferred medium for money launderers, tax evaders, kidnappers, extortionists or bribe givers. Cash has gotten something of a shady reputation. When someone wants to pay cash for a car, we assume that the buyer will underreport its value at registration time to pay lower fees. If we hear that a public official has been found with large quantities of cash in his possession, we assume he is on the take. And no kidnapper to our knowledge has ever accepted a check, even with a check guarantee card and driver's license for identification.

Small wonder cash puts the federal government in a quandary. On the one hand, the world depends on it as an international currency. Plus, the government makes a profit through seigniorage in producing it. Yet cash is a source of problems because it is so easy for criminals to do their deals undetected with cash.

This may be why the federal government has eliminated large-denomination bills. Since 1969 the $100 bill has been the biggest note the government has issued. The faces deleted include that of McKinley on the $500; Cleveland on the $1,000; Madison on the $5,000; Chase on the $10,000; and Wilson on the $100,000. (If you can get your hands on one of these, it may well be worth more than its face value.) Why? Imagine how much money could be transported in a suitcase full of $100,000 bills! In $20 bills, $1 million weighs too much for most people to lift. It's actually harder for drug dealers to transport money than it is an equivalent value of drugs. The physical problem of transporting cash has placed at least some constraints on illegal activities. This is why, as we will see in the chapters on encryption and electronic currency, the government has become apoplectic about the potential these vehicles offer criminals.

The net effect of the ceiling on face value has been to curtail the use of cash for serious business. The $100 bill of 1997 is worth what a $10 bill was at the outbreak of World War II. For those with memories that long, consider what life would have been like back then if the $10 bill were the largest denomination available. It is no wonder that checks and credit cards account for the vast bulk of transactions; the Fed has quietly marginalized cash.

Despite the profit the government makes on cash, it is still expensive to produce and to handle. The $1 bill has to do the work the dime did in 1941. A whole industry has sprung up to adapt $1 bills to vending machines—where coins used to go. The $1 bill gets so much use it wears out quickly, in about 18 months as a matter of fact. It costs the government about $200 million a year to retire, destroy and replace aging currency. And in the private sector, the cost of money includes the people who count it, protect it, carry it around in armored cars and store it in vaults.

### *Counterfeiting*

The biggest problem with cash, however, is that it is under constant attack from counterfeiters, foreign as well as domestic. A businessman visiting the great waterfalls that divide Argentina from Brazil needed to change some of the seven U.S. $100 bills he had brought with him. He went to a nearby money changer, who took out a jewelers' loop and carefully inspected each one. After going through the entire stack, the money changer handed most of them back to the businessman. There were flaws in some of the bills too small for the unaided human eye to see.

According to the *New York Times* (Dec. 3, 1995), the dollar has become "a lingua franca for the safari tourists and business executives who are increasingly criss-crossing Africa." Christopher Allen, regional representative of Catholic Relief Services, is reported to have said: "We keep a jar of 'coup money' at home in case we have to get out of a town in a hurry." And now, because of counterfeit problems with the $100 bill, he keeps it in 20s and 50s. Some banks in Harare, capital of Zimbabwe, refuse to exchange $100 bills for local currency. The central banks of Mozambique and Zambia are now reported to refuse all U.S. $100 bills.

Nor are the Africans alone. Columnist Liz Smith reported in 1994 that "top banks" in London would not give her pound notes in exchange for her $100 bills because of their concern for Middle East-originated counterfeit (see next chapter). Similarly, Sen. Patrick Leahy, a member of the Senate Banking Committee, discovered during a vacation to Ireland in 1995 that his traveler's checks were more welcome than $100 bills.

In Russia, just before Christmas of 1993, four armed men burst into a classroom in the city of Rostov in the southern part of the country. They kidnapped a teacher, a bus driver and a dozen children. The criminals wanted money—not rubles, but real money. They insisted on $10 million to be paid in U.S. $100 bills. The Russian Central Bank scraped up the cash and, after a four-day ordeal, the bandits received five plastic-wrapped packages, each containing $2 million in new bills; only then did they let the hostages go. According to the *U.S. News & World Report* account of the incident, just getting their hands on the cash wasn't enough for the kidnappers. They also demanded equipment that could distinguish between real and counterfeit U.S. money.

"The situation (in Russia) was so bad that German banks would no longer accept $100 bills from Russian citizens," according to Viktor Melnikov, director of foreign currency regulation and control for the Russian Central Bank. He was complaining to representatives of the State Department about an epidemic of forged U.S. currency in his country.

Then there's the friend we'll call Sam, a geological surveyor who travels to remote, relatively unexplored areas to look for deposits of gemstone rough. The company he works for is located in Bangkok, which, along with Hong Kong, is considered the world capital for colored stones, the term gemologists use to refer to gemstones. When Sam goes to survey mineral deposits in a developing country, he is told to report to a local Chinese-owned business for financing, frequently a restaurant located within the target country. On one of his recent trips to Madagascar, he went to the specified restaurant and was taken into a dimly lit back room. Although there was not much light, he was able to see clearly stacks of $100 bills. The man he dealt with counted bills from off the pile and handed them to him.

Having given Sam the needed exploration financing, the local restaurant owner received an equal amount of dollar credits outside the country and beyond local government control. The transaction was recorded in both locations. In effect, what took place was a transfer of cash beyond borders with no money ever actually leaving the country. The key ingredient in such transactions is a common, universally accepted currency. This system would not work well with money that could not be easily spent or converted on either side of any border. That is why the U.S. dollar—especially the $100 bill—is in such big demand overseas.

Because the authenticity of the currency is key to these transactions, these businesspeople require more than cursory assurance of a bill's validity. Each $100 bill is scrutinized, carefully and meticulously; only when it has passed the most rigorous inspection does it receive the imprimatur of this underground economy. Authenticated bills are stamped with a unique mark, the "Bangkok Chop," to validate their worth.

These locals place their own stamp of authenticity on U.S. currency for good reason. Tina Yannazzo of Pacifica, California, learned firsthand about the effects of counterfeiting on an ordinary, law-abiding citizen. In 1995 she closed a $6,000 account with a bank in Daly City. The bank teller handed her 60 crisp $100 dollar bills, which she then tried to deposit at her new bank in South San Francisco.

Unfortunately, one of the C-notes from the Daly City bank was counterfeit. The new bank credited her account for $5,900 and gave the fake $100 bill to the Secret Service. She complained that she deposited good money and expected to receive good money in return. "I don't feel I should have to check my money when it's received from a bank to see if it's counterfeit," she protested. That's not the way either the bank or the Secret Service saw it, though. It's the responsibility of the customer to check the cash before leaving the bank. They told her, in effect, "Once it's out the door, it's yours."

The overall responsibility for fighting counterfeit currency rests with the Secret Service, which operates like a domestic police department. It has done a commendable job in keeping the lid on domestic fake currency by tracking buyers of certain inks and papers, interdicting 90 percent of made-in-America phony money before it gets into circulation. But the Secret Service has no jurisdiction overseas, and that is the source of almost three quarters of the counterfeit seized within the United States. Only a small fraction of the unit's 2,000 agents are deployed outside this country, and these agents are almost completely dependent on the cooperation of host-country law enforcement. Even that small help is not available in the countries where most of the counterfeit is produced, because it is the governments themselves that are the perpetrators.

Tina's problem is every American's problem. Not only is American currency the most counterfeited in the world, but also $100 bills are the most popular target. Because, until recently, it had not been changed for more than half a century, U.S. currency remains easy to counterfeit. Almost every other major currency has more advanced protection against counterfeiting.

There are other, more sinister reasons why American currency is the object of counterfeiters. Though it is the symbol of U.S. prestige and power, it is in fact virtually undefended territory, and therefore an easy target of monetary warfare, of economic terrorism.

### *Foreign Intrigue*

The former Soviet Union's satellites felt the pressure when the rug was pulled out from under them just before the collapse. The USSR had propped up its puppets through an intricate system of barter. Petroleum, armaments and manufactured goods, to give but one example, were sent to Cuba in exchange for cigars and sugar. By manipulating the rate of exchange in favor of a strategic asset like Cuba, the Soviets were able to keep the puppet countries in business. By manipulating the rate of exchange with their more productive European satellites in their own favor, they were able to milk the wealth out of those economies. Taking from the rich and giving to the poor was done for the sake of the advancement of Socialism, but, as colonial exploitation at its worst, it kept everyone pathologically dependent.

North Korea reacted in 1988 when its rival South Korea struck a deal with Moscow that seemed to leave Pyong Yang out in the cold. South Korean President Roh Tae Woo wanted no boycott of the 1988 summer Olympic Games in Seoul. After the U.S. boycott of the 1980 and the Soviet boycott of the 1984 Olympics, he was willing to do anything to make his own international showcase event successful. He was even willing to write the Soviets a check for $3 billion. In July of 1988 Roh Tae Woo declared that he wanted diplomatic relations with all countries, including the Soviet Union and China. He signed the papers with the USSR in 1991 and with China the next year.

Was it a coincidence that Moscow ended barter trade with North Korea in 1989—the year after the Olympics? Not likely. Suddenly, North Korea had to pay cash. Without hard currency, there was no more oil and spare parts for its Soviet-supplied industrial plants, nor for the tanks and vehicles for its military. China also began demanding hard currency for its energy and food exports to North Korea. As a matter of fact, the Chinese parodied the North Korean leader's name: Kim Il Sung was twisted in Chinese to mean "beggar bowl."

For the average North Korean, it meant a drastic decline in an already impoverished standard of living. For the government, it meant taking some drastic action. One route was to intimidate its neighbors with a nuclear weapons program. *Business Week* (July 11, 1995) observed that the world learned of Pyong Yang's nuclear weapons program in 1991, when South Korea and the USSR signed their deal. The article suggests North Korea's sword-rattling was intended to extort the maximum advantage from its neighbors and the United States.

### *The North Korean Connection*

This squeeze for cash also led North Korea to take steps that eventually affected Tina Yannazzo of California. North Korea got into spending counterfeit U.S. currency.

Notorious Japanese Red Army terrorist Yoshimi Tanaka, who had disappeared in 1970 after he and other insurgents hijacked an airliner to North Korea, turned up at the center of a counterfeiting and money-laundering operation sponsored by the North Korean government. After a car chase, extradition and attempted big bribes, the terrorist-counterfeiter was finally brought to justice in Thailand. The forgeries are known in Japan as "Super K" bills and still are produced in a secret plant in downtown Pyongyang. Some of the counterfeit is shipped abroad in diplomatic bags, according to *Newsweek* (June 10, 1996).

Two North Korean-owned trading companies operating out of Macao were caught with $250,000 in counterfeit U.S. currency when police raided their offices and the homes of a dozen of their employees. The companies had made deposits of $50 million, mostly in $100 bills, from the Asia Delta Bank in Macao to the New York-based Republic National Bank office in Hong Kong in June 1994, according to an in-depth *Reader's Digest* report (March 1995). It all seemed like a routine deposit until an observant teller examined one of the notes with a microscope. Under close scrutiny, he could see that the paper seemed to have the correct blue and red silk fibers. The etchings of Ben Franklin looked correct. But a single flaw that was invisible to the unaided eye gave it away as a forgery. Over the next week bank officials found another 1,600 of the fake hundreds, and the Asia Delta Bank accounts yielded another 792.

That discovery turned out to be the tip of the iceberg. It is now estimated that there is as much as $10 billion or more of counterfeit U.S. currency afloat—much of it in $100 bills. U.S. cash now makes up 80 percent of all counterfeit money intercepted by Interpol, and the Secret Service indicates through data revealed in *U.S. News & World Report* (Dec. 5, 1994) that the amount intercepted is increasing dramatically: In 1992 just $29.9 million was confiscated; in one more year the total reached $120 million.

### *Middle East Connection*

When Iraq invaded Kuwait in 1990 they raided the treasury and "liberated" the cash. Upon the arrival of this currency at international banks, inspectors found that four bills out of 10 were fake. The British seized $10.3 million in counterfeit U.S. currency in 1994, which was four times the amount recovered in 1990.

How did North Korea get into the middle of all this? Pyong Yang, though strapped for cash, did have assets, in the form of heavy armaments. North Korea sold several intermediate-range ballistic missiles and launchers to Iran in exchange for oil (once bought from the USSR) and counterfeit U.S. currency.

As a matter of fact, much of international terrorism today is being financed with counterfeit U.S. money. In April of 1992 Syrian agents spent $800 million in counterfeit U.S. money for weapons bought in Czechoslovakia and the Ukraine. And Iran offered to pay $6 million in counterfeit U.S. money to the Irish Republican Army for the assassination of three influential Iranian dissidents.

Iran has been financing its Holy War against the U.S. with forged cash. Not only does using counterfeit U.S. money buy the violence Iran wants, but spending forged U.S. money also weakens the credibility of the U.S., which they refer to as the "Great Satan." Ironically, Iran sees the U.S. as the nation that is morally corrupt and degenerate. Iran also wanted the money because it was broke following its protracted war with Iraq and the U.S. trade embargo. There is some honor, at least, in this ring of forgers. The Iranians don't insist on a dollar-for-dollar exchange of their counterfeits. When they launder money through Syria and then Lebanon, the fake cash is discounted by as much as 60 percent.

*Reader's Digest* quoted a 1992 report from the House Republican Task Force on Terrorism and Unconventional Warfare: "A significant portion of the counterfeit bills are being distributed on behalf of Iran by Hezbollah networks with proven records of success in smuggling drugs, weapons and explosives as well as intelligence operatives and terrorists." And nearly half of the fake cash that goes through Syria is lifted by the military leaders there.

The *New Yorker* (Oct. 23, 1995) maintains that it is Syria itself that is behind the flood of "Superbills." The counterfeiting began during Lebanon's long civil war, according to the report. The Phalangists used skilled Armenian engravers to make the plates, then printed the fake $100 on bleached genuine $1 bills. The counterfeits were passed in Czechoslovakia to buy rifles. Years later, when the Syrians took control of Lebanon, they continued the counterfeiting operation but upgraded it to produce superior counterfeits. The fakes are reportedly transported in trucks on the drug routes through Turkey and Europe, and in ships from the Lebanese port of Juniyah to Cyprus.

In Moscow, where half of personal savings is held in the form of U.S. currency, as much as half of this U.S. currency is now believed to be counterfeit. The Russian Central Bank reports the Superbills to total as much as $4 billion.

Where did Russia get all this counterfeit U.S. money? Iran used the breakup of the Soviet Union as the opportunity to buy up great stocks of conventional weapons, making purchases from former Soviet army depots and from new Muslim republics such as Azerbaijan, Kazahkstan and Turkmenistan. Conventional weapons are not all that is being offered for sale: The "Superbill" may be the currency used to buy weapons-grade plutonium from the former Soviet states for use in deployable nuclear weapons.

Where does Iran get its forgeries? The House Republican Research Committee Task Force on Terrorism and Unconventional Warfare in 1992 accused Iran of printing the fake currency at the mint in Teheran. The Iranians called the charges "wild hallucinations of the extreme right." The money it prints is so good that it came to be known as the "Superbill." It truly does fool both man and machine. The counterfeit bills have sequential serial numbers. They are printed with engravings created by agents of the former East German Republic on two presses identical to those used by the U.S. Bureau of Engraving and Printing.

According to the *New Yorker,* at least one, and as many as three, of those presses is in Lebanon's Bekaa Valley, home also to drug smuggling and international terrorism. The magazine speculates that the presses are in "a barn or a big warehouse," and may be in Syria itself.

In the intaglio process used to print money, an etched plate strikes the paper with such force that it makes the money feel embossed.

"I've done counterfeiting cases, and I know what a counterfeit bill looks like," according to Paul Kelly, a Boston federal prosecutor who spoke to Fredric Dannen and Ira Silverman of the *New Yorker*. "These bills looked genuine. They felt genuine." When minute imperfections were pointed out to Kelly, he said: "I frankly couldn't see the damn imperfections."

As to machines, the "Superbills," complete with magnetic ferrous oxide black ink on the front, were put to the test by the currency scanners at the 12 Federal Reserve Banks. The federal government's scanning machines are so accurate they reject 1,000 genuine $100 bills for every one later found to be counterfeit. But, Kelly told the *New Yorker,* "the Secret Service told me the bills went through the machines."

Continued Kelly, "The Secret Service did believe that this was an effort not just to acquire amazing wealth but also to destabilize the economy of the United States." Robert Leuver, then director of the Bureau of Engraving and Printing, said: "This is an act of terrorism—monetary warfare. The Treasury won't admit it."

### *Just for the Money*

Not all foreign forgeries are part of a conspiracy to undermine our country: Some are made just because the criminals want the money. Take Mexican counterfeit, for example. There has been a flow of Mexican-made forgeries into this country. Because $20 bills receive less scrutiny than $100s, it is easier to pass them, so that is the denomination Mexican counterfeiters have focused on. A batch of these fake $20s were identified in 1994 in Texas and New Mexico, and also turned up in Eugene, Oregon, in 1995. When a Mexican passed a fake $20 at a convenience store, the clerk, who had taken two of them the night before, recognized the forgery and called the police.

"They're good," said Eugene Police Detective Jim Green of the forgeries. "With a cursory glance, if a person is in a hurry, they're probably going to accept them." The problem is, if a person notices something wrong with a bill and passes it along to get rid of it, that person is also guilty of forgery. "Once they recognize that it's counterfeit, they are obligated to turn it in to the police or to a bank," he said.

Then there was "King Kong," a.k.a. Lee Ah-sin, an engraver born in Malaysia who made a superb $100 bill using a converted squid processor for a press. The *New Yorker* described him as "eccentric, obsessively meticulous," and said he had no known grudge against the U.S. Yet he was finally tracked down in 1985 by the Secret Service, with the aid of the Royal Thai Police.

### *Protecting the Currency*

What proportion of cash is counterfeit? According to Federal Reserve Chairman Alan Greenspan, fewer than one of every 100,000 bills of all denominations in circulation is found to be counterfeit. One wonders at this figure. Is it accurate, or is he kidding the troops to preserve faith in the money? Or are we simply counting in all the $1 bills in circulation that no one bothers to counterfeit to be able to come up with this incredible number?

Clearly, the government has been challenged to protect the currency, but is it doing enough? According to *U.S. News & World Report*, the U.S. has assigned only six Secret Service agents on permanent counterfeit detail overseas. The *New Yorker* reports that in March of 1995 the Secret Service was able to convince the Senate Appropriations Committee to press for a significant increase of agents abroad, and in August won approval for the first permanent Secret Service office in the Middle East, on Cyprus.

Until then, the Secret Service presence there had been little more than a handful of agents rotating through by way of offices in Rome, Paris and the States, with help sometimes from the U.S. Department of State and agencies of the Israeli and German governments. This Cyprus task force has supplied information to President Bill Clinton and then Treasury Secretary Lloyd Bentsen about Syria's activities in the counterfeit arena, and this information has been used in negotiations to remove Syria from the State Department's list of terrorist nations.

It isn't now a federal crime to counterfeit U.S. currency abroad. And even if it were, how would we impose penalties on foreign nationals, let alone foreign governments? One option is to bomb the printing presses in Iran or North Korea. Rep. James A. Leach (R-Iowa), House Banking Committee Chairman, said: "We have an obligation to make it clear to any nation that attacks our currency in such a fashion that it will be held accountable." But that's not likely to happen because the U.S. government refuses to make an issue of it. "We have no hard evidence that a counterfeiting plant of high quality U.S. currency is in North Korea," according to Dennis Lynch of the U.S. Secret Service, speaking to *U.S. News & World Report* (June 10, 1996).

Forging the currency of an enemy is not new. The Nazis tried it with the British pound sterling during World War II. As damaging as this assault to U.S. currency could be to the economies of the West, one would hope that national leaders will have the resolve to take military action if need be to neutralize the threat. Another tactic would be to impose sanctions on any country found to be counterfeiting or aiding others found to be counterfeiting. Because the U.S. at this point does not deal with Iran anyway, there is no real leverage here. One measure would call for 15 years in federal prison for anyone forging U.S. currency outside the country. Even this seems a hollow gesture, however, in light of the difficulty of extraditing heads of terrorist states for trial.

A major problem is that so much of this fake stuff is already circulating in Russia that the economy there depends on it. A high official of the Russian Central Bank estimates that between 15 and 20 percent of the U.S. currency in the hands of Russian citizens is believed to be the counterfeit "Superbill."

The Secret Service, for their part, does not even acknowledge that the "Superbill" exists. Richard Rohde, head of the counterfeit division, told the *New Yorker* that the term "Superbill" was a "misnomer," and was not used by the Secret Service. "They are good quality notes, but not that good," he said. He conceded that of the counterfeit cash seized within the U.S. in a recent year, 72 percent was made abroad. And with the help of foreign law enforcement, more is being intercepted every year. In August of 1995, for example, the

Royal Canadian Mounted Police, aided by the Secret Service, intercepted $112 million in counterfeit in Saint-Constant, Quebec.

The U.S. Treasury is mindful that two thirds of the $390 billion in U.S. currency is circulating overseas, and it is unwilling to precipitate a crisis of confidence by recalling the money. "The Treasury has a policy of never recalling existing currency," reports the *New Yorker*, "for fear that the world's hoarders of dollars might switch to Deutsche marks or yen."

And that's the rub for Tina Yannazzo and the rest of us. The important thing for the government is not that some of us will be burned with fake money so much as that we will begin to distrust the currency. It is "our collective confidence in money" that has led to a "mass delusion that has made the United States dollar such a bedrock," asserts the *New York Times* (June 16, 1996).

### *Mind Over Matter*

Counterfeit currency in the end becomes an issue of mind over matter: If you don't mind, it doesn't matter. "Counterfeiting becomes significant to the Fed," the *New Yorker* maintains, "only if it undermines confidence in the dollar.... The Federal Reserve and the Treasury don't fear the Superbill itself as much as they fear a confidence problem that might result if they publicly acknowledge it and countenance a large-scale investigation."

The reason the Fed is so sanguine about counterfeits is that cash is actually a small part of the total money supply, less than 10 percent. Wire transfers, checks and credit card transactions amount to a couple trillion dollars every business day—half the $4 trillion money supply. These accounts are not reconciled by banks shuttling tons of money back and forth. It just would not be practical.

If cash isn't being exchanged for all those wire transfers, and neither is gold or silver, what is going on ... what is money? "Money is the current liability of a bank," Sholom Rosen of Citibank told James Gleick of the *New York Times* (June 16, 1996). "It's as simple as that. It's not gold, it's not silver, it's the current liability of a bank."

If that's what the vast bulk of money is, it is no wonder the Feds are willing to allow these counterfeit hundreds to work their way through the system. After all, if the bill is so good that neither man nor machine can separate it from the genuine, the counterfeit becomes invisible ... except for the unlucky people who wind up holding the bag when a bill is discovered.

Eventually, the new cash will displace the old as it wears out and is removed by the Federal Reserve system. This filtration will take many years, but meanwhile, "we will have two kinds of money circulating at the same time, the old and the new—and they both will be good," asserts Mary Ellen Withrow, Treasurer of the United States.

But as we see it, the truth of the matter is that we will have four kinds of money circulating: the old and the new genuine cash and the old and the new counterfeit. And few of us will know which is which. As the next chapter explains, counterfeit at home comes not from domestic enemies but from the nerds, the computer geeks and hackers who are playing with their latest high-tech toys.

# 5

# The Domestic Threat

*"Systems theory looks at the world in terms of the inter-relatedness of all phenomena, and in this framework an integrated whole whose properties cannot be reduced to those of its parts is called a system."*
Fritjof Capra

Tracking money from a few presses in Iran or North Korea is one thing; watching thousands of small-time operators would be another. "A billion-dollar crop of counterfeit bills produced by thousands of hobbyists making money in their spare time could paralyze enforcement efforts by the Secret Service," observed *Scientific American* in March of 1994.

### *Color Copiers*

Every year since 1989 the amount of counterfeit cash produced domestically on color copiers and personal computers has doubled. The Secret Service has been removing about $25 million to $75 million per year before it reaches circulation, but, by the year 2000, there could be as much as $2 billion of fake domestic currency produced annually.

It's simple to do. Just ask Richard Perez of Phoenix, Arizona, how it's done. He is reported by *PC Magazine* to have counterfeited $1 million on a Canon color laser copier and then to have spent the phony money for 500 pounds of marijuana. Just his luck that the pusher was an undercover agent. Or ask José Martins. He allegedly counterfeited both U.S. and Canadian currency on a Canon copier. He got caught, unluckily for him, because he wrote a bad check to pay for the machine; when the vendor came to repossess, a fake $50 bill happened to be lying under the copier.

It used to take hours of painstaking effort to try to replicate the engravings used to make counterfeit money. Not any more. Color copiers and computers with color printers are so good that thousands of average people may take up counterfeiting as a hobby.

"We have seen a dramatic increase in the sophistication of counterfeiting, but it takes less skill today," observed Jim Bauer, special agent in charge of the Los Angeles Secret Service field office, in a *U.S. News & World Report* interview. A decade ago, he said, it took a skilled printer to produce counterfeit money. Now all it takes is a color copier. The Canon CLC 800, for example, is able to produce virtually undetectable phony money, but Kodak, Minolta and Xerox make copiers that work just as well.

In the three years from 1991 to 1994, the number of U.S. bills counterfeited on color copiers increased by a factor of eight. The favorite target of copier counterfeiters is the $20, because these are in common use and are unlikely to be checked—especially in businesses where the volume of cash is high. This sudden explosion of funny money can be laid at the doorstep of the new, dry-powder copiers. Old liquid toner copiers used to distort the copies when they were made back to back. The copiers today are so sensitive they will even reproduce the red and blue threads in the paper.

The Secret Service has used forensics tests to determine the make and model of copiers used to make the money and would now like a list of those individuals with counterfeit-capable copiers in their possession. The American Civil Liberties Union (ACLU), however, has suggested that it is improper for law enforcement officials to ask businesses for customer lists without a court order. Ed Martone, executive director for the New Jersey ACLU, has suggested that vendors could ask customers to sign disclaimers with their sales agreements if such information becomes critical to law enforcement.

Canon is trying to combat the abuse of its equipment by marketing copiers with a chip that identifies the bills of several countries. When the copier spots the currency, it prints totally black images.

Minolta, according to *Security Management* magazine, stamps every color copy with an almost invisible code that identifies the machine that made it.

If color copiers can be secured, there is not yet such protection for personal computers. With a PC, a scanner and a color printer, counterfeiters don't need a color copier. A March 1990 *Time* magazine article discussed this "desktop forgery." The counterfeiter uses an optical scanner to turn any document into a digital image. High-quality inkjet printers can turn out highly passable counterfeit money—even from a desktop.

Hardware and software costs have fallen so far that these tools are within almost anyone's reach. The price of a color Hewlett-Packard Color LaserJet printer dropped from $10,000 to $5,000 in just one year. High-quality scanners cost less than $1,000. The overall cost of equipment to produce a color document has fallen from $250,000 in the 1980s to less than $2,500 in the mid-1990s.

Software, too, makes counterfeiting easy. Adobe Photoshop used with Adobe Illustrator or Altsys' Freehand make it possible to produce any kind of currency. Technology has placed the ability to counterfeit into everyone's lap. In addition to hate-filled Iranians, law-enforcement officials also must now worry about certain nerds and geeks at the desktop PC, people who occasionally may try to print up a quick fiver to pay for lunch or parking.

### *The Eternal Dollar*

The value of money comes from the level of confidence people place in it. If the volume of fake U.S. money was widely known, the dollar's exalted position could collapse. But counterfeit money is like an inoperable tumor; you can't get rid of it without killing the patient. Which is why we believe the Treasury is simply going to allow the fake stuff to circulate until it is gradually filtered out through the banking system—with hapless holders taking the loss when it is discovered.

Apparently the penalties are not severe enough to dissuade counterfeiting. In this country one could be sentenced to 15 years for producing, possessing or passing phony bills. But in Great Britain between 1697 and 1832, the English hanged more than 300 counterfeiters and transported many others to the penal colony in Australia. Did that stop counterfeiting? Not when it was so easy and just too tempting. What finally ended the hangings was public outcry, along with the demand that the Bank of England make the currency harder to counterfeit. So that's what they did, and it's what just about every country other than the United States did years ago.

"It's odd that, after all these years, the U.S. has such an easily forged bill," the *New York Times* quoted Victor Chando, deputy general manager for international finance of Zimbabwe (Dec. 3, 1995). "You can have a country out in the Pacific with four people on it that has a better currency." Also insulting U.S. money is Yoshihide Matsumura, a Japanese national who manufactures a machine to detect counterfeit bills. He says U.S. currency is so easy to copy and is made so sloppily that many good counterfeiters have to "lower their quality" in order to duplicate it, he told *Newsweek* (June 10, 1996).

Other countries go to far greater lengths than does the U.S. to safeguard their currency. Australia, for example, in 1988 began using bar codes on a plastic substrate and plans to use diffractive optical elements called kinegrams, says *Scientific American*. In addition, *U.S. News & World Report* notes that some Australian money has a clear plastic window that won't copy.

Germany and Great Britain added security threads to their bills scores of years ago. Japan uses special ink that cannot be reproduced on its 1,000- and 10,000-yen notes. Finland and Austria use hologram-like diffraction foils that shimmer and change color. Canadian money has thin layers of ceramic material that changes from gold to green at different viewing angles. Neither the diffraction foil nor the ceramic material can be duplicated on copiers.

Some African countries have had the watermarks and embedded strips for years, and most of them believe their money is prettier than ours, too. One *New York Times* review of the appearance of African cash gives it high marks: "African currency is often quite beautiful, a gallery of lions, elephants, warriors and hydroelectric plants."

Other countries make it a point to remodel the money on a regular basis. Great Britain, for example, has redone the pound sterling note six times since 1914. That's the advantage of changing king or queen: New face, new money, with new seigniorage profits to boot. U.S. currency, by comparison, has looked the same since 1929, when the government reduced the bills in size and made them more uniform in appearance. There was never any serious consideration given to more colorful currency. Mary Ellen Withrow, U.S. Treasurer, said: "Green is the color of prosperity, and black is a good thing too—it shows we're sound and solid and in the black."

For a startling lesson in how seldom U.S. currency is changed, take a $10 bill in your hand. On the face of the bill, Alexander Hamilton smiles enigmatically. On the flip side is an engraving of the U.S. Treasury Building with a number of vehicles cruising by. Even though the bill could have this year as the print date, the cars remain Model T vintage. On the back of the $50 bill is another boxy car from the same era parked in front of the Capitol. One would think that a revenue-starved government would sell that space for advertising when new models come out—at least change the Model T to a Cadillac STS (Terry's personal favorite).

But money is all about confidence, not trendiness. Our money is unchanging and stable, the way people like it. "Many politicians ... have long held that a dramatic redesign of the currency would be highly offensive to the American public—like changing the flag," observes the *New Yorker*. Faith in the U.S. dollar may well be the only permissible state-sponsored religion. The U.S. government is not going to alter the appearance of a winner just to keep up with the times. To take that step is very serious business—a major cause for alarm.

### *Redoing the Currency*

When the new money was announced in 1995, Treasury Secretary Robert E. Rubin, following introductory remarks by an actor dressed as Ben Franklin, explained that the redesign was an effort to "anticipate a problem" and "stay ahead of the curve" because of the "future and potential threat" of counterfeiting through color copiers and personal computers. But the *New Yorker* scoffed at the Treasury Department's stated reason for redesigning the currency. "While the threat of widespread amateur counterfeiting on color reprographic equipment is indeed serious, it is farfetched to think that threat alone prompted the currency redesign."

As far back as 1981 the Secret Service lobbied for a major redesign of the currency because of its perceived vulnerability. They offered a list of a dozen anti-counterfeiting features, such as holograms, chemical markers and multiple colors. Three years later the Secret Service and the Bureau of Engraving and Printing had developed three prototype $20 bills. These new models were not well received at the White House, however. Robert Leuver, then director of the Bureau of Engraving and Printing, informed the *New Yorker* that then Treasury Secretary Donald Regan told him the new bills "didn't float" when proposed to the President. Early in 1985, the new Treasury Secretary, James Baker, and his staff also rejected them. It was only the next year that Baker approved the least conspicuous of the proposed new features—the polymer thread and the microprinting.

The Secret Service grudgingly accepted these initial changes, which were not instituted until 1990. Adding holograms was also considered for the 1990 remake, but, according to *PC Week* (June 1988), the Treasury felt these would not hold up in circulation and also were found to be too expensive. In the 1990 remodeling, the Treasury did insert a metallicized polyester security thread, 1.5 millimeters wide, on the left side of the face in the open field between the border and the Federal Reserve seal. The letters "USA" and the bill's denomination are printed on the strip in an alternating up-and-down pattern. Unfortunately, the strip is easily removed, which defeats its purpose of making the bills hard to reproduce on copiers. If the strip has been removed, it probably has been tampered with, or the bill in your possession is a counterfeit. [Why would anyone remove the security thread? The word among some college students is that airport scanners can identify these strips and come up with an exact total of how much cash is on the person being scanned. True or not, the possibility has many people stripping the thread from their bills at travel time to be "on the safe side."]

Otherwise, $100, $20 and $10 bills issued from 1990 and after should bear the security thread. Series 1988A and earlier bills will not have the strip (there is no 1989 series). According to a 1993 *Nation's Business* article, the $5 and the $1 will not have the strip either, because the Treasury does not think these are in danger of counterfeit. The series year, by the way, is found to the left of the signature of the Secretary of the Treasury.

That strip precipitated an international crisis. Since 1879, the paper used for U.S. money has been made by Crane & Co. of Dalton, Massachusetts, and is sold exclusively to the federal government. It is 75 percent cotton and 25 percent linen with red and blue fibers embedded in it (because most people do not carefully scrutinize cash, even rice paper will sometimes pass). The problem arose when Crane had difficulty embedding the polyester thread, and in 1986 the Bureau of Engraving and Printing looked for another source. The best prospect was Portals Ltd., a British paper manufacturer.

But the Brits were disqualified when Silvio Conte, a Congressman from Massachusetts and a close friend of Crane's late chairman, managed to put through an amendment to an appropriations bill that required American cash to be printed on paper from a U.S.-owned company. Crane continued to work on the process and eventually got it right in 1989. Crane's difficulties in producing paper with the imbedded strip were apparently not experienced by counterfeiters. The *New Yorker* reported being shown a counterfeit $100 by the Secret Service that had the embedded polymer strip.

In the 1990 remodel of currency, the designers added around the portrait the words, "UNITED STATES OF AMERICA," printed repeatedly in letters seven-thousandths of an inch high. The words appear like a thin line to the naked eye and can only be read with a seven-power magnifier. If reproduced on a copier, the words will appear as a solid line. The only problem is, it takes a magnifying glass to tell the difference, and few cashiers are going to spend the time to inspect each bill.

### *New Money for Old*

These changes apparently were a mere finger in the dike, however, in light of the subsequent tidal wave of counterfeit. It took the flood of "Superbills" to convince the Treasury that stop-gap measures were not enough. It wasn't until early in 1996 that the new $100 bills were trotted out. And it will be the turn of the century before smaller denominations are changed.

The $100 bill was first because—after the $20—it is the most passed counterfeit. It is also the most efficient to change: The new bills are expected to cost 25 percent more to produce. The Treasury's Bureau of Engraving and Printing produces more than 9 billion notes per year at a cost of 3.7 cents each and collectively worth $129 billion. Of that, 95 percent replaces worn bills, and 5 percent supports economic growth, according to the Treasury Department.

On the new bills, the portrait of Benjamin Franklin, who pioneered the campaign for paper money, incidentally, is half again as large as before and extends from the upper to the lower edges of the bill. In Franklin's lapel is printed the words "United States of America" so small it takes a magnifier to see it. And in the lower-left denomination is microprinted "USA 100."

Franklin's portrait has been moved to the left of center to make room for a watermark portrait of him in the far right that can be seen when held up to light but does not reproduce on color copiers or color scanners. The watermark, part of the paper, is made by varying the paper density in a small area during the paper-making process. Moving the portrait also means there won't be creases through the face when the bill is folded. Franklin will seem a bit younger in the new portrait because his hair has been made darker for contrast. The likeness comes from a painting in the National Gallery said to have been completed in 1785, five years before Franklin's death.

The bill contains many security features, such as color-shifting ink on the "$100" denomination in the lower right-hand corner: The number is green when viewed head-on and black when held at an angle. The vertical security threads will be placed in different positions on the left side of the bill for different denominations. The words on the thread are visible only in bright light. The thread also glows red under ultraviolet light.

Other changes include a universal Federal Reserve seal that replaces the individual designations of where the bill was printed. There are additional letters and numbers identifying the issuing Federal Reserve Bank. There are concentric fine lines on the front and back of the bills that can be seen with the human eye but are difficult for scanning equipment to duplicate correctly. With all the changes, however, the bill remains the same size, still has black on the front and green on the back, and still says: "In God We Trust."

Revising the $100 bill has given new hope to those who actually like variety in money—the coin collectors. It's not the big bills they're interested in so much, though, as the small change. "This is going to be very exciting," enthused Stephen Bobbitt, spokesperson for the American Numismatic Association, a coin collectors' group, about efforts to redo the nation's quarters. "This is a first step in what we hope will be a redesign for the nation's coinage."

A bill proposed in mid-July 1996 by Rep. Michael Castle (R-Del.) would kick the dour-faced George Washington off the quarters and replace him with a new design for each of the 50 states. These quarters could feature each of the 50 state animals. The pelican of Louisiana and the grizzly of California might represent their respective states, for example. And in Oregon the residents would certainly want their quarters to bear the mascot of the University of Oregon: Donald Duck.

But never assume those coin collectors are fools. The new quarters may be part of a move to make the U.S. Mint "the Franklin Mint of the 1990s," according to Jonathan Locke, president of the Columbia Coin Co. of Portland, Ore. The private Franklin Mint produced a slew of coins and other "collectibles" in the 1970s and 1980s.

One indication that he is right are the commemorative gold pieces celebrating the 1996 Summer Olympic Games in Atlanta. Those coins are not a good buy, according to James DiGeorgia, editor of *Silver & Gold Report* from Palm Beach Gardens, Fla. The proof coins are offered at $259 each but contain only $90 worth of gold. If the U.S. Mint could get that kind of markup on all the money it produced—and then sell it abroad—it could more than cover the balance of trade deficit! A better buy than the Olympics coins, according to DiGeorgia, is a one-ounce U.S. Eagle bullion coin for $400, a coin costing only $18 more than an ounce of gold.

But it's buyer beware for those who are looking to invest in U.S. Mint-produced collector coins. Locke said a survey of the value of some of the Mint's recent commemoratives showed that instead of appreciating, many of the coins actually are becoming worth less than when they were new.

### *Pleasing the Customer*

Current reactions to the new "C-note" are so-so. Many think it looks like "funny money," especially our biggest customers—the Russians, who hold more U.S. currency than the residents of any country outside the United States. According to Angela Charlton of the Associated Press, the U.S. government had to do a major sell job to convince the Russians that the new bill is as good as the old, and the old as good as the new. U.S. bills dated before 1990 are held suspect in Russia, and the slightest wrinkle or stain can cause a bill's rejection.

As mentioned earlier, cash is king in Russia, not only because the people don't trust the country's banks, but also because much of the private economy is underground. The whole idea of private banking, after all, is completely foreign to the many generations of Russians who grew up under Communism. Plainly, they prefer dollars to rubles. People in Russia "have little trust in the local paper and want to be paid in dollars," observes William Safire of the *New York Times*. "Because banks there have difficulty establishing the authenticity of old bills, tellers accept only fresh new American bills for exchange or deposit. As a result, no matter how often our officials assure the world about the continued willingness to honor old bills at face value, Russian investors anticipate a rush to exchange." U.S. Ambassador to Russia Thomas Pickering has told the Russian people: "All old notes … will still be valid at full face value—forever."

Despite the Russians' anxiety about the new $100 bill, acceptance of it is so important to the U. S. Treasury that Washington paid for a telephone hot line there, blanketed the banks with posters and dispatched representatives time and again to reassure the Russians that the new bill would not prompt more counterfeiting or destroy the value of the old bills.

"We have a responsibility to those who put their trust in our currency," the Treasury Department's Howard Schloss told a news conference in January 1996. Despite the assurances, the Russians still preferred the new U.S. money because they regard it as more solid than their own. Pickering said that when the new $100 was introduced, planes flew as much $200 million in cash to Russia daily to meet the huge demand for dollars to exchange for rubles. Russia's Central Bank estimates that 80 percent of the billions in U.S. currency stuffed under Russian mattresses are in the form of $100 bills. Russians with large cash caches that they do not want to explain are already approaching American businessmen with a deal: Turn in the old bills for the new for a 10 percent commission. In the States, gamblers and drug dealers are also scrambling for connections to launder their hidden old bills for the new.

### *How to Tell the Difference*

As Tina Yannazzo learned, if you take counterfeit money, the loss is yours. If you pass it along to someone else, you are guilty of counterfeit and run the risk of a possible jail term of 15 years. It seems prudent, therefore, to check closely each bill you receive and to learn to tell the difference between the good and the bad. For bills produced from 1990 on, there is, of course, the security thread and the microscopic printing around the border of the portrait. If you receive one of the "Superbills" from the Middle East, chances are you won't be able to easily tell the difference from the real thing anyway.

Cash made on copiers and computers is easier to spot, though. It will feel different or it just will not look right. The color may be lighter, and the size and texture may vary slightly. One caveat on the feel of the bill: Some counterfeiters actually are laundering their products in washing machines to give them a "used" feel.

Counterfeiters often bleach $1 bills and overprint them as $100s so they have the authentic feel of real cash. Eventually, though, with much use, even these bills can lose their distinctive look and feel.

In March of 1994, *Security Management* magazine suggested a simple test of money: Rub a genuine Treasury note on a piece of white paper. "It will rub green unless it has been laundered—especially in a wash with bleach, in which case it will not rub any color at all. Photocopied currency will usually rub black. A washed piece of genuine currency will still look the same, except for fading a little. A laundered counterfeit bill will disintegrate." Further, the bill should be printed clearly, without smudges or blurry images. The sawtooth points on the outer edge of the circular Treasury seal should be clear, sharp, even and unbroken. There should be clarity in the scrollwork, crosshatching and outer margins of the bills. All the numbers and letters on U.S. bills have a distinctive style, are evenly spaced and are sharp and clear.

Compare the suspected counterfeit with one you know is real and look for differences in color, size and printing quality. In other words, use the same powers of discernment on cash that you would on a check. If you come across what you suspect may be a fake bill, try to detain the person who passed it to you or write down a complete physical description and call the police.

If humans at cash registers are unable to filter out phony money, one solution may be the development of affordable equipment—such as the magnetic readers that now scan checks—that could recognize counterfeit bills at the point of sale.

Forgers can manufacture fake money as long as the old bills are still in circulation. Sen. Patrick Leahy (D-Vt.) proposed that all $100 bills held abroad be returned within a six-month period after an adequate number of the new bills are available. When they introduced the new bill into circulation, however, Treasury officials emphasized that no currency will be recalled and that all bills now in circulation will remain legal tender. They predict it will take years until all old bills are gone, but that 70 percent of the $100 bills in circulation should be the new model within three years of introduction. After all that work to make a new model, unfortunately, there were reports of counterfeit ones within months of rollout. The new currency is better than the old and harder to counterfeit, but it does not solve the problem of counterfeit.

Meanwhile, law-abiding people like Tina Yannazzo will take a hit every time they inadvertently walk out of the bank with counterfeit cash. And there is a lot of it out there. If Yannazzo had received all the acknowledged $10 billion in counterfeit in circulation instead of just one $100 bill, it would take her 30,000 years to spend it all, even if spending at a rate of $1,000 a day.

Were counterfeit money our only concern, it would be easier to do business with confidence. The problem is, today we must look hard at just about everything of value that changes hands.

# 6

# Is Anything Sacred?

*"All substance is energy in motion. It lives and flows.*
*Money is symbolically a golden,*
*flowing stream of concretized vital energy."*

*The Artist's Way*

Yes, the world is awash in counterfeit cash, but there are times when fake money is worth more than the real thing. British artist James Stephen George Boggs was arrested in 1986 and charged with reproducing the British pound note. He had made actual-size ink drawings of British money and used them as payment for purchases. His total transactions with the hand-drawn bills numbered more than 700, and the goods purchased were valued at about $35,000.

The merchants could either keep the drawings or sell them for a profit, reported *Harper's* in February 1988. According to Boggs, no one ever thought he or she was getting real money.

"At no time have I parted with one of these works when there was any shadow of a doubt about its being a work of art," he protested at his trial. "All the drawings to this date which have been sold in the galleries were purchased from the owners at prices far in excess of the drawn face values and resold by those galleries at tremendous profits of which I have never received a single pence."

The artist was acquitted. Most of us will not be so fortunate as to receive a fake that is more valuable than the real thing. Yet the Boggs incident does illustrate a major truth: It is the intangible value added by people that gives most of the value to a thing, in his case, money that is worth more than money.

### *Soft Counterfeiting*

Counterfeiting isn't just of money anymore. Thanks to the many electronic devices for copying and transmitting data, counterfeiting negotiable instruments such as checks and money orders is a $10 billion problem annually. For financial institutions, it is actually the number one crime problem, according to Ronald Dick, chief of the financial institution fraud unit of the FBI (*U.S. News & World Report*, Dec. 5, 1994).

It works like this: A company employee buys a ream of blank check stock in readiness for payday. On payday, with newly cut paycheck in hand, the employee makes scores of copies of it and cashes them all immediately, before the system has time to react. Or, a bank teller could take copies of checks from companies with large payrolls and reproduce them. *Forbes* magazine once ran an article on creating checks with computer devices and, ever since, according to *Security Management* magazine, financial institutions have been plagued with crooks and fake checks.

"It is not even necessary to be high tech to produce sophisticated looking checks," said Barbara E. Hurst in her "Technology Challenges the Trade" (*Security Management*). "The type style of magnetic ink character recognition (MICR) numbers used on the bottom of a check for high-speed reading is available from many suppliers of desktop publishing or font package software," and it can be installed easily on a personal computer. Most programs come with instructions on how to design your own checks.

Getting blank check stock from a business supply store is no problem. All that counterfeiters have to do is scan a legitimate check onto a computer hard drive and change a few details such as check number and date. The fake check will have legitimate transit and account numbers. Sophisticated crooks may even scramble the transit numbers to slow down the process of presentation and return of the counterfeit checks.

Next time the phone rings and someone tells you you've won a trip or a new car, be careful—especially if they ask for the numbers on the bottom of your checks or other personal information to complete the transaction. The usual excuse is that the taxes on the prize must be paid and a credit card number won't do. If the caller requests your Social Security number and mother's maiden name (as happened to one of the authors recently), you can be pretty sure you're being set up.

These operators can use your account number and create checks charged to you. Disgruntled bank employees have taken customer account numbers to confederates who duplicate the checks. In one case, an insurance company employee passed on copies of premium checks to check counterfeiters. The resulting fake checks were made payable to one individual in the group who deposited them to an account. After a few days the thieves emptied the account and moved on to another bank. It took six months to trace the activity to the employee. An even easier way to get account numbers is to poke through a bank's trash. Information about customers' accounts is still often tossed out at the end of the day along with the garbage.

Most of these counterfeit checks wind up being kited between institutions. A thief will deposit a false check in one bank and draw on that account to deposit it elsewhere, collecting a big balance of fabricated money by repeating the process countless times. Just before the fraud is discovered and exposed, the money is withdrawn.

A few years ago one of the authors was tracked down in a business luncheon to be informed of a number of unrecorded withdrawals from the company checking account. An alert and concerned bank manager for the US Bank of Oregon had been troubled by an increase in the number of payroll checks being processed. They turned out to be frauds, but they were almost perfect.

Three months later, in Everett, Washington, a policewoman was standing in line at a Dairy Queen with her 10-year-old daughter. Looking at a man in the line ahead of her, she mused that he looked somewhat familiar. When it hit her that his picture had come across her fax machine the previous day in connection with possible check forging in Oregon, she pulled her gun, called for backup and apprehended the forger, though not without thoroughly embarrassing her daughter.

The arresting police discovered 14 stacks of business checks drawn against Oregon businesses in the trunk of the forger's car, along with multiple sets of fake driver's licenses and other false identification papers. No one from the author's company had ever met this man and there was no apparent reason to target that particular business. Later it was learned that the forger had simply raided the office building's outgoing mailbox and had removed envelopes, including several containing outgoing checks for payments. When he discovered a check written for a gas card payment, he used it as a master to replicate others. Once the thief had reproduced the checks and was armed with a check signer's signature to duplicate, he generated numbers of false payroll checks. Using his various phony IDs, he drove around town buying small items from large stores that would cash his phony paycheck to cover his purchase and he would pocket the balance. This enterprising and hard-working thief lived in Washington but traveled to Oregon daily to cash fake checks drawn against a number of different companies.

With the technology to produce phony checks becoming more sophisticated and more generally in use, the problem of this type of crime is bound to get worse.

### A Golden Opportunity

If everything were worth what we think it is, we wouldn't have expressions such as "All that glitters is not gold." Sometimes, unfortunately, even things that are made of gold may not be what they are cracked up to be. That's what the Japanese learned in 1988, when the country was introduced to fake gold collector coins. The coins were made of gold, to be sure, but they were only imitations of the 1986 pieces minted by the Bank of Japan to commemorate the 60th year of the reign of Emperor Hirohito.

The authentic coins, the 24-karat, 20-gram originals, were selling for 100,000 yen—more than twice the value of their weight in gold. And that is what led to the counterfeiting. Because the raw materials of the coin cost less than half their face value, there was the potential for 100 percent profit by making copies.

While the government of Japan had minted 11 million of the coins, an unauthorized 103,000 Hirohito coins, worth an estimated $71 million, were also created by counterfeiters. *Time* magazine (Feb. 19, 1990) reported that the coins were so well made that many were accepted by the Bank of Japan itself. Only microscopic flaws revealed the difference. By tracking the sources of the fake coins, the Japanese came to the doorstep of "an undisclosed Middle Eastern government."

Gold and silver are sought-after storehouses of value when people don't feel comfortable with their government. That's because they fear something is going to happen to the currency, that something meaning inflation and devaluation. If paper money becomes worthless, the holder is stuck with paper, while gold and silver will retain at least some value, as will gems and almost any storable food commodity with a long shelf life. The window is open for counterfeiters, however, when value is added to gold in the form of collectors' coins.

### *Precious Stones*

Precious stones have also been a way to store much value in a small package. Many European Jews prior to and during World War II kept a quantity of diamonds so they could take some savings with them when the time came to flee. And in developing nations, people like to wear their wealth, so jewelry is always in fashion. Precious stones, like other stores of value, must be acquired with caution and respect, because things are not always what they seem to be and the value of gemstones can be arguable.

For example, it is beyond the capacity of an appraiser or even most laboratories to tell the difference between a natural or an artificially produced ruby. This gemstone can now be manufactured with such quality that it looks as good as or even better than the natural version. The only way experts can tell a really good manufactured stone from one produced by nature is that the natural stones have imperfections that show up under magnification, while the artificial ones tend to be closer to flawless. The difference to the investor, however, is whether the ruby is worth $1,000 per carat or upward of $50,000. The only way to know whether it is authentic is with a certificate; unfortunately, it is no problem for someone passing an artificial gemstone to also pass a phony certificate of authenticity on it.

Precious stones, it must be added, change in value relative to one another. Alexander the Great, for instance, believed that lapis lazuli was his most valuable treasure. Today, lapis is much less valuable than it was in ancient times. Topaz, once considered the highest concentrated form of wealth centuries ago, is now barely considered valuable.

The four precious stones are diamond, ruby, sapphire and emerald (which is beryl). All other gemstones are generally referred to as "semiprecious." Gemstones are measured in carats, a unit of weight equivalent to about 200 milligrams. A karat, on the other hand (with a "K" rather than a "C"), is the measure of purity of gold. Pure gold is "24 karat," but it is so soft in its pure state that it would quickly wear away. That is why it is alloyed with tin to make 18-, 14- or 10-karat gold for jewelry production. In the past, it was often alloyed with silver. Diamond is actually 100 times more abundant than sapphire or ruby, and yet it is frequently much more costly to buy. There are two reasons for this: Diamond has become a symbol of a man's love for his woman; value was added, in other words, through emotional significance. Plus, value was created in diamond through artificial scarcity. The DeBeers cartel in South Africa sells only enough diamonds to not completely satisfy demand, and that causes prices to ratchet up. DeBeers even bought up Russian diamond mines when the country was still part of the Soviet Union.

A Russian Grade A cubic zirconium has the same characteristics and appearance as a diamond. As a matter of fact, one of the authors owns a ring with several diamonds as a border to a larger cubic zirconium, and virtually no one, not even a jeweler, could easily identify which was real and which was artificial without an electronic device called a GEM instrument. (How come the mixed stones in a single ring? When the center diamond fell out, he had no desire to pay the cost of a replacement.)

Our advice to the uninformed investor is to be cautious when acquiring gemstones. They do have value, but they are not as liquid as promoters may have you believe. Terry once sold a house for a suitcase of gemstones that were appraised at $1 million. It seemed like a good deal at the time. Each stone came with its own certificate of authenticity, and the plan was to ultimately liquidate them for cash. The acquired gemstones, unfortunately, turned out to be worth nickels and dimes on the dollar if he wanted to sell them quickly. The market simply could not absorb that volume of product without destroying their value. If sold off more slowly, however, they were worth dollar for dollar. The gemstones were not phony—it's just that their value was a function of supply and demand and the size of the market.

And it was because of these gemstones that we can impart another important lesson learned: Just because you can't get full cash for something immediately, that does not mean you can't use what you have in order to get what you want. Terry eventually spent some of those gemstones to buy three condos in Hawaii. (It was because of that transaction, incidentally, that he took the course from the Gemological Institute of America to become a certified gemologist.)

Another reason for caution when dealing in gemstones, you will likely pay as much as *four times* the wholesale cost for colored stones if you make your deal through a normal jeweler. To "keystone" is to double the price of a product. In the jewelry business, believe it or not, to double keystone, or charge four times the wholesale price, is the norm.

The only reality in pricing is between a knowledgeable buyer and a knowledgeable seller. Past the hard manufacturing cost of production, value is based strictly on perceived rarity. That's why "knowledgeable" is the operative factor in a market as complex as gemstones.

### *Nuts & Bolts*

Gemstones are not the only non-cash objects counterfeited. Anything of high added value is subject to copying, including industrial products. Airplane parts, for instance, are easy targets. *Time* magazine cited the Flight Safety Foundation's 1994 report that attributed six fatal accidents and at least 20 other incidents to unapproved, or "knockoff," aircraft parts. An estimated $1 billion worth of these parts sit in the inventories of the U.S. aviation industry.

There are 4,000 airplane parts brokers and distributors in the U.S. alone, essentially unregulated and unlicensed. At least one South Florida individual switched from selling drugs to airplane parts because the money was better and he preferred the people he met. Aircraft parts are expensive: A windshield for a Boeing 747 can cost $45,000. A locking pin for the tail section of a Convair 580 turbine can cost $148 if made properly, but a counterfeit can be made from a 50-cent bolt. It was such a false locking pin that was responsible for the death of 55 people in a crash off Norway.

Even mundane goods such as bolts have been the target of forgers. Imitation bolts have been responsible for countless instances of equipment breakdowns and malfunctioning hardware, plus at least one collapsed bridge and the death of a Tennessee construction worker when a girder fell. In May of 1989, *Forbes* magazine reported that the U.S. military was able to reduce the presence of fake bolts from 30 percent of its supply to 6 percent through testing and barring of violating contractors.

### *Everyday Things*

The medicine you take may be a knockoff. Hundreds of millions of dollars' worth of pharmaceuticals produced by people other than the manufacturers are in the distribution system. Javid Naghdi, an Iranian national, was arrested in England in 1988 for trying to sell 100 million bottles of counterfeit tablet versions of the ulcer drug Tagamet (since deregulated) for $27 million. According to *FDA Consumer* (April 1989), he had previously been convicted in the U.S. on charges of conspiracy, manufacture and distribution of a fake version of the arthritis drug Naprosyn and for trafficking in goods bearing counterfeit trademarks. Rather than serve time, he fled to England. Naghdi got caught there because the real manufacturer of Tagamet, SmithKline Beecham of Philadelphia, got wind that someone was offering $700 million worth of their products without their authorization. The Iranian worked with associates in Austria, Mexico, England and the U.S. to copy and distribute these drugs.

In this case the drugs being sold may, or may not, have been chemically identical to the brand-name products. What the counterfeiters were stealing was the value of the research that went into developing and marketing the drugs as well as the credibility established by the trade names. In much of the piracy that has taken place with value-added products, technology has played a major part in making the copies possible. Yet it is in the more mundane things of value printed on paper that the new technology has cut the greatest swath.

### *To Steal a Song*

Theft of artistic properties is everyday business in China. From 1991 to 1993, the number of CD pressing plants increased from three to 26, and most of them churned out pirated music. They either copy entire albums or mix tracks from more than one source. Tourists from Hong Kong to China's Shezhen economic zone find they can buy discs in bulk for $3 each, or about a quarter of the cost in Hong Kong.

Here is where technology has become savior as well as Satan of the artist. In the effort to give the customer ever-superior products, music has been sold on compact discs. The quality on CDs is so good, however, that each one is capable of being used as a master to produce more.

As legitimate CD manufacturers compete for greater efficiency and quality, they sell off their old machines, some of which wind up in the hands of pirates. Add to this China's pressing need to generate hard currency, and it is easy to see how theft of artistic products has provoked an international conflict in relations between China and the U.S. China overlooks, or even encourages, the piracy because much of the product is sold overseas for dollars. The capacity of the 26 factories is estimated to be about 65 million CDs per year. Because this is ten times the number of CDs sold in China, though, it is reasonable to assume that most of them will eventually find their way abroad.

### *A Fishy Deal*

Izabel Lam was a somewhat successful Hong-Kong born fashion designer and sculptor when she met Tim McCarthy at a New York cocktail party. She told him about her frustrations in the fashion business and showed McCarthy some of her designs. She loved to SCUBA dive and was entranced by what she saw underwater—especially the free-flowing seaweed, coral and other aquatic creatures. These undersea forms became the focus of her bronze sculptures. McCarthy realized how beautiful these shapes would look as silverware, and the two joined together in a business to produce them.

Her artistic vision and his practical business sense created unique goods. They had made something from nothing. Objects of artistic origination have the capacity to become the highest value-added products on the market. It's too bad they are also the kinds of value it is hardest to protect.

No American manufacturer would produce Lam's exotic designs, so she and McCarthy took them to a partner in Thailand. He arranged to have her patterns produced and shipped to customers he would obtain. But it seemed to take forever to get deliveries from the factory. Ironically, people kept congratulating him on how well his product was doing in the market.

McCarthy's products were selling briskly throughout Bangkok, but someone else was pocketing the profits: the Thai manufacturer who had appropriated the design and licensed it to fellow bootleg producers. The Thai government was no help, and when McCarthy tried to stop the piracy, his life was threatened, according to a *Time* magazine piece (Oct. 1994). The private detective agency he hired informed him that his designs were going to be marketed big-time in Europe. By the time McCarthy got to a trade fair in Frankfurt, however, the counterfeiters had already blanketed the market with his product, picking up an estimated $6 million that could have been his. Meanwhile, McCarthy has another partner and is trying to sue, but the cream has been already skimmed off that market.

### *Artistic Theft*

The kinds of things most often counterfeited are those in which the major portion of the value comes from some intangible value added, some widely held perception of desirability stemming from unique creation, rarity or association with an artist or other celebrity. That is why works of art can be worth more on a pound-for-pound basis than just about anything else. As with gemstones, however, investing in works of art can be shark-infested waters for the uninformed. A case in point is the vast quantity of artwork on the market bearing the name "Salvador Dalí."

Andrew Decker reported in *ARTNews* in the summer of 1988 that hundreds of thousands of Dalí prints, genuine and otherwise, had flooded American, European and Asian markets since 1980. Called the largest art fraud in history, buyers spent between $625 million and $3 billion on art that was not as it was represented to be. Dalí's wife, Gala, according to Decker, had licensed the rights to make lithographs and etchings of well-known works by the artist. Being ill at the time, the artist wound up selling rights to works he no longer owned.

Sellers of the artwork, in addition, were inaccurately representing reproductions of Dalí's oil paintings and watercolors created years earlier as "originals," which should mean they were personally created and signed by Dalí. Instead, buyers received works that were done by other people and signed by Dalí or by people paid to sign Dalí's name. In the case of works actually authorized by Dalí, he may have supplied presigned paper on which images could be printed.

Another problem is that the same Dalí works of art have been licensed to more than one operator, and many of these have had overruns, which means that more prints than had been agreed to were created, therefore destroying the value of limited edition prints, whose quantity was supposed to be restricted.

"The distinction between the authorized—and arguably original—prints based on new works that Dalí licensed in the '60s and '70s and the authorized lithographic reproductions of old paintings licensed eight years ago is easily lost on collectors," Decker commented. "And sellers have taken advantage of their ignorance by representing lithographic interpretations as original, signed limited-edition prints." Moreover, in addition to the misrepresented reproductions, there were thousands of counterfeit works on the market from publishers in France, Spain and the U.S.

The publishers needed little besides high-quality printing presses, forgers to sign Dalí's name, and false contracts and certificates of authenticity. What they were creating amounted to nothing of more value than a mass-produced poster. The buyers, unfortunately, expected these works to appreciate in value. When the scandal blew up, Dalí washed his hands of it: "This is not my problem," he is reported to have said. "This is a problem of society, of greed, of naïveté. If people want to produce poor reproductions of my work and other people want to buy them, they deserve each other."

### *Plentiful Picassos*

Even when works of art are genuine and authentic, the value in them can be moot because of the illiquid nature of art. Take Picasso, for example. He was one of the most successful and most prolific artists of all time. During the last decade or two of his life he earned between $10 million and $15 million a year, and over his lifetime he had sold $250 million worth of artwork. Unbelievably, he was more productive than the market could absorb. When he died, he still owned and had stored at four villas two thirds of everything he had ever painted, and there are 150,000 works of art bearing his name.

Because there is so much, Picasso's estate has been valued at $3 billion, or 12 times the worth of all the art he had ever sold when alive. If the heirs tried to dispose of these paintings all at once, though, the art would lose most of its value. Practically everyone knows Picasso's name, yet most of the people who own one of his works could not sell it today if they wanted to. A $200,000 Picasso once couldn't be sold for cash in a roomful of millionaires.

Sotheby's held an auction of Picasso, and, out of 200 originals, submitted only 40 for sale to a room filled with 220 collectors. A mere 18 paintings were sold that day. And yet, the 18 that sold set the value for the remaining ones. This is the remarkable thing about the value of art. If you have 100 paintings and put two on the market and they sell for $250,000 each, then the remaining 98 in your garage are each considered equal in value. The next time a piece from the same artist is brought into the marketplace, an appraiser will look at the price paid for the last pieces.

One artist we know of learned that a philanthropist was about to donate $100,000 to a charity. Thinking quickly, the artist convinced the philanthropist to buy at auction a painting he had donated to the charity. Thereafter, the artist had documentable evidence that his paintings sold for as high as $100,000 for a single piece. Then the artist spread the rumor that he was dying of cancer. The value of his painting skyrocketed, he sold out his stock and went underground. Winding up eventually in Thailand, the artist changed his name and style, and hired scores of Thai artists to crank out artwork under his new identity.

Does this mean that art is a bad investment? Not necessarily. Does it mean that anyone, and especially the uninformed, should exercise great caution when "investing" in art? Absolutely. But as we shall soon see, artwork and similar collectibles have uses other than hanging on a wall; they are excellent vehicles to exit from illiquid assets.

Why all this attention to counterfeit currency and other things? It is to create a new way of understanding regarding the exchange of value. Too often people wrongly place their trust in things that seem real but are not, and disdain the things that seem unreal but are very real indeed.

SECTION

# New Money—New Questions

TWO

# 7

# Bill Gates Versus the Luddites

*"The chief characteristic of the volitional act is the existence of a purpose to be achieved, the clear vision of an aim."*
Robert Assagioli

"As I have said many times in my sleep, 'To Hell with Bill Gates'." These are the words of writer Kurt Vonnegut, explaining why he refuses to get rid of his typewriter and buy a computer. Vonnegut speaks for many people. He represents those whose VCR continually flashes "12:00." He stands for everyone for whom "going on line" has something to do with fishing. He speaks for the computer illiterate.

Vonnegut's reaction to technology is mild, though, compared to some. Kirkpatrick Sale, for example, an environmentalist and historian of the Luddite movement who lives in Manhattan, smashed a personal computer with a sledgehammer before he gave a lecture at the New Jersey Institute of Technology, according to the *Wall Street Journal* (April 12, 1996).

Who are the Luddites? They are everyone to whom advancing technology is a threat. They were originally a group of English workers who, between 1811 and 1816, tried to halt the introduction of labor-saving equipment by burning factories and destroying machines. They are said to be named after Ned Lud, an imbecile who broke two mechanized knitting machines.

Today they are the millions who are not marching to Bill Gates' cadence. They even held a Luddite Congress in Barnesville, Ohio, in 1996, and attendees were encouraged to travel there by train. Vonnegut has correctly identified Gates as the Luddites' enemy, because more than any other individual, he is setting the pace for the advent of the future. "Get comfortable with computers," Gates advises. "Those who don't will be left behind."

Bill Gates is head of Microsoft, the corporation whose programs run 85 percent of the world's 150 million personal computers. At this writing he is also one of the two wealthiest men in the country, and he came to that fortune faster, younger and using fewer natural resources than any other individual in the history of mankind.

More important than the money he made for himself is the change he made in how wealth is created. He sells tools that others have, in turn, used to make themselves rich. He constantly creates new tools we simply have to have. He calls these "killer applications," or "killer aps" for short. These are uses of technology "so attractive to consumers that it fuels market forces and makes an invention all but indispensible." It is this indispensibility of his products that has given Gates a form of world control.

There is no software company in a position to challenge Bill Gates, but the neo-Luddites emerge as his opponents. In his book, *The Road Ahead*, Gates writes: "A Luddite might ask, 'If Churchill had used a word processor, would his writing have been better? Would Cicero have given better speeches at the Roman Senate?'

"Such critics have a notion that because great things were achieved without modern tools, it is presumptuous to suggest that better tools might elevate human potential." As Gates sees it, "Informational tools are symbolic mediators that amplify the intellect rather than the muscle of their users." In other words, software makes it possible for minds somewhat less than Churchill's or Cicero's to achieve more than they would have unassisted.

"How many have the talent to become a Steven Spielberg, a Jane Austen, or an Albert Einstein?" Gates asks. "We know there was at least one of each, and maybe one is all we're allotted. I cannot help but believe, though, that there are many talented people whose aspirations and potential have been thwarted by economics and their lack of tools. New technology will offer people a new means with which to express themselves." Gates' tools are for more than expression. "Because the most efficient businesses have an advantage over their competitors, companies have an incentive to embrace technologies that make them more productive." His tools mean wealth, power—even survival.

But every action produces a reaction, and the people Gates said will be "left behind" are coalescing into an anti-technology movement. The neo-Luddite manifesto was published in the early 1990s in the *Utne Reader*. Several of its followers practice a back-to-the-land, anti-modern lifestyle. And their models are, naturally enough, the Amish (see Chapter 4) who, with their black clothing and horse-and-wagon existence dispense with just about everything of the modern age. "The Amish are in some sense an ideal, because they combine a rejection of technology with a spiritual attachment to the land that I think is essential," according to Sale. The Luddites held their convention in a rural area of Ohio where many Amish live.

To the Luddites, the pace Gates is setting is unbearable. Sale said, "The control of technology at this moment is absolutely undemocratic," in that it rests with corporations rather than individuals and communities. The *Wall Street Journal* commented, "The sense that people are serving machines, and not the other way around, is what most irks Luddite sympathizers. To describe what, in her view, are technology's ravages on both mind and body, Chellis Glendenning (a psychologist in New Mexico) has coined the term 'technoaddiction.' And with a nod to 12-step programs, she exhorts the stricken to 'recover from Western civilization'."

But recovery from the addiction is not very likely when technology's "pusher," Bill Gates, is driven like a missionary to spread the gospel of the future. So, it's either keep up with Bill Gates or be left behind. That is true not just for companies, but for everyone in the workforce, and there's the rub. The Software Revolution is to service workers what the Industrial Revolution was to manual laborers. Both kinds of work lose market value because they become cheap and abundant. This is not an issue to Gates in the larger sense, because people no longer needed in one area can work in another, and the net result is that "more gets done." But the displacement brings stress to those left out—those who may lack the energy and imagination to retrain, let alone to become entrepreneurs.

Gates has teams of programmers writing software to help experts such as financial planners, for instance, do their work better. It is just as likely, though, that the software he develops will wind up in the hands of consumers who no longer will need those financial planners. It's not just secretaries who have to fear for their jobs now. Bill Gates' goal is to give everyone the same access to information that is available to the heads of the wealthiest corporations. He can produce software that will enable consumers to replicate professional services, from writing wills to picking stocks.

### *A New Napoleon*

It is no wonder that some identify him alternately as the Anti-Christ or the Messiah. There was even a rumor in the mid-1990s that Microsoft was buying the Roman Catholic Church. In junior high school, Gates studied Napoleon, and, like the great French emperor, Gates came to power through leading a revolution.

"Small businesses arguably have been the greatest beneficiaries (of personal computers), because low-cost hardware and software have permitted tiny outfits to compete better with large multinational corporations," he wrote in *The Road Ahead*. Gates empowered small business; he gave the little guys the ability to turn the tables on the big boys.

Before Gates, in the mid-1970s, financial writer Andrew Tobias suggested that giant corporations would dominate the economy. In that era, why would anyone have thought otherwise? When the Fortune 500 list was compiled in 1954, such companies accounted for 37 percent of Gross National Product. By 1979, a quarter century later, they accounted for 58 percent, observed John Case, writing in "The Wonderland Economy" for *Inc* magazine. Big corporations had increased their share of the manufacturing workforce from half to three quarters in the same 25 years.

Could the trend ever swing the other way? Could any force on earth possibly halt and reverse this immutable, glacial movement toward bigness? At their apex in 1979, the biggest manufacturers employed 16.2 million workers. But by 1993, that number was down to 11.5 million. The largest service companies increased employment only slightly.

And yet, there were 20 million new jobs created at the same time, mostly in small businesses. The decline in manufacturing jobs came from foreign competition rather than from personal computers, which happened to come along just in time to give marginalized workers the opportunity to become self-employed.

Many small businesses acknowledge their champion. "Gates leveled the playing field," said John Boone, co-president with his wife, Lori, of Employment Trends, a Beaverton, Oregon-based temporary help service. The Boones were able to build their business successfully under the noses of older, bigger competitors, thanks to tools provided by Gates' Microsoft.

"A national company would have no cost advantage over us" in the data processing necessary to operate the business, Boone said. Employment Trends began with a single personal computer that allowed the Boones to make professional presentations so they could get business. As their company grew, they added power through client-server computing, rather than by buying an expensive mainframe computer. Consequently, they have been able to expand their information capability incrementally, and at a fraction of the cost. Boone has spent about $80,000 for a number of PCs and a server—all operating together with Microsoft programming—that give capabilities that would until recently have cost hundreds of thousands or even millions. "We couldn't have done this 15 years ago," he said.

### *Microsoft Network*

"The information highway will open undreamed-of artistic and scientific opportunities to a new generation of geniuses," writes Gates. And the Microsoft Network gives an entryway to the Internet through Windows 95. Gates has given a new opportunity to entrepreneurs. Kevin Andersen of Accounting and Consulting Firms International (ACFI) refers to his association as "a conglomeration of local accountants with global coordination in a strategic alliance." And that has been made possible through the Microsoft Network (MSN).

The 30-plus firms in Andersen's alliance are based in the U.S., Europe, the Pacific Rim and Latin America, but they can be reached at the click of a mouse through MSN's Entrepreneur's Forum. This forum offers selected small firms icon positions on the MS Network screen, and for those seeking accounting, ACFI is the icon that is available.

That's valuable positioning—like being the Howard Johnson's on the turnpike—and Andersen got it for his band of accountants by convincing the people at Microsoft that MS Network users were better off dealing with entrepreneur-level accounting firms than they were Big Six conglomerates.

Through ACFI, a business person in Denver can have any necessary accounting and business service performed in Europe, let alone anywhere else in the world, and everything can be conducted by way of a desktop computer and modem. The business person can e-mail the accountant in the desired country, or even communicate in real time in a private chatroom. Records of transactions will be automatically captured electronically and transferred to the right departments. And all of this with no long-distance charges.

Compare that speed and flexibility with the current way of doing business: figuring out the hour of the night or day overseas, long-distance phone calls, letters that can take several days, travel. It seems archaic by comparison. It would be possible to find accountants on the Internet, but it would be much more difficult. Gates has made it easy to do business his way.

"Small companies don't need to go to a Big Six accounting firm that is more expensive and gives worse service," Andersen maintains. With such a network of local accounting firms, small businesses can strike up personal relationships on the other side of the world.

ITEX Corporation, operator of the ITEX Trade Exchange, also has its own position on the Microsoft Network. "This means that anyone using Gates' Entrepreneur's Forum who wants to do business through barter will find us," says Michael T. Baer, ITEX president.

"Of course, those wanting to find ITEX on the Internet have only to go to our home page: http://www.itex.net. Our BarterWire electronic trading service makes it possible to do business around the world without cash." (More about that later.)

### *Gates and the Balance of Power*

The world has not seen the likes of Bill Gates in a long time, perhaps not ever. If he continues to be successful, he may be remembered as one of those towering figures of the 20th century, certainly in the history of money. He has held private meetings with Jiang Zemin, president of China. Their pictures have appeared together, as if they are chiefs of state convening a summit conference.

Gates has met with the leader of China at least twice as of this writing, which is once more than the President of the United States. Perhaps that's because the pragmatic Chinese know what real power is. The President of the U.S. is an elected official, a public employee who could be fired at the whim of the voters. But Bill Gates leads the company that is transforming the world.

The irony of this obeisance is that China was the country from which sprang the maxim: "Power grows from the barrel of a gun." Thanks to Gates, it is truer to say: "Power springs from the software of a computer."

"Like one of the great sea powers of old, Microsoft today controls access to the modern lanes of communication," wrote Thomas L. Friedman for the *New York Times*. "Microsoft operating systems run 85 percent of the world's personal computers. Microsoft doesn't need Washington to open doors for it because foreign governments are begging Microsoft to come in and translate Windows 95 into their languages, so they can get on the information highway."

Steve Ballmer, who is second to Gates at Microsoft, told Friedman: "People say, 'You have this technology. We hear it's changing the world. Tell us how it can help us.' "

Gates is changing the balance of power between generations. He is, at this writing, in his early 40s, and the median age of his 18,700 employees is 27. Contrast this with the finding published in the

*Indianapolis Star* that about a third of white males over the age of 54 are unemployed.

One finding of historical economist Claudia Goldin, whose work was reported in the *Wall Street Journal*, is that rapid technological change helps some workers while hurting others. The article described the advent of the computer as "an era in which the premium that employers pay to workers with skills, education and computer know-how has been rising and wages of people without those advantages have been receding."

Goldin learned that in the decades before World War II, the most high school graduates were attracted to the new industries as well as by businesses that sold or serviced relatively new products, such as autos. Today the new frontier is computers and the Internet. Because of the rapid changes, the balance of economic power between generations is being upset. In the past, the experience of older workers was rewarded with job security. But if that experience is with outmoded technology, it is actually a detriment, which is why workers over 50 now are displaced by younger, more technically adept employees.

Familiarity with computers empowers the young and divides the generations. "Just tell kids, 'We're going to take your computers away,' and see what happens," Gates says. As he shifts power between generations, he does the same between companies.

### *Gates the Pioneer*

As kids in suburban Seattle in the '60s and '70s, Bill Gates and his pal Paul Allen were fascinated by the new personal computer kits becoming available. The two became friends in high school and hung out in the computer lab, where Gates wrote his first program to play tic-tac-toe.

The earliest computer kits were little boxes with 48K and 64K of RAM. Few of them could share any software. An application written for one brand was used on that one only. It was like the early days of automobiles, with gasoline, diesel, electric and steam all running around together at once and no interchangeability of parts.

Even as school kids, Gates and Allen sensed there was money to be made from computing. One of their first projects was to make a device that counted traffic. In 1975 they wrote BASIC for the MITS Altair 8800 computer—the first language for computers. It was the beginning of a new age.

One of the easiest of the computers of the '70s was the Apple II, and one reason it was good was that the company Gates and Allen founded, Microsoft, provided the software for it. And when IBM decided to launch its Personal Computer in 1980, Gates and Microsoft produced the operating system for it. That programming has become the near-universal standard for all subsequent PCs: MS/DOS, or Microsoft Disc Operating System. It is cumbersome to use and requires knowledge of arcane codes, but it was more useful than anything else that had been written to date. Gates could see MS/DOS potential to standardize PC machine languages, and he kept the right to syndicate it.

The new tools put older companies at the same disadvantage as older employees. They couldn't keep up with the changes. Back then, IBM was the corporate giant that seemed to control the world. But even IBM was outsmarted by Bill Gates, then a kid in his mid-20s. Gates teamed up with Intel Corp., which produced the microprocessors that are at the heart of most personal computers, to encourage other entrepreneurs to create clones of the IBM PC.

The rest is history. Clones were cheaper and, many say, better than the IBM PC. The public loved them, and applications writers produced a cornucopia of programming for them. All this was not on the agenda for IBM. The giant computer company had treated software more as a service than a product, according to Brent Schlender writing about Gates in *Fortune* (Jan. 16, 1995). IBM, Hewlett-Packard and Digital Equipment Corp. charged an annual fee for use of their software and maintenance, upgrades and modifications. But Microsoft sold the software outright.

"In the 1980s the Justice Department spent years investigating IBM, only to find that the rise of the PC had left the firm a shadow of its former self," notes *The Economist*. As a matter of fact, in 1983 *Business Week* ran a cover feature proclaiming: "The winner is ... IBM." And yet a mere decade later, *Inc* magazine noted a milestone:

"In case you haven't noticed, Microsoft is fast closing in on IBM in total market value. As of April 14, the market value of Microsoft stock came to $24.9 billion, compared with $28 billion for IBM. Microsoft, you may recall, was an Inc 500 company in 1984 and 1985. It will thus become the first Inc 500 company to overtake IBM—although not necessarily the last."

While Microsoft was growing, IBM was downsizing. A large body of IBM expatriots are now entrepreneurs, probably using the tools devised by Bill Gates. The young, imaginative entrepreneur ate the lunch of the old, established corporation.

Gates' competitors are often pleased when the U.S. Department of Justice investigates Microsoft for unfair competition. Microsoft's Windows program embedded MS/DOS within itself. It also incorporates many programs—from word processors to disk utilities—that used to be stand-alone products from other companies, some of which went broke, observed *The Economist*. Because Gates controls the operating system, he can include competitors' functions as part of Windows.

One of the tactics Microsoft is accused of is writing its software to disable that of its competition. Microsoft Plus!, a companion to Windows 95, places Microsoft's Internet Explorer icon on the screen. But in the process, it is said to overwrite Internet software of competitors such as Prodigy and Netscape. When that happens, it becomes simpler to enter the Internet with Microsoft's own on-line service. According to Mike Elgan, editor of *Windows* magazine, Microsoft competitors are "just looking for anything they can find.... The Justice Department action is absolutely absurd."

Or is it?

### *The Quest for Security*

Evan Simonoff, editor-in-chief of *Financial Planning* magazine, in his October 1995 issue, recounted a conversation between an individual and an official of Merrill Lynch about that company's competition. "While I haven't confirmed it with the Merrill's CEO, this source says Merrill ranks Microsoft number one and Charles Schwab & Co. number two" as competitors.

Simonoff observed that Microsoft ranks high on the list of many companies' competitors. Microsoft is to software what Xerox used to be to copiers. Microsoft dominates the software industry (an industry that grew by 11 percent in 1994, making it the fastest growing service business in America, according to *The Economist*, July 1995).

Gates would like to have the repeat business IBM used to have. To be able to buy software meant independence for the purchaser, but for Gates it meant every sale was closed-ended, and without steady income.

"It's not like it's an overnight crisis or something, but in the long run, Microsoft's got to get most of its revenue from repeat customers rather than new ones," Gates told *Fortune*. To sell again to the same customers, Microsoft expanded from operating systems to applications such as word processors and spread sheets. Microsoft also introduced planned obsolescence into software with products such as Windows 95. But Gates could see a new horizon.

That's what led him to a grand ambition: "This new, electronic world of the information highway will generate a higher volume of transactions than anything has to date, and we're proposing that Windows be at the center, servicing all those transactions." With his domination of the software scene, Gates is poised for one of the biggest nonmilitary power grabs in history. If he is one of the richest men in the world now, it is only small change compared to what could be on the horizon.

Gates tried to buy Intuit, the maker of Quicken, for $1.5 billion—at a 50 percent premium over its stock price. Quicken is the software used by millions of people to manage their finances, from balancing their checkbooks to conducting banking and paying bills. It is an application so universally useful that people simply have to have it; it's the classic "killer ap." Gates' competitors pressed the Justice Department to intercede, and, under threat of anti-trust action, he withdrew from the deal.

Why is this important? Because if Gates, with his control of the Windows operating system, can also make it easy for people to use his financial management software and his gateway to the Internet, and can become partners with banks and credit card companies, he can control commerce.

This means that not only every time an individual pays a monthly bill, but also every time a factory, retail establishment, corporate database, stock exchange or credit card company pays its bills, Bill Gates will be there—*taking a cut!* This possibility turns even bankers into Luddites. The banking industry takes the Microsoft challenge very seriously, ever since Gates called banks "dinosaurs." Hugh McColl, the CEO of NationsBank, warned that banks could go the way of railroads unless they meet the challenges of online banking services. The day is coming, he said, when consumers might identify financial services more closely with technology companies such as Microsoft than with banks.

### *Gates and Change*

In the end, Gates is the apostle of change in a world that would prefer to be comfortable. Gates has said that many people predicted 150 years ago that farm mechanization and the industrial revolution would eliminate most jobs. "That same misprediction can be made here. That's not to say there won't be some people whose skills or location won't match the way things change." But, he said, "We all have to deal with change, and the U.S. is in a better position to do this."

Perhaps he's right. Maybe it is the destiny of the United States to lead the charge into the future, into the new frontiers of electronic currency and the Internet, with our own Bill Gates as the one blowing the bugle. Yet it is also true that it is human nature to resist change, no matter how appealing. And as long as that is who we are, there will be Luddites who can't or won't keep pace. The young will continue to gain dominance over the old; newer, smaller businesses will upset the more established ones.

Gates has seen the future, and to him it is the Internet. Therefore, he has reorganized his company to focus on new opportunities there. "Microsoft goes through this every few years," according to Richard

D. Owens, a securities analyst. "They reorganize, refocus, restrategize—whatever you say. It has proven successful."

The head of Microsoft plans to make access to the Internet so easy and inexpensive that almost anyone can go online. If he truly succeeds in that effort, Gates may even win over the Luddites. If not, they will be left even further behind—their cash stolen from them as happens to the Amish—because the Internet is intimately involved in the future of money, as we shall see.

# 8

# The Meaning of the Internet

*"People find new information distinctly threatening, because if they incorporate it they will have to do a good deal of work to revise their maps of reality, and they instinctively seek to avoid that work. Consequently, more often than not they will fight against the new information rather than for its assimilation."*
M. Scott Peck, *The Road Less Traveled*

The Internet could become a more important development than the telephone or television. The authors believe the impact will be more like the telephone *multiplied by* the impact of television. Understanding the Internet is critical for anyone who wants to know the future of money.

"No communications medium or consumer electronics technology has ever grown as quickly; not the fax machine, not even the PC. At this rate, the citizens of cyberspace will outnumber all but the largest nations," according to *The Economist* of July 1, 1995. "PCs put computing power in the hands of ordinary people; the Internet gives them something compelling to do with that power."

If the Internet is frontier territory, how can it be defended? It is an international medium with no central company, country or standards body exercising anything more than symbolic authority. If you outlaw something in one country, it can spring up in another. "It's what technicians call a distributed network, and it's a censor's worst nightmare," according to Gina Smith, writing in *Popular Science* (Jan. 1996).

### *Treasure Chest or Pandora's Box?*

Pandora, as Greek myth has it, was the first mortal woman sent to earth by Zeus; her arrival was to be a curse for the theft of fire by Prometheus. Zeus gave her a box and, like Eve, Pandora yielded to temptation and opened the box. Out of it flew all the evils of human existence, and no one could put them back into the box. A later version of the myth suggests that Pandora let all human blessings escape and be lost, leaving only hope.

There are many government officials around the world who, for a number of reasons, think the Internet has become Pandora's Box. Out of it have sprung pornography and hate material, and new enemies who dislike more about the Internet than its content. The Net, quite possibly, is the best example of Marshall McLuhan's pronouncement in the 1960s, "The medium is the message." More on that later.

Beginning life in 1969 as the Pentagon's Advanced Research Projects Agency (ARPAnet), the Internet came into being as a sword beaten into a plowshare. It connected Defense Department computers around the country into a system that decentralized national security data. Decentralization meant the enemy could not stage a preemptive strike by destroying a single U.S. military headquarters. The network of computers was too vast for nuclear bombs ever to completely destroy.

Eventually the Department of Defense connected its research team with those at half a dozen universities, and in short order the early Net was a tool of communication for academicians. For years, most people with access to it had some connection to a university. Personal computers gave access to businesses and individuals.

Vinton Cerf, a former Stanford professor, has been called the "Father of the Internet" for co-inventing the Internet's computer language, which was introduced in 1974. He was the one who persuaded network users around the world to adopt common standards to make information exchange easier. He eliminated barriers between hardware and software, wired, satellite or mobile access.

The World Wide Web is the European-invented segment of the Internet featuring a Windows-like environment with graphics, 3-D, text, video and audio, enabling companies and individuals to create their own Web sites. Finally, in 1993, when the Mosaic browsing software hit the market, the World Wide Web became usable by the population at large. It was the addition of graphics and "search engines" that lowered the barrier to entry to the Internet so that any reasonably intelligent person could use it.

Unfortunately, the Internet soon became like a party where anyone is invited, and the undesirables didn't take long to show up. Pornography became available in the Alt (for "alternative") section of Newsgroups. And hate and racist organizations put the Net to use to proselytize and even transfer homemade bomb recipes. The Net, in other words, turned into a Pandora's Box, allowing all sorts of evil into the world.

The Net, however, can also be employed for internal control, and has already been instrumental in a Secret Service sting operation. Setting up a "swag shop" in cyberspace—a place where stolen goods are traded—the Secret Service advertised illegally obtained cellular telephones and credit card data, and, after eight months of investigation, arrested half a dozen people.

One service company, Commercial Information Systems, Inc., in Portland, Oregon, offers to use the Internet to research public records everywhere about potential employees' backgrounds, including criminal/civil court records, assets, vehicle registration. This type of service can make it virtually impossible for anyone to outrun the past.

### *International Strife*

The Internet has become a major bone of contention around the world. "As foreign governments come to understand the power of the Net, they will search quite unapologetically for ways to control it," said Stewart Baker, former general counsel of the National Security Agency in *Wired* magazine in 1995. As online services expand abroad, he asked: "What will stop foreign governments from regulating their content, both directly and indirectly? And since the Net is a seamless whole, what will prevent such censorship from limiting our own access to information?"

We don't think his worries have much substance. When the French tried by sending police to shut down two Internet providers whose users spread pedophilia material, other Internet services went on strike. As recently as May 1996, France was temporarily cut off from the rest of the world to prove the key point: Internet providers are like telephone companies that are not liable for obscene telephone calls sent across their lines. Telecommunications Minister François Fillon was forced to agree that Internet providers should not be held liable for words and pictures placed there by users.

The Internet has only a minor presence in China. Estimates are that by the middle of the 1990s, only 30,000 Chinese had e-mail addresses, while others estimate that as many as 100,000, mostly university students, may have been online. The government of China is hindering this growth. As authorities tighten control over computer access, even something as innocuous as an Internet club is suspect, reports Seth Faison for the *New York Times* News Service. Participants in Chinese Internet clubs meet in secret and discuss how to avoid government interference.

"The Internet is still very sensitive in China," Faison quotes a 24-year-old Chinese computer technician as saying. "We're not trying to do anything illegal, but if the government finds out about us, we're finished."

The government seeks to control the flow of information over the Internet, the way it monitors telephone and fax transmissions. Any Internet service must be supervised by the Ministry of Post and Telecommunications, so that there will be "healthier development of the exchange of international computer information," according to the New China News Agency. It also said, "Neither organizations nor individuals are allowed to engage in activities at the expense of state security and secrets. They are also forbidden to produce, retrieve, duplicate or spread information that may hinder public order."

But Internet users in China have access to information from many groups of Chinese outside the country who are opposed to government policies. It would be easy to dismiss China's opposition to the Internet as merely a repressive government trying to keep control of its people. We think, to the contrary, that there is more to it than that. Opposition stems from the very origin of the Internet itself as well as to what that origin means.

### *Spreading Ideas*

Now merge Marshall McLuhan's well-known statement, "The medium is the message," with the existence of the Internet. The result is that the most powerful of the Internet's ideas are the ones considered most offensive by an authoritarian regime.

Just as the Internet is decentralized, it is likewise decentralizing. It is structured such that packets of information go from server computer to server computer, taking circuitous routes to reach the final destination. If one link in the chain is broken, the information will simply find another route, like water flowing downhill. There is no headquarters or owner of the Internet. If the Internet is built to withstand nuclear attack, then how can any single government have the power to regulate it?

The Internet now has a life of its own, and is, therefore, impossible to control. That is anathema to authoritarian governments, which believe those in charge know best, and that the general welfare is enhanced when decisions come from a central source and are implemented by those downstream. The Internet, on the other hand, empowers the individual to gather and disseminate information, make contacts and decisions. More than that, the Net challenges the individual to access it. Except for having to meet requirements in educational settings, no one is forced to surf the Net. The individual must decide and act alone to become involved.

Going online takes a lot of initiative, work and investment. In other words, the Net insidiously seduces people into acting like entrepreneurs; it creates in them the souls of Americans. No wonder it poses such a threat to the authoritarian powers of the world.

"America's popular culture is overwhelmingly dominant in the global lifestyle department," observes John Naisbitt in *Global Paradox*. "American music and television and books and magazines, and especially movies, seem to stick out of every corner and nook and cranny of the world, becoming universal." And as he further points out, all this exposure to Americana means that "people want genuine authentic American stuff." Which is to say, American culture is the lifeblood of American business—and therefore prosperity—and the Internet is a powerful way to spread it.

The Internet is the historic heir of the Roman system of roads. For good reason did they say: "All roads lead to Rome." The Roman military built their early highways to conquer and defend territory, but this transportation system became the cement that welded the empire together by stimulating trade. The Internet has similar origins as a military tool, and is similarly becoming the highway for international commerce. Just as the Roman roads ensured Roman dominance of its time, the ARPAnet turned Internet turned World Wide Web gives the coming age an American stamp. And if the centuries of prosperity that stemmed from the Pax Romana, or Roman Peace, are a precursor of what lies ahead for us, then the Internet could indeed usher in a time beyond belief for the United States.

### *Decentralization on the Micro Level*

The Internet is one component of an electronic communications revolution that could literally change the landscape. Understanding how each of these systems functions and how individuals might profit from them is different from understanding how together they might re-create society.

The Marxists used to say of economic conditions that: "A quantitative accumulation results in a qualitative change." What this means is simply that after enough electronic tools have been introduced—"a quantitative accumulation"—there is a "qualitative change"—which means the world becomes a different place. And unlike a political revolution, no one hoisted a flag and proclaimed, "This is it!" Around the world, wherever technological innovations have had an impact, individuals have recognized that their lives have changed.

Millions of people realized it during the storms of the winter of 1996, when workers stayed home in the Northeast U.S. but continued to function through their phones, faxes and computers. There were so many people online, the telephone system could not keep up. It was like everyone who owned an automobile was driving on the same turnpike at the same time.

Bad storms can make the phone lines half again as busy as on ordinary days. But the storm-born crush only speeded up the expansion in telecommunications to serve home-based businesses. The number of Americans working from home increased more than sevenfold between 1984 and 1994, according to the National Association of Home-Based Businesses. The association said there were 45 million home-based workers in 1994 compared with 6 million in 1984. This included corporate employees with a home office in addition to businesses run from home.

"With telephone services the way they are, you've got everything you need at home," association president Rudy Lewis said. "The growth has exploded." He runs his association, representing 200 types of business ranging from software to balloons, from his own home, of course.

There was a time when working at home was what employees wanted. Now employers are demanding it. In 1993, for the first time, involuntary telecommuters outnumbered voluntary ones because companies can avoid the expense of office space in urban centers. Telecommunications also allow routine clerical tasks to be performed anywhere in the world, instead of near the corporate center.

Peter Greis, a consultant for the Ernst & Young accounting firm, said the company is trying to create a mobile corporate structure, with fewer corporate offices. When he goes into a corporate building to work, he is assigned an office for the day as if he had checked into a motel. "We're focusing more on becoming a virtual organization," said Greis, who works out of his home in Dayton, Ohio.

He's not alone. Stuart A. Harrington uses e-mail to operate with one foot in Japan and the other in the U.S. His is a global office, connected to everywhere he needs to be in real time. He is a contract resale distributor in Japan working for OrCAD Inc., a developer of software for electrical engineers. If the Japanese take a liking to a particular program, OrCAD can quickly sell 10,000 copies at $5,000 each. On a busy week Harrington will pass messages and revised versions of software back and forth across the Pacific on electronic bulletin boards. Company executives formerly communicated via air mail and telephone calls, but now those ways are not only too expensive, they also took twice as long to get things done.

Individual businesses have been able to move away from population centers because of faxes, e-mail, Web sites and other tools of the electronic age. This quantitative accumulation of individual decisions eventually makes for a qualitative change in the nature of cities. The full account of what the future may hold for cities awaits you in Chapter 18.

### *Destabilization*

The spread of the technology, in other words, does not bring calm in its wake—quite the contrary. It brings upheaval and change, loss and gain, not just physically but also at the spiritual level. The pornography issue that dominated much of the outcry about the Internet is only the tip of the iceberg and misses the point. At the core of the controversy is not so much what is transmitted on the Internet as that any information be transmitted at all.

To China, the ideas suddenly available to its citizens include information from Human Rights in China and China Spring, New York-based groups; the Center for Modern China, run by the dissident writer Liu Binyan and based in Princeton, N.J.; each offering reports via the Internet available in China and each beyond the ability of the Chinese government to control.

It is instructive that the Internet came to prominence at the same time as the American Militia and Patriot movements, anti-government and decentralist groups who focus on the right to keep and bear arms, who use the Net as a means of communicating and attracting adherents.

The Internet has "unprecedented potential and scope" to give people "incredible power to promote violence, threaten women, denigrate minorities, promote homophobia and conspire against democracy," according to Rabbi Abraham Cooper, associate dean of the 425,000-member Simon Wiesenthal Center. The Los Angeles-based organization seeks to encourage Internet providers and universities to refuse to carry messages that "promote racism, anti-Semitism, mayhem and violence."

Rabbi Cooper sent a letter in early 1996 to America Online, Compuserve, Prodigy, the Microsoft Network and dozens of Internet service providers, in which he said "Internet providers have a First Amendment right and moral obligation not to provide these groups with a platform for their destructive propaganda." And indeed, some of these providers have begun dropping clients who post offensive material.

But these sources of hate can simply establish their own servers. Mark Weber, director of the Institute for Historical Review, which denies that the Holocaust ever happened, said pressure had been brought to bear on his Internet access provider to drop his Web service. "If need be," he said, "we could conceivably set up our own service provider."

And the very fabric of the World Wide Web would be torn if free speech, no matter how dangerous, is abridged, according to the Electronic Frontier Foundation (EFF) a civil liberties group that focuses on computer networks. "The Wiesenthal Center should realize it is not possible to make anti-Semitism or historical revisionism go away by censoring it," according to Mike Godwin of the EFF. "The best response is always to answer bad speech with more speech.... On the net, it's quite clear that whenever anti-Semites or Holocaust revisionists surface with an attempt to purvey distortions or untruths, individual citizens spontaneously respond and correct the record with documentation and facts."

Dozens of Web pages have emerged that directly challenge the hate pages, and some even link their pages to the hate sites. The Internet empowers fringe groups and radicals because it gives them tools with which to communicate that they could not otherwise afford.

The Internet is an electronic projection of early American frontiersmanship, where anything goes and anyone can stake a claim to his or her own domain and have virtual elbowroom. The Net has been called the closest thing to "a functioning large-scale anarchist society that human culture has yet seen." (Jay Kinney, *Wired,* 1995)

The Internet upsets the established order. The White House has bypassed the news media on occasion to deal directly with citizens through Internet forums. At the grassroots level of politics, such as local school affairs and in city government, the Net offers people the opportunity to debate issues.

Activist Jamie Love said, "In 1991 I started posting notices on the Internet, and all of a sudden we were reaching 10,000 people." And it cost them nothing. The Net gave "a tiny group like ours an opportunity to shape the debate." Because the smallest group can have as much exposure on the Net as the largest, "it all looks the same, so the only thing that matters is the merit of your argument," Love told *Common Cause* magazine in the spring of 1994.

The Internet holds the promise of challenging the need for representative democracy. If each citizen can be informed about issues and can express wishes via the Net, why go through the process of electing people as representatives? Internet visionaries dream of a future in which digital communications create a virtual world free of national borders. "Class, hierarchy and even physical location count for nothing on the Internet; in cyberspace, everyone is more or less equal," reports *The Economist* for Jan. 14, 1995.

The goal of the Electronic Frontier Foundation, begun in 1990 by Lotus software founder Mitch Kapor, is to retain the freedom of the Net by keeping government regulations away. These Internet pioneers, according to *The Economist,* "loathe the notion that government, having lost control of the Internet, might regain it simply by enacting new laws. If a single set of beliefs can be said to dominate the politics of cyberspace, it is radical libertarianism—i.e., a belief in keeping the government out of building, running and above all regulating what happens in this chaotic domain."

If someone wants to post a page on the Internet, there is no government agency to issue approval. You just do it. If you want your own domain name, you simply register it with a private organization. If you want to take part in discussion groups, you simply sign up. The message of all this freedom is freedom itself. The message of this new medium is not that the Internet disseminates rebellion, pornography or hatred. The message is not the content of the ideas, debates, contention, disagreement. The message *is* ideas, debates, contention and disagreement.

Clangor, glitz, novelty, excitement, freedom—that's America's stock in trade—that's what we sell. If the Roman roads transported people and goods, then the Internet transports ideas and attitude. Roman roads made the world Roman; the Internet makes it American. It's a wonder more countries don't fight it.

### *On the Plus Side*

The invention may transform the creator. The 1968 movie *2001: A Space Odyssey* began with the image of apelike creatures learning to use bones as tools and weapons. The scene cuts away to a space station in the year 2001. That scene would be completely incomprehensible unless one were familiar with some "current events" of the day. Some anthropologists in the 1960s, for example, held that man's brain evolved from the use of weapons and tools. We are who and what we are, they hypothesized, because our early ancestors learned to kill using weapons.

If that were true then, is it possible that the electronic revolution is having a similar effect on us now? It has become a standard joke that it takes a teenager to figure out how to set the digital clock on a VCR. They have grown up with computers, VCRs, camcorders and video games as well as cable television with remote controls.

It is noteworthy, then, that IQ scores have risen 27 points in Britain since 1942 and 24 points in the U.S. since 1918, with comparable gains throughout Western Europe, Canada, Japan, Israel, urban Brazil, China, Australia and New Zealand, observes Sharon Begley in the *New York Times* News Service, 1996. New Zealand political philosopher James R. Flynn first noticed the phenomenon, commenting that "there is not a single exception to massive IQ gains." Concurring is Yale University psychologist Wendy Williams. "The increase in scores is real, it has been empirically demonstrated, and it is widely accepted."

This shoots holes in the "nature" side and bolsters the "nurture" side of the argument presented in *The Bell Curve*, the controversial 1994 book that argues strongly in favor of the heritability of intelligence and the strong correlation between IQ scores and income.

Height is genetically determined, yet it has been rising, as has intelligence. "Similarly, intelligence may have a genetic basis yet still be subject to environmental influences," writes Begley. "These influences would shape the form that intelligence takes in a particular society."

The environmental influences most likely to have led to increased intelligence have been technology disguised largely as entertainment. Radio and television increased basic vocabulary, but it was video games that improved the ability to assemble a puzzle, a common trait measured on IQ tests. Video games full of action require the player to navigate through space, which is training for the mental paper-folding skill assessed in the Stanford Binet test. UCLA psychologist Patricia Greenfield has said the spread of these image-intense technologies could explain the spurt in IQ scores in the U.S. between 1972 and 1989.

Real world intelligence,which is the ability to learn faster or make creative leaps or do any of the other things we understand as intelligence, is not rising as fast as IQ scores. This is called "the broken link" between IQ scores and intelligence, but those IQ scores do measure intelligence nonetheless, and gains are gains.

The Internet has quietly spread throughout America's schools. At this writing half the nation's classrooms had access to it, up from a third just a couple years ago, and well ahead of the general public. President Clinton set a goal for wiring every classroom in the nation to the Internet by the year 2000.

If the technologies of the 20th century indeed have been responsible for raising basic human intelligence, one can only wonder which is the creator and which the created. It is interesting that human intelligence rises in almost direct proportion to the requirements to operate and create the new tools. How we will become transformed in the future through using the Internet is anyone's guess. And we can hope that the adage from economics, that a quantitative accumulation results in a qualitative change, may someday prove to be true for humanity as well. That is, unless we have become nursemaid to our own creations.

Those reading this book at some time distant from the end of the 20th century will have the luxury of knowing what to call this era, when business just began to be done on the Internet. Will our age become known as the Electronic Revolution, the Communication Age, the Age of the Internet? It was only 20 or 30 years after the fact that historians characterized what was going on at the end of the 19th century as the Industrial Revolution. Observers in the midst of the action saw parts of it, and called it the Age of Steam, or the Machine Age, or the Railroad Age. What will be the overarching reality that will characterize and define the meaning of the entire age?

"Even in this relatively late state in our transition from labor-intensive to information-intensive production and management, the range of options for naming this historic revolution is still wide open," notes David Pearce Snyder, lifestyle editor of *The Futurist* magazine. In other words, until someone tells us otherwise, your name for this period is as good as anyone else's.

Perhaps it will be known as the Digital Revolution, as Nicholas Negroponte, also of *The Futurist*, maintains. "Like a force of nature, the 'digital age' cannot be denied or stopped. It has four very powerful qualities that will result in its ultimate triumph: decentralizing, globalizing, harmonizing and empowering."

We can agree with Negroponte on some of the qualities he observes, but the jury is still out on whether those things are good or bad.

# 9

# Making Money on the Internet

*"The system IS the solution."*
AT&T

Hyperbole, thy name is Internet. Is there anyone alive today who has not heard of this system that allows computers to communicate with and access information from one another? The Internet or the World Wide Web, its more graphic side, has sparked the imagination like nothing else in recent memory.

### *Who Is Making Money on the Web?*

Is there any real substance to the World Wide Web? More important, is anyone making money on it, and if so, how? "Corporations, smelling a land rush of another sort, are scrambling to stake out their own claims in cyberspace," reported *Time* in the spring of 1995. "Every computer company, nearly every publisher, most communications firms, banks, insurance companies and hundreds of mail order and retail firms are registering the Internet domains and setting up sites on the World Wide Web. They sense that cyberspace will be one of the driving forces—if not the primary one—for economic growth in the 21st century."

This sounds so melodramatic we can't help be a little dubious. Maybe it's just that our vision does not reach far enough into the future. "The information superhighway may be mostly hype today, but it is an understatement about tomorrow," according to Nicholas Negroponte, writing for *The Futurist* (Nov.-Dec. 1995). "It will be beyond people's wildest predictions … the access, the mobility, and the ability to make change are what will make the future so different from the present."

Vinton Cerf, president of the Internet Society, was quoted in the *Wall Street Journal* (June 17, 1996), "I'm not at all shy about predicting that by 2005, the Internet will be as big as the telephone." And there are about 660 million telephone lines installed worldwide. If even a fraction of that is true, it is no wonder there is so much excitement. Dan Udoutch, president of Netscape Communications Corp., said he expects 300 million Internet users by the year 2000, with 20 to 30 million users being added each year in the mid-1990s.

Negroponte is not the only one filled with hope. Some grasp at that hope with the desperation of the drowning. George E. Curry, editor of *Emerge* magazine, sees the Internet as the "only chance" for blacks to enter the mainstream of the American economy. "We must seize the opportunity now," he told the National Association of Black Journalists. "This is it—the only way out. If you don't have a computer and aren't online, how are you going to compete?"

Agreeing that computers offer African Americans a unique opportunity is Tony Brown, a black television commentator. "The 21st century will not be a century of black and white. It will be a century of haves and have-nots. The haves will have a computer; the have nots will not." Blacks are not the only ones who feel the pressure the Internet is causing, however. A Time/CNN poll of 800 Americans in 1995 found that 57 percent did not know what cyberspace meant, but 85 percent were sure information technology had made their lives better.

"They may not know where it is but they want desperately to get there," *Time* reported. "The rush to get online, to avoid being 'left behind' in the information revolution, is intense." And well they might feel this way: "A working person who is able to use a computer earns 15 percent more than someone in a similar job who cannot," said *Time*. Wealthy and upper-middle-class families form the bulk of the 30 percent of American households that owned computers in the mid-1990s. And statistics indicate that the United States is already sifting itself out along ethnic lines in computer ownership.

The most recent study, done in 1994 for the National Telecommunications and Information Administration (*The Oregonian*,

March 10, 1996) found that the U.S. population group with the highest household penetration of computers—39.1 percent—was Asian and Pacific Island households, including Japanese, Chinese and Korean families.

Whites, on the other hand, had a much lower percentage of households with computers—28.6 percent. The percentage for Native Americans, including Indians, Aleuts and Eskimos, was still lower—20.7 percent. For Hispanics, the penetration was 13.1 percent. And of African American households, only 11.1 percent had computers, less than a third the percentage of the Asians.

With this knowledge, and with the awareness of how greatly computing can magnify productivity and therefore power and wealth, it's small wonder people feel desperation, as if they were seeing the last helicopter leaving the roof of the embassy, as if the last boat were leaving the dock.

### *Reality Check*

Maybe the desperation is premature, though. Maybe all the hype about the Internet, at least for the time being, is overblown. Mark Stahlman, an interactive-media consultant, dared suggest that the king had no clothes when he proclaimed at the 1995 Aspen "Cyberspace and the American Dream" summit of the Progress and Freedom Foundation, "There is no revolution."

A spokesperson for the foundation cut him short: "People here accept there's a revolution. If you're saying there's not a revolution, it gets us into an old debate we're not going to have." Stahlman did not raise the issue again, the *Wall Street Journal* reported.

To some, the age of the Internet was dead before it even started. "Internet commerce deemed dead: Consultant says businesses can't justify cost of maintaining public presence in cyberspace" was a headline in the January 11, 1996, *Globe and Mail* of Toronto. The article maintained that the Internet as a place to do business has failed and will be replaced by a web of members-only special interests.

"There will be a continued academic and hobbyist environment and then there will be hiving," according to Stephen Arnold, president of Arnold Information Technology of Harrods Creek,

Kentucky. By "hiving" he means commerce will be conducted through the Internet, but in highly active clusters of locations open to narrow constituencies.

"It's over, the party's over, the plane is landing," Arnold is quoted about his assertion that business has not yet figured out how to exploit the Internet for profit. "When companies do an assessment of the payoff of their Internet site, there'll be no proof, no sales, nothing but anecdotes. There will be a backlash against that."

The *Wall Street Journal* cautiously came down on the side of the debunkers in "Future Schlock: Today's Cyberhype has a Familiar Ring" (Sept. 7, 1995). The writer, Daniel Pearl, lampooned the hoopla boosting the Internet by reminding readers that overblown predictions about new technologies have been made in the past. "Claims about the wonders of 'cyberspace' sound all too familiar to those who know the history of the plain old telephone," he wrote.

"Every period has its set of people who are saying, 'There's never been any change like this before,'" observes Carolyn Marvin, communications professor at the University of Pennsylvania at Philadelphia and author of *When Old Technologies Were New.* She observes that "People forget all the predictions that didn't come true." When the telephone was introduced, for example, it was expected to bring peace on earth, eliminate Southern accents, revolutionize surgery and preserve agriculture by saving farmers from loneliness.

A "futurist" of his day, technology watcher S.C. Gilfillan predicted in 1912 that picture phones were coming soon and that "home theaters" would arrive by the early 1930s. People would be able to dial up symphonies, Presidential speeches and Shakespearean plays in three dimensions. And, he predicted, only the best material would survive. H.G. Wells forecast that the telephone would help eliminate traffic congestion by pulling people out of cities. And sociologist Charles Horton Cooley said that "an intricate mesh of wider contacts" would turn people's geographical neighbors into strangers. Novels, orchestras and movie theaters would vanish, and government as we know it might not survive either, he wrote — all because of the telephone.

From our vantage point several decades after the fact, we know such predictions did not come true. The question remains, however, whether these forecasts were merely premature, awaiting some other development for their fulfillment, or whether new technologies simply take us down paths we could not have imagined.

Early advertising for the telephone, it may be pointed out, claimed that the average man would have "the power of ancient emperors" to summon anyone, simply by placing a call. People in power, of course, are no more accessible today than they have ever been, telephone or not. Their answering machines and caller ID and a host of other devices sequester them from "the average man." And even though both Bill Gates and Al Gore are potentially reachable by widely publicized e-mail addresses, it doesn't mean they will click the "reply" button and answer.

One of the Internet debunkers is Claude Fischer, a University of California professor whose research has shown that the telephone has not isolated people from their neighbors. As a matter of fact, 90 percent of telephone calls nationwide, he found, are local. Predictions about revolutionary social change resulting from technology, he maintains, have a shelf life "roughly equivalent to that of a Big Mac."

### *Why the Problem?*

Demonstrating how difficult it is to shop on the Internet, Louis Ericson, writing for *Popular Science* in January 1996, went on a virtual shopping spree looking for, among other things, a house and a sweater. In his search for a house he found that the Web "more resembles a crazy quilt than a carefully woven spider's web. There is no directory or table of contents, much less a real estate section." (As a matter of fact, no single source claims to have the entire Internet catalogued.) And when he finally found a sweater he wanted, he couldn't order it online. He had to disconnect and call an 800 number and talk to a woman who "had no clue what this Web thing is." He said the company's Web site later disappeared. "Many of these Web sites seem to have the shelf life of bananas. Or grow like weeds."

It isn't that the products are not on the Web; it is just too difficult, at least as of this writing, for most people to find them and to buy them. This has kept the Internet below the critical mass of selection it will take to lure large numbers of shoppers. Vinton Cerf believes, however, that Net commerce will grow in a nonlinear fashion. "What will happen, I think, as people sort out how to do commerce on the Net and software supporting it," he said in the *Wall Street Journal* of June 16, 1996, "is you'll see a very fast growth spurt that will look small at the beginning and will therefore be apparently dismissable, only to overwhelm you with a tidal wave when it finally catches. Because it's exponential, the absolute numbers can start out small and get astonishingly big."

### *What Does Work*

The businesses that do well on the Net are those that offer goods hard to find elsewhere. Jeffrey Bezos, founder of Amazon.com (http://www.amazon.com) is a prime example. As the Web's largest bookseller, his company was on its way to posting $5 million in sales its second year in existence. Amazon.com boasts 1.1 million titles, which is five times as many as those stocked in the garden-variety book superstore. Customers can search by author or title, can read reviews of books or offer their own. The *Wall Street Journal* (May 16, 1996) reported that Amazon.com will flash the titles of related books when you select one. If you tell Amazon.com about your favorite authors, it will send you by electronic mail a constant stream of recommendations.

"Although it is a relatively small company, Amazon provides a singular case in which the frequently hyped Web is actually changing consumers' lives," according to *Journal* writer G. Bruce Knecht. "It also suggests how online retailing could change the way publishers market books."

Passport Travel Guide (http://www.webnights.com) developed an interactive Web site under Netscape 2.0 that offers loads of free information and makes money by selling advertising. David Neal, managing director, looks at webnights.com as an independent media source similar to radio and television. "People come to the site, read the listings and then are exposed to the advertising," he said. "If we make the site interesting enough, the advertisers will get good results."

What the guide lists is more than 50,000 hotel, motel and bed & breakfast properties in Mexico, Canada, the Caribbean and the United States. Many of these pay a nominal fee to secure their property's continued listing on the Passport Travel Guide. Plus, there are expanded listings with photography and graphics; for an additional fee to advertisers, the guide arranges direct hotlinks to hotel chain home pages. A user wishing to visit Boston could click on the Marriott at webnights.com and see the hotel both inside and out, and could click on the weather for a five-day forecast. The same user can also click on special events to see what's going on in the Greater Boston area—all free of charge. Said Neal: "We have to make it as interesting as television, because that's who we're competing with."

Michael Sullivan-Trainor of International Data Corp. studies Internet commerce. He said the Web has attracted more than 100,000 retailers, with some spending more than $1 million each on their Web sites. In 1995, though, total sales on the Web amounted to just $324 million, or a little more than $3,000 in sales per retailer.

People shopping the Web in the early days have been looking for specialty items or incredible bargains, according to Charles Legg of Discount Laser Disc (http://www.teleport.com/~dld), a part-time business he runs from his home when he isn't working his day job as a mail carrier. He has found that "The day of doing garden-variety retail on the Web is still a long way down the road." It does not yet draw enough customers for most businesses to use it as an exclusive sales vehicle. Legg says of the $15 monthly charge for his Web page: "It's the best bargain I've ever seen," but he follows that up with the cautious observation that the Internet is not the path to sudden fortune.

"If a company is hoping a Web page will catch some surfers and gain some business from them, I don't think they will have much success," says Jeff Irwin, president of Kaspia Systems Inc., a firm that develops monitoring software for computer networks. This is such a new way of doing business that many sites are still tagged, "Under construction." Businesses using the Web just hope they will have enough time to get it right before a flood of potential customers finds them.

### *Profitable Niches*

The early days of Internet marketing offered exceptional opportunities to niche marketers. No specialties have been too obscure. Kaspia's Irwin told a reporter for Portland's *Oregonian* (Feb. 4, 1996) that when he needed a solenoid to repair his pinball machine, a browser on the Web found 12 pages that mentioned pinball repair. "Within an hour I found a guy in Boston who had the part I needed," he said.

Kent Frutiger sells decorative and vintage plumbing products such as claw-foot bathtubs and pedestal sinks in his A-Ball Plumbing company (http://www.a-ball.com). He stays involved in sites related to plumbing and old-house renovation, and sees the Net as one more way to position himself as a source of decorative plumbing and as an authority. He spends two or three hours a week at it and attends gatherings of business people interested in the Net. His products are obscure, but his Net activities to date yield six to 10 daily requests for information.

Tom Atiyeh of Atiyeh International Ltd. (http://atiyeh.com) is a wholesaler of oriental rugs. While he doesn't sell directly to the customer through the Net, he does have a colorful Web page to steer potential customers to retailers he supplies.

It is easy for niche marketers to get on the Web. One such enterprise, ipd Co., Inc., which sells after-market parts for Volvos through a catalog business, had long contemplated a Web site. Theirs is such a specialty business that it made sense to reach out that way, but they had no idea of how to go about it. "This guy just showed up and said he had scanned our newsletter into his computer and showed it to us, on the Web," according to Scott Hart of ipd. The company had their Web site online, complete with domain name and hotlinks to pages of parts, done for them on speculation, and the entrepreneur charged them $2,800. "It was so inexpensive we couldn't say no," Hart said.

Real estate seems to be doing well on the Web, at least anecdotally. Despite the frustration experienced by Louis Ericson, many home buyers are having success shopping the Web, and agencies are flocking to it. It is possible on the Web to shop for castles in Germany and villas in Italy, not to mention condos in Hawaii and beach houses in Southern California. In cities such as Portland, Oregon, practically every major real estate agency had a Web site by the mid-1990s.

One of them, Reekie Properties, used the full potential of the Web to make its site attractive to potential customers: Reekie's Web site offered the evening's television listings, current weather and ski conditions. With a sound card and Microsoft Explorer Internet software, the house hunter could even listen to music while browsing.

"I want people to look at our real estate Web page not just for real estate but as a resource," said owner Ian Reekie. "Every time they do that, they're being programmed with Reekie Properties. So when they're ready to buy, I hope they'll think of us."

Other agencies' Web sites offer the telephone numbers and addresses of employment agencies, mortgage companies, banks, colleges and universities. There is also information on calculating loan payments and locating a lender. Some list the open houses along with addresses and sometimes pictures. Most Web sites allow the user to type in information about the kind of house they want, including location, number of bedrooms and price range. House shoppers in the New York market can enter a price range and be told how many corresponding properties are available.

Many real estate firms report several thousands of hits per month on their Web sites, often from people out of the area seeking to relocate. Portland, Oregon, agents Barbara and Bob Ramirez report selling homes to customers from Texas and as far as away as England who found what they wanted on their Web site. One of their home buyers even landed his new job through the Web.

Other electronic innovations have revolutionized real estate sales. Instead of the old Multiple Listing three-ring binders, agents now use laptop or notebook computers. They even provide potential homebuyers with discs that can be browsed on their own computers.

### *Where Money Will Be Made*

Debunker Stephen Arnold calls the post-Internet world the

"Intranet," and says the way to make money is to forget about the Web surfers and focus on narrow constituencies.

"I don't want a public user," he said. "I only want members of my constituency who are loyal enough to give me their credit card numbers." He sees a group of services, each with a narrow emphasis and each so desirable that the target market will pay well for them. And advertisers will also pay well because the constituency is so focused.

"The new Yukon gold field is the Intranet," Arnold said. "It's the greatest money-making opportunity in electronic information that has ever been. It looks a lot like the Internet except I'm going to charge you to get in and I'm going to charge you for every mouse click, and you're going to love it." (See Chapter 12, "Electronic Currency.") He hopes that car racing enthusiasts will pay as much as $20 per month to gain access to a Web site where they will be able to hear or see thousands of car race broadcasts each year. He said that more than three quarters of the people he has queried said they would be willing to pay for the information. Half of those people said they did not have Internet connections but would be willing to get them simply to be able to receive his service.

Such select-audience services already exist. Starware Corp. of Bellevue, Washington, offers a premium subscription service with ESPN Sportszone, a sports Web site with audio and video feeds. It hopes in the future to make available to subscribers their choice of any broadcast sporting event in the U.S.

One company, Necx Direct, has become one of the most successful distributors of software by charging a subscription fee for access to their Web site, where new programs can be downloaded. Another "killer ap" for the Internet is an electronic crystal ball. It's called Document Retrieval using Linguistic Knowledge (DR-Link), a software package developed by Syracuse University that will allow online users to ask about the future, such as which companies Microsoft is most likely to buy. If it proves successful, money will be no consideration for those using it. Imagine the profits to a stock brokerage whose employees all make deals like inside traders. "It's so technically sophisticated that buyers don't even ask how much," Arnold said. "The value of the service is such that price isn't even an issue."

Even the information available on the Internet without such a high-powered service can mean money to those willing to use it. That's what one nun learned, as she invests funds from her sisters with information she gains from the Net.

"This is how the individual investor can get information that will help them get a level playing field with the big guys," observed Sister Rene Foster of the Benedictine Sisters of Mount Angel, Oregon. Sister Rene has mastered a program that can give her 100 stock prices per minute from Compuserve, and she also uses Prodigy's investment forums. This nun will be one of the millions expected to be investing over the Net before the turn of the century. Trading is available online through Portfolio Accounting World Wide or PAWWS (http://pawws.secapl.com). This site offers a comprehensive set of services for the would-be online investor: portfolio accounting, securities and market research tools, and stock quotations at 15-minute delays or, for an extra charge, real time. How the investor can feel secure using such an online service is the subject of the next chapter, "Encryption."

Some online services require traders to fill out a few forms online and download the filled-out client agreement. After signing it, traders fax the client agreement to the brokerage office and wire in their money. With the advent of electronic currency, however, even these formalities will become things of the past. Stay tuned for Chapter 12.

### *The Web and Big Money*

The World Wide Web is attracting the kind of money it will take to make something happen. The *Wall Street Journal* (May 26, 1996) reports that Microsoft and Wal-Mart Stores, Inc., have entered into a joint venture, one that could finally find the fabled El Dorado on the Web. So far, unfortunately, the Internet has been a big disappointment for major retailers. Home shopping on the Net has not materialized—at least not enough to satisfy Sears, a joint venturer with IBM in the Prodigy online service. Launched in 1984, Prodigy was a pioneer in online services. "Sears originally invested in Prodigy because they believed home shopping would be a tremendous driver, but that home shopping segment never really took off," according to Peter Krasilovsky, senior analyst for Arlen Communications, a consulting firm for new media.

Later, when Sears announced in 1996 that it was willing to take a $300 million hit on its initial investment in Prodigy in order to unload it, Krasilovsky said it "really was to tell shareholders Sears knows it has a dead fish on its hands, and they're going to dump it and never look back." The announcement sent Sears stock up more than 62 cents.

"For all the hype about the online world, almost no one is making money in it," according to Evan Ramstad of the Associated Press. It takes big money to compete, and those with the money are unwilling to risk it out of fear that an unexpected technological advance could render their investment worthless.

Someone, surely, must be making money online. Organic Online, a San Francisco Web site developer, succeeded in luring such mass marketers as McDonald's, Levis and Colgate-Palmolive. Early presences aimed at consumer information (*Mediaweek*, Oct. 9, 1995). Organix has done sites for Volvo, Saturn, Microsoft and MCI. While there is no information yet on how well these advertisers did on the Net, there is information on the company that put them there. It took only two years for Organix to become one of the top developers of Web sites for major marketers. The firm doubled its 1994 gross revenue in January of 1995 alone. Although the company may not continue to grow that fast, executives do expect Organix to continue its "exponential" growth.

### *What It Will Take*

The Internet is not going to truly take off as a money-making engine until two things happen. First, there has to be a safe way to pay for things online, and this topic is so important it has chapters of its own coming up. And second, the barrier to entry to the Internet must be lowered to admit as much of humanity as does cable television. Computers, according to Bill Gates, "need to be much simpler and hassle-free than PCs have ever been before." His goal is to make using the PC more like turning on a stereo, with no training needed.

The "Set top box," or "Internet Appliance," holds the promise of making surfing universal. Such a single-purpose unit does not offer word processing or most of the other features of a conventional computer. As a matter of fact, it uses a television screen as its monitor. As to price, the box cost only $500 or so when it entered the market, and is, consequently, within the reach of just about everyone. This appliance has no hard drive; all the computing and Internet browsing are done through a central computer to which it is connected by telephone. Gates is talking about something more sophisticated, but still simpler than a full PC: a sealed box to which no circuit boards can be added. Instead, extras are simply plugged in. He calls it the "Simply Interactive PC" or SIPC. It will have new hardware and software that will increase the reality of 3-D graphics, provide theater-quality sound and play movies. The SIPC will have an "instant on" feature that keeps the computer ready to go as soon as it is turned on.

Faster access to the Net will also increase its use, and that will come when the Net comes through cable television—instead of passing through telephone lines. One of the first such experiments took place through Cox Cable in San Diego in 1995. About 150 customers got to access Prodigy there without tying up their phone line or disrupting their television. And it is possible to download large files containing sound or video much faster than with the fastest modem on telephone lines. One user is so spoiled he won't even bother using the World Wide Web with a mere 14.4-baud modem.

It doesn't take much of an investment on the part of the cable company either, Joe Waz, vice president of external affairs for Comcast Corp., told *Popular Mechanics* (June 1995). "We can be the first to the market with a bigger pipe to the PC, so why not do it?" The telephone companies can keep their lead by making access cheaper, and that's just what AT&T has already done. When in 1996 they offered their customers free access for the first five hours per month and unlimited access for $19.95 per month, they received half a million orders, so many they couldn't produce the software fast enough to keep up.

### *Net Telephony*

Using the Net for free long distance calls ought to attract consumers' attention. It has already caught the eye of telephone long distance companies, who have lobbied hard to stop it. With a sound card in one's computer, it is possible to transmit and receive telephone messages over the Internet from anywhere in the world. ITEX used the technology as early as 1996 to communicate with its offices in South Africa and Australia.

It was a primitive way to communicate, however. Unless the computer's sound card is fully duplexed, sound can go only one way at a time. That means users held down the keyboard space bar to talk. And they had to prearrange through e-mail with their voice partner when to be online. "They're more than curiosities, but far less than practical business tools," suggests *Netguide* magazine (June 1996). But free is a very good price, so Internet telephony offers the potential to attract millions more people. "Internet phones scare traditional telecommunications companies silly," according to *Netguide* writers Kevin Reichard and Nelson King.

"Think of it: for the price of a local call on either end, two $15 per month net accounts, and a little advance planning, two people anywhere in the world can talk as often and for as long as they want. Compare that to international telephone rates that climb upward of $1 per minute, and Net phones look pretty good, even with all the logistical and operational difficulties."

It looks so good that several small long distance carriers tried a preemptive strike against it through a petition to the FCC to force regulation of software developers. The America's Carriers Telecommunications Association (ACTA), with 130 members who buy wholesale long distance time and remarket it to consumers, have tried to block Internet long distance calls or require the FCC to control it. What makes this struggle so fascinating is the vast amount of money at stake. Long distance calls are a $75 billion per year market. The ACTA calculates that a call placed over one of its carriers costs seven times as much as a call to the same place for the same time as an Internet call, according to *Netguide*. No wonder the FCC was asked to rule that software companies are long distance carriers. These software products include VocalTec Inc.'s Internet Phone; Camelot Corp.'s DigiPhone and Quarterdeck Corp.'s WebTalk. In addition, Netscape has built voice software into its Navigator program, and Microsoft plans a phone product as well.

Despite all these features and advantages, the Internet is not going to achieve its potential on its own. It will simply not be able to attract the number of users it needs to become a viable mass-market tool unless it is properly promoted. And for that to happen, someone with vision and ambition has to get behind it and promote it.

That can be no one other than Bill Gates. Microsoft restructured itself with emphasis no longer on Windows, but instead on providing content for the Internet. Gates' interest in the Net means that it will eventually achieve its potential. Of course, it also means he will achieve his. Before the cash can really flow over the Net, however, there must be some form of electronic currency, and there must be some safe way to transfer it, all of which is about to be described.

# 10

# Encryption

*The estimated annual cost to U.S. taxpayers for keeping government documents secret is $20 billion per year. That's $6 billion more than the entire NASA budget.*

Source: *The Great American Bathroom Book III*

The problem with the Information Superhighway is that it is a two-way street. This truth must be understood to make sense of the controversy about encryption, which is the technology that makes it possible to send information in secret. The military created the Internet, and its vast potential to generate wealth. But the road to riches can just as easily become the road to ruin, and that is the problem. The technology needed to do business on the Internet is also what makes it possible for the bad guys to wreak havoc.

### *The Secret Weapon*

If the net can be used for commerce, why can't it also be used for crime, terrorism and war? "On the telephone, law enforcement agencies can eavesdrop on suspected criminals," observes *The Economist* (Jan. 14, 1995). "On the Net, messages can be encoded in a way that is virtually unbreakable, shielding them from prying eyes."

Which is why a great struggle has been going on behind the scenes. At the government level, the conflict is between the proponents of controls over encryption—the Department of Defense, the F.B.I. and the National Security Agency—and the forces putting their weight behind the Departments of Commerce and State. Pressuring Commerce are computer and software industries that seek profits from selling encryption products; businesses that want to sell goods and services via the Internet; and other organizations that want to use the Internet as a secure conduit for communications.

The profit potential of all this is mind-boggling. The problem is that the computer programs and chips needed to make the Net safe to do business are also classified for export purposes by the Department of Defense and the National Security Agency as munitions, forbidden for export without a license; and that means they are tightly controlled. The Department of Defense and the National Security Agency have forced the Departments of State and Commerce to seize almost every patent application for cryptographic inventions.

"They do not want America's enemies, criminals or terrorists to be able to communicate in complete secrecy," according to *The Economist*. "Since the Oklahoma bombing the Federal Bureau of Investigation has joined the calls to keep encryption under wraps." Indeed, one former neo-Nazi reported in the *New Yorker* that it was via the Internet that his group transmitted files on making bombs. Because information on the Net is uncensored and available for anyone, individuals on the violent fringe of society can act in concert with their fellows and yet maintain no direct, traceable connection with each other.

If the Internet has been useful for the U.S. military, imagine the power it could give to terrorists, criminals and foreign enemies. They could use it to communicate their plans all over the world in secret and act on those schemes without knowing the actual identity of the others. Malcontents could commit mayhem in the total absence of an organization to track down, leaving no leader to arrest, no headquarters to blast. Is there any question why governments want at least to be able to intercept and read the material such individuals transmit?

After the Oklahoma City bombing in 1995, the U.S. Congress held a hearing on terrorism. Sen. Edward Kennedy (D-Mass.) brandished a 76-page "Terrorism Handbook" his staff had downloaded from the Internet. It contained recipes for a variety of bombs, including the fertilizer bomb that killed 167 people in Oklahoma.

"Right now we're considering a telecommunications reform bill in the Senate that is trying to do something about porn on the Internet. We should do something about this terrorist information, too," said the Senator. But what? If you regulate the service providers in one state or even one country, undesirable information will simply be placed online elsewhere. How do you get the genie back into the bottle? Where is there a plug to pull? Government has lost control of its own creation, the Internet. And that is precisely why it is absolutely essential at least to be able to monitor what goes across it.

### Greater Vulnerability

As we noted earlier, U.S. currency is seen by foreign enemies as a vulnerable target of economic warfare. If enemies can undermine confidence in U.S. currency by flooding the world with counterfeit money, they can damage the U.S. economy. Unfortunately, a few billions in fake $100 bills is no more than a mosquito bite compared to the potential for havoc the U.S. faces through Internet terrorism.

We also saw that the strength of the U.S. monetary system stems from the credibility of the country's military. Because of budget constraints, however, the U.S. Army at this writing has only 1.1 million ground troops, which makes it only the eighth largest in the world. To keep its military edge, the U.S. relies increasingly on high technology. If the technology is vulnerable, though, so is its superiority. The larger issue facing the U.S. armed forces is developing the capabilities to defend the increasingly electronic backbone of the economy.

"In the Gulf War the military made extensive use of the Internet for its communications, and it would have suffered had the Iraqis decided to take it out," according to computer security expert Steve Kent in *Time* for August 21, 1995. The magazine reported that mercenary hackers offered to do the job for Saddam Hussein, but he turned them down.

Not only the military, but the entire infrastructure of the U.S. is vulnerable. Computers that control banking, stock exchanges, air-traffic control, telephones and electric power are all open to computer-generated attack. "We're more vulnerable than any nation on earth," Vice Admiral John McConnell has been quoted in *Time*.

This country could be brought to its knees by an enemy who never physically crosses the borders; more frightening yet, we might not even know who it was, nor have the ability to retaliate.

Mindful that America is the most open of all countries to such attacks, the U.S. military is preparing for such an electronic war. *Time* has said that the Bush administration at one point considered disrupting the Iraqi computers that controlled government financial transactions, but the CIA was against it. "Every time screwing around with financial systems has been discussed as a covert action, people have walked away from it," a former CIA official is quoted by *Time*. "Messing with a country's money represents a fundamental attack. No CIA director has ever recommended it."

That doesn't mean that America's enemies have the same scruples. "Groups of electronic intruders, if organized and funded by interested adversaries, have the capabilities to launch sophisticated, widespread attacks," according to the Pentagon's Defense Science Board. "A Third World nation could procure a formidable, modern information warfare capability virtually off the shelf."

Those who remember their history know that the Nazis lost the war when the British cracked their encryption code. The Allies knew just about every move the enemy was going to make before they made it. Secrecy is key to survival; for that reason the debate about encryption is without question among the most important issues of the end of the century.

### *What's at Stake*

Because of the dangers, the U.S. government has banned export of strong encryption technology, and the F.B.I. and other law enforcement agencies want to expand their access to transmission of information not just on the telephone lines, but also on the Internet.

"Internet users, fearing invasion of their privacy, have mounted the virtual barricade," observes *The Economist* (July 1, 1995). "But the battle has slowed the deployment of encryption technology in general, ironically making it even easier for criminals already online to steal information."

U.S. companies want to sell encryption overseas. Half the business done by the software and computer companies is abroad. The market for U.S. computer systems was expected to hit $200 billion by the turn of the century, but federal laws prohibiting the sale of encryption products could cut that by as much as 30 percent, according to a report prepared by 13 U.S. technology companies, known as the Computer Systems Policy Project, which includes IBM Corp. and AT&T.

Shortly after the industry report was released, the Department of Commerce came out with its own report. Conducted in conjunction with the National Security Agency, it concluded that U.S. companies were being hurt by the ban on encryption exports enforced by American and other governments. The late Secretary of Commerce Ron Brown once said: "If your foreign competitors are exporting products with encryption capabilities and you are not, that puts you at a tremendous competitive disadvantage."

Said Kathy Kincaid, manager of information technology security programs at IBM, about the anticipated easing of restrictions: "They are finally understanding the industry view, and that's a positive step. The global view is so important to our business as the Internet and electronic commerce take off and grow."

### *The Breakthrough?*

Many people have feared that someone could get their credit card numbers over the Internet or figure out who they are doing business with and what they are buying. They have been right to fear this. Take the experience of Vladimir Edelman, a writer for *Inc.* magazine. He was checking his e-mail one day in 1995 when he came across a message from the industry-forecasting manager of IBM's Europe branch. The message was not intended for him, and his e-mail address was nowhere even close to an IBM address. He learned that a malfunctioning server somewhere could misroute anyone's important messages elsewhere.

Another *Inc.* writer, Phaedra Hise, said sending important data through a public online service is like sending secrets on a postcard.

"Users transmitting privileged information electronically have no fool-proof way to protect against a document's being peered into, altered or forged." Already, system operators on the Internet can read the e-mail of others, and hackers can get into e-mail boxes as well.

Edelman believes small companies deceive themselves by thinking they will be overlooked by electronic vandals and the thieves known as hackers. As a matter of fact, smaller firms become tempting targets precisely because they are less likely to have the built-in security of a larger organization, so hackers are less likely to be caught. Novice hackers go after small companies and identify them as "penetration test sites" on hacker bulletin boards, according to Edelman.

Clearly, confidence is the issue, and misgivings about the Internet are not going to be purged overnight. But a major step forward—time will tell whether it was indeed *the* breakthrough—was Security Electronic Transactions (S.E.T.). This software standard was put into service in 1996 by MasterCard and VISA to protect online credit card transactions by encrypting account numbers. With S.E.T., people can buy items from a store in cyberspace as securely as they could in one at the nearest mall.

The industry standard ended the jostling between Microsoft and Netscape, the two most powerful Internet software companies, about how best to protect online transactions. The Internet needed "someone to provide a payment solution that everyone agrees on," remarked David Weisman, an analyst for the market research firm Forrester Research Inc. His company expects online sales to reach $22 billion by the turn of the century. And it is predictions like these that have all potential players anxious to play ball. "IBM hopes this will speed up electronic commerce on the Internet," said Marke Greene, a vice president at IBM.

More than 60 banks and most credit card companies have a Web presence, but only a few have announced secure, automated Internet-based transaction approval services. Even the most sophisticated security codes have been broken. Netscape Navigator browsing software has integrated its Secure Sockets Layer, or SSL protocol. And yet, in August 1995, a French student at Ecole Polytechnique cracked the exported version of Netscape Communication's secure Web server. One highly publicized case like this with S.E.T. might be all it would take to bring down the whole house of cards.

### *Huge Potential*

Domestically, encryption devices are already in common use. "Industries from cellular phone services to cable television use encryption to ensure correspondents privacy and to authenticate identities of trading partners," according to *The Economist*. The Chicago Board of Trade (CBOT) has a Web site that offers information and news to CBOT traders. It is eventually intended to present a virtual storefront where third parties offer fee-for-service information to the futures trading market. CBOT is using Netscape's secure Web server and will clear payment information automatically through Bank of America.

"Several years ago, most businesses wondered why they would ever need encryption tools," commented Bob Stratton of the Internet service provider UUNET Technologies of Fairfax, Virginia. "Now, most major businesses want encrypted security tools," he said. This is particularly true for companies with distributed client/server computing. "We consider customer information extremely confidential," said Bill Chang of Fidelity Investments. "Moving that data over open communication lines is not doing everything we should to protect our customers."

The Internet also offers companies the opportunity to replace costly leased lines. All manner of data, files, transactions and e-mail can be transmitted over the Internet essentially for free, and will be, provided it can be done securely. Private lines can be replaced by virtual private networks through the Internet infrastructure.

UUNET's LanGuardian is designed to replace leased lines. Public key encryption is used to direct data over the Internet to another LanGuardian site, and it is decrypted at the destination. Encrypted "tunnels" over the Internet allow a company with facilities all over the world to view and interact with its various parts and those outside the company would never see what's going on.

Companies that want to encrypt only certain mail messages on a case-by-case basis can use a software package from IBM called Lotus Notes. One of the options is to encrypt only outgoing mail, or to encrypt incoming mail before it is stored on an in-house computer, so the sender does not have to be the one to encrypt it. Alternatively, various parts of the message can be encrypted. For example, if an organization has a number of levels of security clearance within itself, parts of the document can be cleared for certain members, while the rest remains secret. This capability has already been used in a private New York psychiatric facility, where patient files are partially encrypted to prevent administrative workers from gaining access to sensitive information about patients.

Another issue: How do you know the person at the other end of the screen is the person he or she claims to be? There needs to be some way to verify that each party to a sale is who they claim to be. This is called "authentication," and is addressed in a number of software applications.

A step forward was technology that divided sensitive information such as credit card data into 1,024 bits of information instead of the 128 that had been the norm. The theory is that this makes it much more difficult to pilfer the information. VISA International and MasterCard acted together to develop encryption technology currently being incorporated into software offered by Netscape-Veriphone, and, in doing so, broke an impasse between Microsoft Corp. and Netscape Communications Corp. over how to prevent theft in Internet commerce. This standard may be the catalyst that causes Internet commerce to explode.

### *Solving the Problem*

This is why encryption has become the heart of a modern-day dilemma. On the one hand, national security depends on government agencies' capacity to intercept the information flow via its own creation, the Internet. On the other, the fact that the government has this capacity undermines confidence that transactions can be conducted in privacy on this new means of communication.

Daniel Bernstein, a University of California student, wanted to give his Snuffle encryption program to the world free via the Internet. Then the State Department interfered and told him he would first need a munitions export license, and he has not been able to get one. Bernstein and the Electronic Frontier Foundation say his First Amendment rights of free speech have been violated.

All attempts to regulate export of encryption have been awkward at best. Take the example of Phil Karn, an electrical engineer from San Diego who succeeded in getting the State Department to give him a license to export a book called *Applied Cryptography* by Bruce Schneider, but was forbidden to include a disk containing codes that were identical to those in the book.

The F.B.I. in particular requires access to tap telephone lines. The bureau estimates that some future emergencies may prompt it to tap as many as one phone line out of 1,000 in some areas. While telephone calls are fairly simple to tap, they can be less easy to understand when they are encrypted. Philip Zimmermann, a Colorado programmer who has devised a program he calls PGP for Pretty Good Privacy, offers the private citizen a level of secure calls previously available only to the government. The program digitizes the human voice and recalculates it so that it is unintelligible to even the most sophisticated eavesdropper. The voice quality may not be perfect and there is a second or so delay, but it is security that is now free.

A friend of Zimmermann, according to *The Economist*, got ahold of PGP and made it available through MIT on the Internet (http://web.mit.edu/network/pgpphone/). Described by *The Economist* as "a stinging affront to the government's power to control the dissemination of cryptography," this action by his friend got Zimmermann in trouble with the feds, who prosecuted him.

According to *Client/Server Computing* (October 1995), both the sender and the receiver have a unique public key and private key. Public keys can be freely distributed, but private keys do not have to be shared with anyone. Public-key encryption affixes a digital signature to unencrypted and encrypted messages, to encrypt messages, and to initiate encrypted sessions that will be carried out with private key encryption.

"Here's how it works," reports *Client/Server*. "The sender encodes the message using his or her own private key and the recipient's public key. When the message arrives, the recipient decodes it using the sender's public key, and a private key. By decoding the message with these two keys, the recipient confirms the identity of the sender, and the sender is assured the message can only be deciphered by the intended recipient. None of this requires sharing private keys."

IBM, AT&T, Motorola, Microsoft and other large and small companies use it; as of this writing it is part of 3 million installed software packages. Other users include the Web browser and server from Netscape of Mountain View, California, as well as CyberCash Systems secure payment system. A commercial version of PGP is distributed through ViaCrypt, of Phoenix, that had purchased a general license from RSA for the algorithms of which RSA holds the patent. ViaCrypt also offers a commercial encryption product for text that includes a signature recognition feature. This digitized "signature" verifies that the sender is the true originator.

PGP uses public-key encryption devised by RSA Data Security of Redwood City, California, whose public-key encryption is the most widely used. RSA President Jim Bidzos said his company in the past had blocked efforts to incorporate the software into the free version of PGP. His company gives away RIPEM, a simple program similar to the shareware of ViaCrypt, but which can process files no larger than 48 kilobytes. It can be downloaded at http://www.rsaref@rsa.com.

### *Too Late?*

Is the government trying to stuff the evil spirits back into Pandora's Box? Is it trying to close the barn door after the horses have run off, so far as encryption is concerned? The encryption devices the government is trying to ban are already widely available in Japan and Europe. Barry D. Bowen of the Bellingham, Washington-based Bowen Group wrote, in *Client/Server Computing*, that "U.S. software firms develop and include high-strength encryption in their domestic products, (but) they get export approval only for very weak algorithms."

He said that these restrictions make the U.S. look "silly" because U.S.-based companies have their hands tied behind their backs while foreign firms can sell encryption products both overseas and in the U.S. The telephone company NTT of Japan and the Japanese subsidiary of RSA, for example, have created a two-chip encryption system that is reportedly uncrackable (*The Economist*, June 8, 1996). These chips have been exported to at least 15 countries around the world with impunity, but it is unlikely governments will simply drop controls of encryption as a result. The most sophisticated encryption code that can be exported legally is known as the Data Encryption Standard. Devised in the 1970s, it can probably be defeated by any garden variety hacker.

A compromise offered by the federal government is the so-called Clipper Chip, which would enable users to encrypt messages—while the government would retain electronic access so it could eavesdrop if necessary. The question is whether banks would accept this solution, unless the access codes could be held by a third party from which the government would have to gain access, and which would be financially responsible if the codes were misused.

What is exportable is the partial encryption package offered by CyberCash. The company distributes software free to consumers and vendors, and takes a fee paid by the bank card clearinghouse. CyberCash gives the consumer a plug-in for Web browsers such as Netscape or Mosaic, while the vendor gets more sophisticated software.

When the consumer wants to buy something, he or she selects, from on-screen choices, the credit card to be used; the seller, the amount of the transaction and the approval are also shown onscreen. The data, which gets encrypted and digitally signed, then goes to the seller. The seller never decrypts this information, however, according to *Client/Server Computing*. All the credit card data is stored in the customer's computer, not the seller's. CyberCash decrypts both parts of the transaction, compares information such as the amount and vendor identity, obtains the bank clearinghouse's approval and notifies the vendor, all within seconds.

The only part of the transaction that is guaranteed privacy is the payment envelope, which means the credit card information is protected, but what is purchased and the fact that the customer was in contact with the seller is not. Even though encryption, especially for export, is likely to remain controversial for the foreseeable future, commerce is and will be conducted over the Internet. Let's look at that next.

# 11

# Smart Cards

*"Is it not strange that we fear most that which never happens. That we destroy our initiative by the fear of defeat, when in reality, defeat is a most useful tonic and should be accepted as such."*
Cyrus H. Curtis

It looks like a credit card, but isn't. There is no "credit," no paying later. It looks like a debit card, but isn't. There is no account that is being accessed. These Smart Cards are cash, in every sense of the word, and they represent a major step forward in the history of money. Pay the restaurant with them and the bill is taken care of immediately. Spend the money on the card at the grocery store and there is no authorization, no signature, no waiting. Give the value on it to your daughter at college and there is no record of it. It's cash on a card.

It works through a tiny computer chip embedded in plastic. The chip contains as much as four kilobytes of memory, which is about 80 times as much as the typical magnetic stripes on credit cards. For reasons you will see, banks want to promote the Smart Cards, but people aren't sure they want to use them. A survey reported by the American Banking Association (ABA) found that only 40 percent of Americans want a card that stores money, while 61 percent would like to have a card that stores medical and insurance records. Part of the reluctance may be that people realize it will be too easy to spend money on a card. VISA cites studies that indicate people will spend more with a cash card than they would with ordinary currency, from 5 percent to 25 or even 40 percent more.

Combining functions on a single card was introduced in the mid-

1990s. As a matter of fact, the ITEX Barter Express card is a prime example. The card accesses the barter exchange member's trade account through special Point of Sale terminals so he or she can spend Trade Dollars like cash at participating merchants. In 1996 the Barter Express card also added VISA/MasterCard and debit card functions, the first card in the barter industry to do so.

Multifunction cards for the general public may be nearer than we think, according to Bob Gilson, executive director of the Smart Card Forum. Gilson told *Popular Science* (July 1995) that his group's market surveys indicate that "there is a higher level of technical sophistication" among people than there was when magnetic stripe cards were introduced.

"Most people have some mind's-eye view of what a Smart Card can do," he said. "Fifteen years ago they had no perception at all. They are interested in information access and security features. These are not intimidating." And he predicted that in addition to a microprocessor, Smart Cards will also have magnetic stripes and bar codes and will eventually replace the driver's license, medical insurance cards, debit and credit cards.

Not everyone is pleased with that prospect. "I want to know what the risk is," said Marc Rotenberg of the Electronic Privacy Information Center (EPIC). "When they swipe my card at the health club, are they also getting my insurance information?"

### *Small Change*

Where there is money changing hands, the banks want to be in the middle of it, no matter how small the transaction. Because nickel and dime spending amount to a lot of money—$526 billion in cash purchases in the U.S. under $20, according to an ABA report of the MasterCard calculation. Which is peanuts in the global cash market. VISA said all cash transactions accounted for $8.1 trillion of the $14 trillion of total world personal spending in 1993.

Why all that cash when there are credit cards? Because most people are not credit-worthy, says the ABA, pointing out that 68 percent of Americans do not have either a VISA or a MasterCard, let alone a debit card. These are prime Smart Card customers. All transactions involving plastic, whether credit cards, debit cards or Smart Cards, accounted for 9 percent of consumer transactions in 1994 and were expected to be 15 percent by 2001 (*Time* 1994). And many people distrust credit cards, fearing that someone will run up a bill on their account. When celebrated hacker Kevin Mitnick was arrested, he had a list of 20,000 credit card numbers in his possession.

Smart Cards, on the other hand, do not open your credit line or bank account to thieves. And they don't require online authorization like credit or debit cards. The wait time for processing is closer to two seconds than two minutes. That means they can zip you through a convenience store check-out line. It is actually faster to use a Smart Card at a pop machine than fumbling for change and plugging in quarters. Tests have proven that Smart Cards make cafeteria lines move faster.

Smart Cards and other forms of E-cash give consumers greater freedom to move value. Frank Trotter III, a vice president at Mark Twain Bank, said, "You will have the ability to send a friend e-mail with money at the bottom of it. You can transfer that to a card, walk into your local retailer and use it to pay for something. You will even be able to transfer money from card to card, or directly into your computer."

And Smart Cards open new opportunities to spend money: in home shopping from TV, it is awkward and risky to dial an 800 number and read a credit card number over the phone. With a set-top box, on the other hand, you could merely swipe the card and make the purchase.

A Smart Card is also useful in watching the budget. "If a family had a college student, they could allow her to load a certain amount of money a month," according to Diane Wetherington of MasterCard, as reported in *Newsweek* (Oct. 30, 1995). And they could even limit what the money could be spent for—okay items such as books and food, but not beer.

### *Where's the Beef?*

Will there be 100 million Smart Cards in the U.S. by the year 2000, as is predicted by Joseph F. Schuler, senior vice president of business development at Stored Value Systems of National City Corp., Cleveland? Will all ATM cards in the U.S. be Smart Cards by the year 2004?

Don't start counting those hundreds of millions; not, at least, until the banks figure something out. To start with, although the costs are dropping, at this writing each Smart Card costs between $2 and $10, while the price of magnetic stripe cards runs between 25 and 50 cents. Many banks find the investment is justified by the fact that electronic stripes are relatively easy to counterfeit or tamper with, compared to microchips, which are very difficult to fool with.

But not impossible. In early 1995 a New York transit clerk was caught creating fraudulent Metro Cards with which to ride the subways. He had figured out a way to load the cards without the computer subtracting an amount from the central depository. Looking specifically for atypical events in operations, the system's software spotted the discrepancy and led to the clerk's arrest, according to *Popular Science* (July 1995).

Then, there would be the cost of retrofitting all those ATMs: There are 125,000 to 130,000 magnetic stripe-reading ATMs in the U.S. and about 375,500 magnetic stripe-reading Point of Sale (POS) terminals. Retrofitting a single ATM costs $2,000 to $5,000, representing hundreds of millions of dollars that banks and merchants would have to absorb. It is true, however, that newer ATMs from the largest manufacturer, Diebold, and POS makers Verifone and Hypercom are all Smart Card-compatible.

Of course, banks are not the only ones investing in Smart Cards. Catherine A. Allen, vice president of Citibank's technology office, remarked: "Now we've got critical mass in the Smart Card area. Transit authorities, parking lot operators, telecommunications companies, health care providers, banks and such software companies as Intuit and Microsoft are all looking at Smart Cards. These players will get the infrastructure in place, then you're going to see a lot of creative application."

More important than the costs, though, is the question of how the bank makes money from Smart Cards. Credit cards are no-brain-ers: The two percent charged to the merchants, together with the service charges from people who don't pay their bills on time, make a substantial cash flow. But where's the profit in putting money on a card being spent for 30- or 50-cent purchases?

The ABA says there are seven ways banks could make money on Smart Cards. Banks will:

1. Reduce their cost of handling cash. To count it, to store it, to move it and to protect it are all expensive activities. Which is to say, Smart Cards give banks the opportunity to further downsize staff.
2. Reduce the costs of credit card fraud, which amounts to millions each year. "Credit card fraud," according to a quote in the *Great American Bathroom Book*, "costs consumers $6.74 per year for each card they carry. The total cost of fraud to issuers in 1993 was one billion dollars."
3. Charge merchants a fee. That is, unless they adopt the Mondex model, which charges the consumers.
4. Charge consumers a fee. That is, unless they pay attention to the Mondex experiment, in which consumers resisted paying fees.
5. Acquire new customers and gain their loyalty.
6. End up with the pool of unused money created by the people who don't spend all the value on their cards. (This is an income source the barter industry refers to as "breakage.") This is especially true for the Mondex model, where the money on the card is kept by the bank if the card is lost, even though it can't be spent if the card is locked, but more about this later.
7. Have advertising space on the cards that can be offered for sale.

None of these possibilities for making money on cards is based on anything more than an educated guess, except for the one possibility that most American banks apparently had not even considered.

### The Danmont Phenomenon

For an entertaining glimpse of the future of at least some modern money, go to the collectors' services bulletin board (www.teledanmark.dk/english/telekort.htm) for Tele Danmark, the Danish telephone company. Tele Danmark first introduced telephone cards in

1983, and ever since has done something decorative with them. One released in 1996, for instance, is made of birchwood, the country's first wooden chip card (Telia of Sweden introduced the first wooden chip card in the world, the Web site proclaims). The newest card is called "Sunflowers," and is a reproduction of a painting by Charlotte Thymark. Tele Danmark keeps these cards valuable by making many of them limited editions.

The little cards are so pretty that, after the money on them is spent and sometimes even before, people collect them. As a matter of fact, they are such a hot item that Tele Danmark maintains a bulletin board at its Web site specifically for collectors to advertise what they have, what they want and to discuss current card values. From time to time the company announces new editions and anticipated production runs. The possibility of credit cards being bought and sold as collectors' items is so intriguing that VISA plans to introduce "commemorative" cards of its own.

The phone cards evolved into coin cards through Danmont, which is owned equally by Tele Danmark and a banking company, Penginstitutternes Betalings Service (PBS). The coin cards are used for small purchases, such as in vending machines. In operation since 1992, Danmont has dispersed more than half a million disposable cards in 60 towns and cities, according to *The Economist*, and, in August 1995, introduced a rechargeable version. The company hopes that half the population of Denmark will use the cards within seven years of introduction. Danmont's technology is so impressive that VISA even bought the rights to it, a fact to be recalled later in this chapter.

Once banks and credit card companies saw the potential, Smart Card tests began to be conducted in many places around the world in the mid-to-late 1990s. In March 1996, for example, MasterCard announced a trial involving 10,000 customers in Canberra, Australia, to test a combined cash, credit and debit card issued by three of the country's big banks. At the same time, VISA in the Gold Coast area, and Transcard, a locally developed prepaid Smart Card for travel and shopping, were being tested in Sydney.

Most digital cash trials are single-currency projects run by groups of domestic banks. As many as 24 countries are currently running or have planned such projects. Those most interested in Smart Cards or E-cash are countries such as Russia, Brazil, South Africa and even Zambia, where robbery and high inflation make carrying around a pile of cash a concern.

In the United States, Citicorp and Chase Manhattan joined VISA and MasterCard in a six-month pilot program to introduce Smart Cards on New York's upper West Side. DigiCash of Amsterdam, the Netherlands, is developing a Smart Card for Internet payments. Squaring off in readiness for a turf battle of gigantic proportions, the various card projects are competing for nothing less than international acceptance. According to Richard Poynder, chairman of the Smart Card Club, an independent trade association, the big firms are waging a "purse war" to decide the industry standard.

On the one side is British Mondex, along with Wells Fargo and six other banks that have begun testing the Mondex model; on the other is Citibank with its view of the future. But we're getting ahead of ourselves.

### *Going for the Gold*

The world was watching athletes from around the world competing to bring honor to their countries; behind the scenes, a struggle with potentially much higher stakes was being fought out. America got its first big exposure to Smart Cards during the 1996 Summer Olympic Games in Atlanta. Issued by a consortium of banks—First Union, Nations Bank and Wachovia—a Smart Card was given by VISA to each athlete to spend at the cafeteria or wherever they were accepted at the games. This move, with coverage by the media, helped familiarize the world with this new form of money.

The cards the banks distributed to the athletes were disposable; rechargeable cards came next. In addition, banks around the country, such as U.S. Bancorp in Portland, Oregon, issued the cards to customers who requested them for their trips to the games. Once the customers were in Atlanta, their cards were as convenient to use, and in many ways more so, than cash. People took them to terminals where they could convert major currencies such as Japanese Yen and Deutsche Marks into electronic deposits that could be stored on the cards. Once they had spent all the value on their cards, they went back to ATMs, inserted the cards as if making a withdrawal, entered their PIN (personal identification number) and recharged the value on their cards.

Competition is what drives athletes on to great achievements. The same is apparently true of Smart Cards.

### *Mondex Takes the Lead*

Smart Cards appeared on a large scale in July 1995, when the 170,000 residents of the British community of Swindon spent their first E-cash on Mondex cards at about 750 of the city's 1,300 businesses. Everyone who lived, worked or shopped in the Swindon area, from age five on up, could apply for a card. After planning to distribute as many as 40,000 of them through two British banks, Mondex wound up issuing only 8,000, according to *Newsweek*. It was a small beginning, but then, so was *Sputnik*. This rollout of Smart Cards in England had the same smelling-salts effect on the world financial community that the Soviet space satellite did on the U.S. military establishment.

Mondex is the brain child of Timothy Jones and Graham Higgins, who, as executives of National Westminster Bank (NatWest) in London, came up with the idea. They applied for their first patents by spring of 1990, and in the next couple years teamed up with such electronics companies as Dai Nippon, Hitachi, Panasonic and Oki. They also did thorough market research on more than 5,000 consumers in the United Kingdom, the United States, France, Germany and Japan. The reaction indicated that people were very ready for E-cash. Researchers found that 94 percent of those polled like the idea of a Smart Card, and 75 percent of them said they wanted one even if they had to pay for it.

"It's probably the most positive financial services research that any of us have ever seen," according to Ann Adams of Mondex, as reported by Seth Godin in *Presenting Digital Cash* (sams net publishing, Indianapolis). Reality, unfortunately, was somewhat less than the hype predicted. *The Economist* reported that use of Mondex was below expectations. After planning to charge a monthly fee to card users for the privilege, Mondex ultimately decided to postpone that idea.

What is it? The Mondex card is *not* like a credit card with which the recipient of the funds has to be paid eventually in real cash. It's *not* like a check, either, that has to clear a bank. With the Mondex system, consumers insert a credit card-size Smart Card into a card reader in a retail terminal. Funds are transferred immediately from the card to the terminal with no need for signatures or authorization. Small businesses such as coffee kiosks or news stands can use a battery-powered terminal that doesn't have to be connected to a telephone line or a computer modem line. For more detail, check out the Mondex Web site (www.mondex.com/mondex/home.htm).

The card can be recharged with electronic money at special ATMs or by phone. At the ATM, the user can recharge the card's value, pay value into the bank, check the balance remaining on the card and, with some banks, get a statement of the last five transactions. A Mondex-compatible phone can also recharge the card, acting like an ATM machine at home. The phone can also check the balance of the bank account, and can transfer money across the telephone lines and make payments to other Mondex card holders anywhere in the world.

The Integrated Circuit (IC), or small microprocessor embedded in the plastic, is what makes the Mondex card a Smart Card. The microcomputer is programmed to function as an "electronic purse" that can be loaded with "value" that remains stored until it is used as payment for goods or services at retail or service outlets that use it.

To find out how much value is left on the card, users swipe it through a key fob-size balance reader and the balance is displayed on a small screen. *Newsweek*'s Daniel Pedersen was not impressed with the balance reader, though. "This gizmo is much easier to ignore than the haunting sight of an emptying wallet," he wrote.

Mondex also offers an "electronic wallet"—a pocket-size device with a keyboard and screen that can store a large balance of value and transfer it to the Smart Card. That way if the card is lost, only the value stored on the card is gone; the bulk of the value can be kept with the wallet and stored securely at home or in a hotel safe if you're traveling.

This device Pedersen found too bulky. "Luckily, you don't need to carry it all the time. It's so heavy, you half wonder if that guy dropping his coins wasn't ahead of the game after all. Mondex's best minds agree, and they are working on a lighter model."

As we said, lose your Mondex card and it's as if you lost money. You don't get it back. The card has an electronic locking system, though, so whoever finds it can't spend the value remaining on it. This means, in theory, that it is more likely to be returned if lost. To lock the card, the owner simply presses a button and unlocks it with his or her chosen PIN.

Even so, Tim Jones took heat from Phil Donahue's audience when he appeared on the show in 1996. Because Mondex is only a card with electronic codes, they argued, why should Mondex retain the stored value on the card instead of returning it to the cardholder? Even Donahue himself asked the question again and again. It is precisely this customer resistance that has led Mondex to keep the card as simple as possible. "Getting people to accept as abstract an idea as digital dough will be hard enough for Mondex without confusing the issue with more bells and whistles," commented writer Seth Godin.

By the way, Mondex claims their system was designed as a global product that can function in any country where the Mondex system is used. The Mondex Smart Card holds five different currencies at any given time in separate "pockets" on the embedded microchip, so users can take their domestic Mondex card abroad.

The Mondex card is a way to get around the encryption problem in making Internet purchases. Mondex calls their card "a vital link between the physical and the electronic marketplaces." On the other side of the world you can receive money via the Internet and spend it back at home at your local mall. Each time a Mondex card is used, the chip on the card generates a unique "digital signature" that can be recognized by the other Mondex card involved in a transaction. This "digital signature" is the guarantee that the cards involved are genuine Mondex cards and that vendors are dealing with untampered Mondex signals. The recognition process also identifies the card for which the cash is intended, so funds cannot be intercepted by a third party.

### *Worldwide Scramble*

When Mondex reared its head, it got the competitive juices flowing around the world, perhaps just what it took to move Smart Cards forward. With any new territory, whoever gets there first and hangs on is the one whose language is spoken. The same is true for Smart Card technology, which is why there is such a scramble among the players to set the standard.

This is also why, despite the initial problems, Mondex was encouraged enough with its Swindon experiment to introduce its cards to the rest of the United Kingdom in 1997. Mondex pushed forward globally with regional franchise agreements. A British banking group, HSBC, bought Mondex's Asian franchise, which encompasses China and India. Mondex trials were conducted in both the U.S. and Canada and were planned for Australia. And a group of Japanese banks and technical companies were in talks for franchising in their country.

Credit card companies such as Europay, MasterCard and VISA paid attention. *The Economist* said these companies tried to shut out Mondex by forming a common technical standard known as EMV for stored-value cards. The idea is that merchants can install a single terminal that accepts the banks' different cards, but not those of Mondex. The likelihood is, however, that rival terminals will be developed to deal with several different standards at once, not just EMV—at least that's what Mondex executives hope.

VISA is reportedly working with NatWest's domestic competitors, including Barclays and Lloyds, on a possible rival British system to be called EPUK. One banker said, according to *The Economist*, that VISA "is adding its badge to anything that moves as a spoiling tactic against Mondex." MasterCard had the opportunity to buy

Mondex when it was still an idea, but declined. That's not to say it couldn't change its mind, especially if the experiment conducted by Wells Fargo and half a dozen other banks in the U.S. is successful.

Then there is the issue of acceptance. Mondex appeals to merchants because it is free to them, while VISA and MasterCard want to charge the merchant. On the other hand, early tests of Mondex showed customer resistance to the charges—the equivalent of plain, old-fashioned seigniorage. Add to that the issue of tax reporting. Because electronic money is anonymous and easily sent abroad, how is it to be reported? Daniel Pedersen, the *Newsweek* reporter who reviewed Mondex in England, found at least one tavern that did not take it. Will those businesses used to "skimming" cash before it is reported find electronic currency helpful or a hindrance? This is all new territory. At this writing, anyone in the United States can issue a Smart Card; in Europe that privilege is reserved for banks.

The U.S. banking industry is aware that the Federal Reserve is looking at who should be able to issue Smart Cards here, as well as what other regulations ought to apply. Why doesn't the Fed simply jump in and regulate Smart Cards? Or produce their own? Philip Diehl, director of the U.S. Mint, suggested that idea at an October 1995 Congressional hearing. Appearing at the same hearing, though, Alan S. Blinder, Federal Reserve vice chairman, testified against government involvement for now, fearing that it might "stifle the innovative impulses of the e-money community," according to *Newsweek*. Government is not apt to acquiesce in something so vital to its own survival as control of currency, however. Most likely the Feds will wait for the dust to settle, for technology to be developed, for standards to be set, and for the public to accept E-cash—and then move in and take over.

Ironically, the technology for Smart Cards, like the Internet itself, grew out of the government's security needs, according to *Popular Science*. The U.S. Marines who train at Parris Island, S.C., are paid with a Smart Card that can be used at base facilities or the local fast-food joint or bowling alley. The Corps estimates it saves as much as $40,000 per year with the cards.

Meanwhile, financial institutions are forming alliances with technology and telecommunications firms. In Japan, VISA has linked up with Toshiba, and Mondex with Hitachi. *The Economist* has indicated that these alliances give a clue about how digital money might develop. "The problem is too large for one bank or institution to develop a winning scheme alone." Eventually, two or three global operators may triumph.

Citicorp, in April 1994, filed a patent on its Electronic Monetary System (EMS), said to be technically superior to Mondex. One of the main ways it differs from Mondex is in allowing banks to keep track of the money they are issuing. As users fill their electronic wallets with money, the bank creates digital bank notes that are passed along from person to person as the funds are spent. These digital bank notes may become smaller or larger as the value moves through the economy, but each portion of it carries an electronic tag that allows the issuing bank to identify its money.

The bank may or may not know who is using it, but to Mondex advocates, the anonymity for the user actually makes Mondex more valuable. For the bank, however, the advantage of having the information is that if the source of the electronic money can be determined, it should be easier to verify whether payments have taken place.

Another consumer benefit in the Citicorp EMS? It is allied with a software agent that enables users to seek out the best prices for products they want.

EMS could have its greatest impact among banks themselves. Citibank believes EMS is an ideal way to transmit large amounts of money to other banks in real time with no risk of armored car hijacking. In addition, EMS can handle any number of foreign currencies and exchange them at agreed-upon rates, something Mondex can't do, according to *The Economist*. At last report, Citibank was trying to strike deals with other institutions, corporations as well as banks, to get EMS into use.

Novel as they seem, Smart Cards are not a dramatic new development in money. Catherine A. Allen, vice president of Citibank's technology office and chair of the Smart Card Forum—a group of banks and vendors interested in smart cards—put it this way: "Smart cards are ... part of the broader shift to electronic delivery, to making ATMs more functional, to using PCs and the Internet to do home banking, to going to Point of Sale terminals to get cash back, to getting electronic benefits transfer off of a card," she told the American Banking Association magazine. They are an important development, but not revolutionary.

How long will it be before Smart Cards catch on? "It usually takes about 15 years for consumers to accept anything," observed Laurie Yoler, head of worldwide financial services marketing for Sun Microsystems of Mountain View, Calif. Her company makes a security device for encrypting and authenticating information that is invisible from the network it protects.

Joseph Cady, a consultant with CB Consulting in San Diego, said: "One of the biggest challenges strategically is how quickly is (E-cash) going to be embraced by the consumers.... If you roll it out too soon, you run the risk of alienating your customers. The technology actually ends up driving customers away from the office."

The future of Smart Cards as a new form of money was assured, however, when they caught Bill Gates' attention. In May of 1996, in secret, Microsoft and Hewlett-Packard began working on a way to integrate Smart Cards and personal computers. Through the system they announced months later, the user inserts a Smart Card into a new computer slot—just as a floppy disk is inserted—and makes purchases and sends or receives money over the Internet.

Microsoft, in fact, is redoing Windows and its Internet products to accommodate Smart Cards. And H-P is building Smart Card readers into its computers. Together, they have set standards they hope will be used by other manufacturers. Also involved in the deal are Schlumberger Ltd. and Groupe Bull of France. These firms will produce the cryptography and secure the storage services required to use Smart Cards on personal computers. And Siemens AG of Germany will also integrate Smart Card readers into its Windows-based PC products.

Whose standards will prevail—those of Danmont, Mondex, VISA and MasterCard, or Microsoft? There is so much at stake that the early entries in the field are not going to roll over just because Bill Gates has entered the fray.

But if Microsoft wins the struggle for standards with Smart Cards as it did with software, will the transfer of funds become as easy as it is to use a personal computer? And if so, will this have the same stimulating effect on business as the PC did? (See Chapter 7.) On the other hand, can the world tolerate so much power concentrated in one pair of hands? Gates was able to get away with setting the standards for PCs because no one saw him coming—and everyone underestimated the potential of the market.

That's decidedly not the case with money. This is a game everyone wants to control; and everyone now knows the kind of impact Gates is capable of generating. There are already some strong contenders in the ring—as we will see in the upcoming chapter on electronic currency.

# 12

# Electronic Currency

*"With money in your pocket, not only are you wise and good looking, but you sing well, too."*
Yiddish proverb

Smart Cards employ sophisticated electronic technology, but they remain tangible objects. The big leap in the evolution of money is purely electronic currency—when things are bought and sold with no money in your pocket. Electronic currency may indeed be "the biggest revolution in currency since gold replaced cowrie shells," according to *Business Week* (June 12, 1995). In some ways it is more of a revolution than cowrie shells yielding to gold, because at least each of these were tangible. But one has less of a chance of grasping the electronic impulses of electronic currency than one does of holding onto the wind.

Just how big of a deal is electronic currency? It seems to invite prophesies of the Apocalypse. James G. Cosgrove, vice president and general manager for business multimedia services at AT&T, was quoted in *Business Week*: "Electronic commerce will literally change the way business is done worldwide." That's pretty big talk, but not as big as came out of Eric Hughes, president of Open Financial Networks, a Berkeley, California, consulting firm, who said: "The retail banking market will collapse and give way to global competition."

Howard Anderson, managing director of the Yankee Group of Boston, said: "Banks are worried because they realize intuitively that they are buggy whips" (*Upside*, Jan. 1996). Or, how about the prophesy coming from Bill A. Frezza, president of Wireless Computing Associates and co-founder of the advocacy group DigitaLiberty? He declared: "Over the long haul, this is going to lead to the separation of economy and state."

Is the advent of electronic currency really the trumpet blast heralding the destruction of such temples as banking and government? Or will this phenomenon become woven into the fabric of the financial system as we know it?

### *Frontier Spurs Invention*

In the mid-19th century the American frontier was expanding so quickly that the stagecoaches and buckboards of the day could not transport currency quickly enough to meet demand. The Western Union Telegraph Co. introduced the novel idea of the wire transfer of money, allowing credits to be transmitted instantly across the vast young country. Following World War II, America entered an era of protracted economic expansion. The credit card, invented in 1956 by Bank of America employee Joseph Williams, helped fuel that growth. Credit cards became widely popular in the mid-1970s and grew to be one of the main cauldrons in which banks cook up new money. Each new credit card represents thousands of dollars. All the recipient has to do is use it, and the ensuing liability becomes part of the money supply.

One individual we know has collected all the unsolicited credit cards that have come to his home; when he added up the credit limits, the total came to more than $200,000. He could take the cash advances and leave the country, but issuers of cards have learned that only a small fraction of people abuse the credit. They have also learned that it is far less expensive to give cards to members of associations than it is to check each credit application individually; the card issuers benefit from the organizations' screening of prospective members.

The number of cards in circulation worldwide with magnetic stripes that allow consumers to pay for goods and services and obtain cash is expected to almost triple in less than a decade. The *Nilson Report* (June 1996), which covers consumer payment systems, predicts that the 3 billion cards in circulation worldwide in 1996 will become 8.6 billion by 2005. Even though more than half the cards in existence are held in the U.S., some 50 million Americans, not deemed creditworthy, still don't have credit cards.

Although we use the term "credit card," the piece of plastic we are referring to is actually electronic money. Order takers at the other end of the telephone or over the Internet do not see or touch your card; they want only its number and expiration date. This electronic payment system has eliminated the need for C.O.D., because the goods are paid for when ordered.

The credit card system is, in effect, a tax on the uncreditworthy. The two percent charged to merchants by the credit card companies to handle transactions is reflected in higher prices for everyone, as just part of the cost of running the system. And "cash or credit, same price" has replaced "discount for cash." Everyone pays, whether they use a credit card or not.

Next came debit cards, which directly access bank accounts, and automatic teller machines (ATMs). As with credit cards, there is a cost—a fee for use. It seems ironic that banks have the gall to charge for ATM use, considering that their cost for an ATM transaction is a fraction of what it would be for one employing a teller (see "Home Banking and the Internet," coming up). When Quicken and similar proprietary software gave people access to their accounts at home through personal computers—allowing them to pay bills without ever writing or mailing a check—direct banking was a viable possibility.

But it is the Internet that is the next frontier for money. Like the Old West, the Internet is open and wild, abounding in opportunities—and aching for a medium of exchange. As with frontiers of the past, government has been slow to provide the currency needed for commerce, and entrepreneurs have filled the void.

A U.S. Commerce Department/Killen & Associates' study has predicted a huge growth in electronic purchases in the early years of the 21st century. Electronic commerce, including retail, wholesale, service and mail-order purchases, accounted for 4.5 percent of all purchases in 1994; in dollar totals, this amounted to $245 billion, while $5.15 trillion was spent for traditional purchases. By the year 2000, it is estimated that electronic purchases will amount to 16.2

percent of all purchases—a total of $1.65 trillion compared to $8.5 trillion for traditional goods. And by 2005, the study predicts that electronic purchases will amount to 19.7 percent of the total. In dollars, that would be $2.95 trillion compared to $12 trillion for traditional purposes.

Of that growth in electronic spending, far and away the fastest growth will be via the Internet, the study concludes. From a standing start in 1994, Internet purchases are expected to reach $600 billion by 2000, and $1.25 trillion by 2005, which would be 10 percent of total purchases. Small wonder the Internet has captured the imagination, and why no one wants to be left out.

### *Are New Currencies Required?*

What will be required to facilitate this expected flow of commerce? New forms of money, perhaps?

"There is nothing intrinsic about the Internet that demands new means of exchange," according to Debora Spar, an associate professor at the Harvard Business School (*Harvard Business Review,* May-June 1996). "There are no technical obstacles to routing and recording even nontraditional transactions through established routes; nor are there demands for new levels of financial oversight or regulation."

In other words, commerce can be conducted on the Internet now, in her opinion, and the U.S. dollar and the banking system can handle the business. But is she right? Many buyers seem to have agreed with her. Despite warnings about losing control of their credit card number, they have used their plastic to make purchases on the Internet anyway.

The turning point was the security feature in Netscape Navigator 2.0, which is the most popular software for finding and manipulating information on the Web. With Secure Sockets Layer (SSL) to encrypt data, this browser enabled online banking. Other Web browsers offer similar security. With the apparent protection offered by the latest browser encryption features, buyers were finally overcome by their desire to buy the things offered on the Web. In 1996, among goods in great demand, they could get tickets to Olympics events. "We didn't know what to expect because the technology was so new," according to Donna Jonsson, deputy managing director of communications for the Atlanta Committee for the Olympic Games. "We were very pleasantly surprised."

Gateway 2000 Inc., which has become one of the country's leading producers of PCs, sold thousands of them within months after they put an order form on their Web site. Amazon.com of Seattle sells several thousand books a day from its Web site. More than 80 percent of its customers complete their transactions online (see Chapter 9, "Making Money on the Internet").

"We are seeing an almost complete turnaround," according to Michael Wolff, who publishes the NetGuide book series. "There is a perception that technology has improved and the security is there. And it's also the fact there is so much out there for sale and so the compulsion to buy is growing."

Besides, consumers think, security on the Internet is no worse than anywhere else. How, after all, is a hacker supposed to find their credit card number and their name out of all the data on the Net? And what's the difference between exposing your number online and giving it over the phone to a telemarketer or a waiter? And if a crook did get your credit card number, federal law limits an individual liability in credit card theft to $50.

"The fears about credit card numbers on the Net haven't moved me that much, since I give my credit card to people in restaurants all the time and they take it out of my sight where I can't see what they're doing with it," observed Dave Hatunen of Daly City, Calif., as quoted by Evan Ramstad of the Associated Press (May 28, 1996).

People have shown they can be weaned away from cash and even checks. Electronic transfers and credit card transactions now account for 18 percent of the trillions that consumers, corporations and governments spend. The number of electronic transfers increased 200 percent between 1986 and 1993. By comparison, checks and cash transactions in the same seven-year period rose only 17 percent. More than 37 percent of consumer payments are made by check. That comes to about 55 billion checks written annually by consumers, business and government. The average American's total is 270 checks per year, compared to 10 for the average German.

Also, checks are expensive to process, with financial institutions paying about $1.30 for each transaction. Banks end up losing money on about half of all checking accounts because handling costs often exceed the interest earned on the money in them. "It takes $150 billion a year just to run the U.S. banking system. That's a crazy number at the end of the day," remarked Colin Cook, senior technology officer of Citicorp, to the *New York Times*.

Electronic transfers, on the other hand, cost about 15 cents each. Is it any wonder banks want to move us in that direction? By the time banks add up all expenses, such as real estate and staff, they calculate it costs them $10 to have a customer come into a branch to check an account balance with a teller. Talking to the customer on the phone costs $3, and automated Touch-Tone telephone access costs 40 cents. That is why the authors question the bank practice of charging a one or two percent fee for customer use of ATMs, which represent a substantial cost savings to banks. We especially challenge an extra charge for Internet or other electronic banking. The banks ought to be paying their customers, which is exactly what we predict some will soon do.

Electronic bill paying saves money not only for banks, but big check writers see savings as well. The U.S. government, for one, saved $133 million in 1993 by paying close to half its hundreds of millions of bills by computer rather than by mail. It's not just big mailers that save through electronic commerce.

Confidence in Internet transactions was the missing key. Once the comfort level rose high enough, the money began to flow. To complete the loop, it took a familiar vehicle for the transfer of money; and that vehicle, of course, was good, old credit cards. Other means of transferring value on the Internet that have evolved may or may not survive. The final outcome will depend on their appeal, and on how well the U.S. dollar/ banking combination serves the needs of Internet commerce.

### *First Virtual*

First Virtual Holding Company (http://www.fv.com) has introduced a way to hold your credit card number in escrow, so to speak. First Virtual stands between the buyer and the seller until the transaction is complete. In other words, rather than giving the credit card number to a vendor over the Internet, you furnish a Virtual Personal Identification Number (PIN), which is used instead of the credit card number. To do this, you register your credit card with First Virtual over the telephone, not over the Internet. All you need is VISA or MasterCard and an e-mail address.

First Virtual's management team includes people experienced in developing Internet mail protocols, such as Nathaniel Borenstein, Lee H. Stein, Einar A. Stefferud and Marshall T. Rose. Their system is a simple approach to transferring money by e-mail messages. To buy, you give the vendor your Virtual PIN. First Virtual gets back to you by e-mail to confirm the purchase. Your response will be "yes" to confirm the purchase, "no" to cancel, or "fraud" to immediately cancel your Virtual PIN. "Fraud" is the cry that your Virtual PIN is being used without your consent. There's no getting around the inherent basic problems of doing business this way: Parties to the transaction can't see each other, the buyer can't see the merchandise, and the seller can't see the money. Trust is still the issue.

To sell on First Virtual you must have an account that accepts direct deposit, you complete an application and send $10. Sellers will find it is not cheap to do business on First Virtual, but it is a lot less expensive than maintaining a real-world store. When you make a sale, First Virtual charges a transaction fee of 29 cents, plus 2 percent. At the time they settle with you, First Virtual deducts an additional $1 for processing.

First Virtual's Web site offers this example: If you sell something for $1, First Virtual charges 31 cents and credits you with 69 cents. If you sell for $10, they charge 49 cents and credit you with $9.51. If you sell for $100 they charge you $2.29 and credit you with $97.71. If you did each of the three preceding transactions, you would receive $107.91 minus the additional $1 processing fee and would net

$106.91. Then, there is a "nominal storage fee" of $1.50 per month per megabyte of data. One megabyte is the electronic equivalent of 600 typed, double-space pages of text.

Add to that the 8 percent First Virtual charges for each transaction you do in their InfoHaus virtual shopping mall. Those fees are charged directly to your credit card rather than being deducted from the sales revenue deposited into your bank account. Which is to say that if your deal somehow went sour, you would still be out the money, in real cash. If you sold $111 worth of goods, First Virtual would charge you 8 percent ($8.88) plus $1.50 to your buyer's Virtual PIN, which is $10.38 charged to your credit card. Nonetheless, many companies find this cost of doing business competitive, including Apple Computers, Reuters and National Public Radio, which sells electronic transcripts of programs.

To avoid such fees as seller, you may sell from your own server, collect the buyers' Virtual PINs and send the transactions to First Virtual yourself. The process can be automated with software you can install on your own server. If you have a problem, though, don't call them; they take only e-mail. (See Mark Twain Bank for a story of real helpfulness!)

For the buyer, especially those buying files, software or other information, this shopping experience is not like going to the local bookstore. In a real store you can examine the merchandise and decide whether it is worth your money. In a virtual store, on the other hand, unless there is a sample online, you are buying a pig in a poke. To build confidence, First Virtual urges its participating merchants to let buyers "try before they buy." That is to say, let them have the information or file and hope they will like it enough to pay for it later. There is the danger that some may not pay for it, but, says First Virtual, "you lose little or nothing. After all, it costs you nothing to 'manufacture' a new copy, and you don't have to worry about restocking or repairing 'returned merchandise'."

So, we are back to ground zero—back to "shareware" because of the inherent problems of selling things on the Internet. "Of all the philosophies for Internet information commerce," First Virtual says, "'try before you buy' is the most compatible with the unrestricted flow of information that now governs the Internet." And if one of the customers becomes too abusive about taking material without paying for it, their "tight controls" ensure that individual's Virtual PIN will be suspended or terminated.

First Virtual's creative approach does not require special software or hardware; for that reason it may have a future for people reluctant to give out their credit card numbers directly over the Internet. Still, with its three-steps-per-transaction, it is cumbersome, and as new security software gains acceptance, the need for the intermediary approach may fade.

### *DigiCash*

The next stage in the evolution of electronic currency is not based on credit cards, but on real money. And to prove it would work, the developers invented a completely fictitious money dubbed the Cyberbuck. If you could just get your hands on a Cyberbuck, you might have a real collector's item. But, alas! It was an electronic currency, with no physical manifestation and not redeemable for any real money. The Cyberbuck, however, did prove a very important point: People are willing to trade goods and services in exchange for what amounts to nothing that is backed by nothing.

The Cyberbuck was the unit of electronic currency issued by DigiCash (http://www.digicash.com) and its founder, David Chaum of Amsterdam, the Netherlands. Chaum, who received his Ph.D. in computer science from the University of California at Berkeley, teamed with his colleagues at a government-funded institution in Amsterdam called the Center for Mathematics and Computer Science, came up with a "blinding" technique that allows numbers to serve as electronic cash. To demonstrate its viability, Chaum launched an experiment in October 1994 that eventually led to the Mark Twain Bank, through which real money is now flowing.

Chaum issued 100 Cyberbucks free to each of the 30,000 people who participated in his experiment. The Cyberbucks went into participants' DigiCash bank accounts. Although these Cyberbucks could not be exchanged for real money, their relative scarcity and the goods and services behind them gave them value.

People set up shops at the DigiCash Web site and sold things like books and pictures and software, mostly things that could be transmitted online, goods most people could live without. In time, a true small economy evolved and, a year after it was launched, Chaum cut off enrollment in his experiment. If anyone wanted in on it, he or she had to buy someone's Cyberbucks, and it cost a real dollar to get the e-mail address of the person advertising them for sale.

The experiment turned into a real business, and E-cash™ came into being. E-cash is not fictitious money but rather the electronic representation of real cash—primarily the U.S. dollar and a number of other currencies as well. The advantage to users is that this is real money; simply notify Mark Twain Bank you want your cash taken out of electronic currency and it will be sent to you in a check.

DigiCash says that because "E-cash offers full payor anonymity, it is perfect for controversial applications," leaving it to the imagination what those might be. The company explains that the identity of the payor is not revealed automatically, so the payor stays in control of personal information. The payee, however, is identified to the bank. Which is why E-cash is not good for money laundering, tax evasion, black market activities, extortion or bribes, according to DigiCash. The reason is that all money the payee receives must eventually be funneled through the bank. "It's not possible to hide from the bank the fact that you received money from it (and thereby hide it from the authorities). So tax evasion is definitely out."

DigiCash offers online consultants to help would-be merchants set up a cybershop. These are a combination of a Web page and the E-cash payment software that automatically collects money from people choosing certain links when visiting your Web page. To have an online shop costs an introductory fee of $150, $250, $350 or $500, depending on how much business you are going to do. Monthly fees slide downward; the smallest entry-fee shops pay $25, the next pay $20, then $10 and $5. And DigiCash takes a sliding percentage of sales; for the smallest entry fee shops the percentage is highest, 3 percent of the first $500, then 2.75 percent, 2.5 percent and 2.0 percent.

These fees may sound steep, but DigiCash suggests you compare them with credit card discounts, and reminds the seller that there is no per-transaction fee.

No wonder DigiCash believes other banks will want to license their software and build a system. The technology behind DigiCash is at the heart of CAFE, a project sponsored by the European Community to develop a pan-European currency system.

Those anxious to jump on the DigiCash bandwagon face the same risks of collecting arrows in the back that any pioneers do. When you cut through the hype, you find an ingenious setup through which DigiCash has put itself in a no-lose situation, but one in which it warns its customers: "Caveat emptor," buyer beware. The disclaimers throughout the DigiCash Web site are not conducive to building consumer confidence. All transactions made through DigiCash are at your own risk, they warn you. "If you pay to download something and it turns out to be a fake, then that's your bad luck, I'm afraid, though if you let me know, I will delete it," the DigiCash Web site warns. And if the vendor takes the money and runs, there is nothing DigiCash can do but delete the offer.

Not only are the vendors not guaranteed, but neither is the sanctity of your money. "DigiCash has developed a system that according to reviews is secure and potentially safe. There is no way to guarantee you that there is no chance of a successful attack on the system, or your personal copy of the software," the Web site warns.

"As a result, you should treat all funds transferred out of your Mark Twain Bank World Currency Access Account to the E-cash mint or further to your hard drive as cash. This cash should be protected as though you were walking down an unfamiliar street that a friend has told you is safe. Your friend may believe this to be true, but can not guarantee the result of a random attack.

"Minimize the amount of cash you carry in the E-cash mint and on your hard drive to an amount that you can afford to lose."

To spend money on the DigiCash system, you sign up for an account online, and DigiCash transmits a form on screen that you run off on your printer, sign and mail, along with your check, to

Mark Twain Bank of St. Louis. Your money goes into a World Currency Access Account, which is a traditional bank account with no minimum deposit.

You receive software so you can work the system. It does help to be computer-literate, though, because the Web site warns you: "If you have any problems during the process (of installing the software) please do not call the bank!!!!!!" Again, they advise the user: "If you have a problem, remember Rule Number 1, do not call Mark Twain Bank right away if you have a problem!! E-mail us at support@mark-twain.com."

Once your money is in your World Currency Access Account, you can notify Mark Twain Bank that you want some of it moved to the E-cash mint. Like a cash withdrawal, this money is then no longer in your account. With the software provided, you issue instructions to the mint to "coin" some of your money and place it on your hard drive. This can be all or only a portion of the money you have moved from your bank account into the E-cash mint. The money you have on your hard drive you now can spend in the online shops or e-mail it to a friend on the other side of the world. When you're on the Web, E-cash software runs in the background. It appears on the screen as a small box showing the amount of money stored on your hard drive, with a five-button tool bar in which every button is a mini icon for the basic functions: One button is for transactions with the bank and another is for transactions with other E-cash users; the third shows you your payment history for payments made as well as received; the fourth and fifth buttons give a current status report and a personal settings dialog box.

As soon as a payment is required, a dialog box pops up and you are asked to confirm the requested payment. A click on the "yes" or the "no" button is enough to make or refuse the requested payment from the digital coins on the hard drive. When an E-cash withdrawal is made, the PC of the E-cash user calculates how many digital coins of what denomination are needed to withdraw the requested amount. Next, random serial numbers for those coins will be generated and the "blinding factor" will be included. "Blinding" is the bank's way of issuing an electronic note without tracing its receiver. This makes the E-cash as anonymous as paper currency.

The result of these calculations will be sent to the digital bank. The bank will encode the blinded numbers with its secret key (digital signature) and at the same time debit the account of the client for the same amount. The authenticated coins are sent back to the user and finally the user will take out the blinding factor that he introduced earlier. The serial numbers plus their signatures are now digital coins, their value is guaranteed by the bank.

When the user makes a purchase, the coins go to the receiver, who in turn sends them to the digital bank. The bank verifies the validity of these coins and that they have not been spent before (every coin is used only once). The account of the receiver is credited. Another withdrawal is needed if the receiver wishes to have new coins to spend.

### *Breakage and Float*

If you use the DigiCash system, you had better hope your hard drive doesn't crash, because you could lose the money in your computer. And you'd better watch the expiration date on your screen, because your e-cash eventually expires. Like the Mondex system, in which a lost cash card means money found for Mondex, the DigiCash scheme is bound to pay the bank handsomely in money either lost or expired: breakage. Even if you don't lose your money, the bank still makes out by lending your money without paying you interest: float.

Breakage and float are two tantalizing and related sources of income for providers of electronic currency. Float can be defined as money on hold; breakage as money you lose and I find. Float is what sellers of travelers' checks enjoy when buyers do not cash them. That money is loaned out at interest, just as providers of electronic currency will do with the money they hold as deposits or which is on your hard drive waiting to be spent.

DigiCash earns float by requiring a monthly minimum balance in non-interest-bearing accounts, or by requiring that users pay a monthly fee. For example, setting up an account with Mark Twain Bank costs $11 if you're just trying it out, $25 for a frequent user.

There is also a monthly fee of $1 for trying it, $2 for frequent users and $5 for heavy users. To waive the monthly fees takes a monthly balance of $500 for light users, $750 for frequent users and $1,500 for heavy users. You receive no interest until you have a deposit of $2,500 in your World Currency Access Account, which means the bank gets float on hundreds of dollars held in thousands of accounts, not to mention the money "coined" and resting on hard drives.

Breakage is float that has hit the ground, a source of income known to every issuer of certificates, coupons or scrip. When someone pays in advance for goods or services, such as restaurant meals or hotel rooms, and receives a certificate in exchange, a percentage of the holders of the paper will never redeem it. They will either lose the cards or simply forget them until after they have expired. The people who sold those certificates keep the money.

When a telephone card company sells cheap calling time, they are banking on the fact that a substantial portion of buyers, anywhere from one to 10 percent, will not use all the time on the card before it expires. The question is, will states enforce their escheatment laws, which require found or unearned money to be turned over to state treasuries? And if states set that ball in motion, where will they stop? Will the money behind lost travelers' checks wind up in state coffers?

### *Where Is Government?*

Where is the federal government while electronic currency is inchoate and aborning? Well, the burgeoning industry would like nothing more than for government to stay on the sidelines and keep hands off. And that is precisely the role government seems willing to take, for now.

When the U.S. quashed private currency during the Civil War, the Supreme Court subsequently reaffirmed that Congress has the capacity to suppress "the circulation as money of any notes not issued under its own authority." The question for the beginning of the 21st century is, what is money? If the new forms of exchange on the Internet are considered money, what will government do and when?

The U.S. mint views electronic currency as "substitutes for

coinage" (*New York Times*, June 16, 1996). "Government-issued electronic currency would probably stem seigniorage losses and provide a riskless electronic payment product to consumers," according to Alan Blinder, who, as vice chairman of the Federal Reserve, spoke at a Congressional hearing. The intention now is to wait and see, it would appear. Said Lawrence Summers, Deputy Treasury Secretary, "I think we should maintain an enormous presumption in favor of letting people participate in markets and compete and do all those things, while insisting on a whole set of regulatory safeguards that insure that electronic money is not marketed by people who are then going to default."

"I don't think that setting up the Government Electronic Money Corporation is particularly attractive. That is the philosophy that brought you the world's state-run airlines, the world's state-run telephone companies and the world's state-run electric companies, and by and large it hasn't been successful." These are reassuring words to an industry investing its genius and effort to create new media of exchange. History has shown, however, that government eventually gets into the act. As suggested earlier, government either closed down or bought out competing currencies in the past, and there is no reason to believe it won't eventually do the same with electronic currency.

### *Banks Enter the Fray*

CyberCash Inc., of Reston, Virginia, and giant banking company Wells Fargo are also experimenting with their own electronic currency. It works much like a checking account. Clients put real money into their electronic money accounts using proprietary software provided free by CyberCash. They spend their money on the Net and, at the end of the day, CyberCash clears all transactions and converts the electronic currency back to money.

CyberCash was founded in 1994 by William Melton and Daniel Lynch. Melton had also founded Verifone, which makes equipment to authorize credit card transactions. The two managed to convince the U.S. government that their encryption software could not be used to transmit secrets, so it is exportable (see Chapter 10 on the issues of "Encryption").

Banks' interest in the Internet stems from a fateful discovery they made when they introduced Automatic Teller Machines (ATMs) as a convenience for customers. Banks learned that the cost of handling an ATM transaction is a fraction of the cost of a traditional one. It made financial sense to move away from bank branches and tellers and in the direction of automating as many transactions as possible at ATMs. To accelerate cuts in expenses, banks have moved branches out of separate buildings and into grocery stores. As early as 1990 many bankers were worried that customers would not accept handling financial matters in a grocery store. The customers, however, apparently preferred it. Cathy Haffner, U.S. Bancorp vice president and manager of in-store banking, said an industry survey of grocery shoppers showed that a bank was the third most requested service behind only a bakery and a deli.

Each retail center is likely to draw an estimated 35,000 visitors per week, which is an attractive base of customers. And in-store branches are inexpensive: $200,000 to $300,000 compared with nearly $1 million for a stand-alone branch. And some of the grocery banks can be operated with a single employee. Stand-alone bank branches generally need deposits of $25 million to break even, while in-store branches need only $6 million to $8 million, according to Jay Tejera, a Dain Bosworth analyst specializing in bank stocks. He said when banks look at the numbers, "it's surprising it hasn't happened faster."

One reason is the lack of enough suitable grocery store chains. And this has set banks scrambling for the best ones. U.S. Bancorp has arranged to have branches in Albertson's stores, the fourth largest grocery chain in the country. U.S. Bancorp did it by acquiring West One Bancorp of Boise, Idaho. Albertson's, which is also headquartered in Boise, is a big borrower from West One; in addition, Warren McCain, chairman of Albertson's executive committee, was on the West One board of directors. U.S. Bancorp has considered grocery branches as a way to expand. But other banks, such as Wells Fargo, are closing stand-alone branches in favor of the grocery store outlets.

### *Home Banking and the Internet*

Electronic technology also helps banks close branches. The Federal Reserve predicts that American Banks will close as many as half their branches by the year 2000, a reduction of 30,000 branches. There will still be bank branches nonetheless. "I don't think we're going to see everyone do their banking online," according to Harvey Radin, a spokesperson at Bank of America's San Francisco headquarters. "We don't believe it's going to be all one or the other. We strongly believe in giving our customers a choice," he told Fran Gardner of Portland's *Oregonian* (Oct. 8, 1995).

Banking from home is so far a tiny portion of the potential market, accounting for just 1 percent of transactions in 1995, according to Jupiter Communications, a New York-based marketing firm. Those who do bank this way enjoy the luxury of avoiding dealing with cash, as well as its attendant risks of theft and loss. They use Intuit's Quicken or other software and their PC's communications program to work with their banks.

Banks want people to move in that direction, and are doing what they can to "encourage" people. Some bank customers are charged $3 every time they deal with a teller. One bank offers inexpensive checking to customers if they are willing to pay $1 to use a teller.

Unfortunately, banks feel they can charge the customer for the "service" of banking at home or using an ATM, even though these transactions cost the bank a fraction of those executed by a real teller. "The banks need that technology to drive their processing costs down," according to Joseph Cady, a consultant with CB Consulting in San Diego.

"We're not trying to force anyone to switch to ATMs or PC banking," according to Linda Parker, vice president and manager of emerging delivery services at U.S. Bank in Seattle. "We're offering those because there's another segment of customers who prefer to do their banking that way."

Wells Fargo is the first major bank to offer online transfers directly through its Web site (http://www.wellsfargo.com) and at this writing is the only bank to allow transfers between credit and deposit accounts. Wells Fargo Bank of San Francisco and Los Angeles is the eighth largest bank holding company in the country. Rival Bank of America announced it is right behind with online banking. Wells Fargo had offered home banking through personal computers since 1989 for customers with a modem, connecting either directly with the bank or through Prodigy. Through Quicken or Microsoft Money, customers have been able to access account balances and history and download the information. With the protection of the encryption offered by Netscape Navigator's secured browser, however, Wells Fargo has now been able to take the final step: Internet banking.

"Internet transfers is the latest enhancement in Wells Fargo's evolving Internet banking strategy, which is focused on giving customers the ability to manage their finances conveniently and securely, anytime and anywhere," according to Gailyn Johnson, senior vice president of Online Financial Services. The service allows Wells Fargo customers to transfer money between their Wells Fargo accounts, including checking, savings, market rate, Money Market Access, credit card, equity line and other lines of credit. Their customers can pay balances on credit card, equity line and other lines of credit accounts by transferring money from a deposit account. They can also advance funds by moving money from a credit account to a deposit account. Also online, customers can find the location of the nearest ATM in Wells Fargo's 13-state territory.

To arrange Internet access to accounts, customers call an 800 number to get a secured password. Besides a personal computer, modem and access to the Internet, customers need to have the Netscape Navigator secured browser to view their account.

The bank maintains their customers will soon be able to make payments over the Internet at anytime to anyone, as mentioned earlier in their arrangement with CyberCash. "Customers can do business through Wells Fargo on the Internet with the same confidence that they have whenever they deal with Wells Fargo," Johnson said. Wells Fargo was rated "Best Online Bank" by *Smart Money* magazine, and its Internet site was awarded "Best Overall Site by a U.S. Financial Institution" by the Online Banking Association. It also received a four-star rating by Yahoo, the highest rating given by the Web site locator.

Other banks will follow, but many will wait and see. "We have to assume electronic money will be the subject of sustained attack from all kinds of people," said Colin Crook, senior technology officer for Citicorp.

### *Barter and the Future of Money*

Banks, in their rush to downsize, could find they have lost their hold on customers. "E-cash will be offered by both banks and nonbanks," remarked DigiCash's Chaum. If Internet commerce swings in the direction of an electronic currency, DigiCash or CyberCash could just as well work with Microsoft and its 70 million Windows users as it could with banks. And that is a prospect that may well fit with Bill Gates' long-range objectives.

Banks could find themselves "buttons on a network operated by other entities," according to William M. Randle, senior vice president at Huntington Bancshares. If that seems unlikely, look at what happened to credit card processing. In the mid-1970s, banks owned that business. Twenty years later, 80 percent of card transactions were processed by non-banks such as First Data Resources Inc.

Just as the banks don't have a lock on Internet commerce, neither does the U.S. dollar. Chaum's DigiCash hopes to base its E-cash some day on a blend of currencies and precious metals. Today, there is nothing preventing big players from issuing their own private money—provided they are willing to relocate the way Chaum did to The Netherlands—or other countries where it is permitted. The only question is whether people believe in the integrity of the one issuing it.

Chaum showed in his initial experiment that thousands of people are willing to buy and sell over the Internet using a fictitious currency based on absolutely nothing. It may seem surprising that people are willing to do that, until you think about the world economy. The U.S. dollar is the preferred medium of exchange, but it can't be exchanged for anything, either.

But what if there were an electronic currency backed by goods and services produced by thousands of businesses? Of course, we refer to trade dollars, which are the accounting unit of the trade industry. Trade dollars don't expire. Trade dollars are impossible to counterfeit. The trade exchange is a clearinghouse, or marketplace, governed by trading rules which all the members of that particular marketplace have agreed to honor. Trade dollars are, in effect, a private money, the only genuine electronic currency.

Professor F.A. Hayek, in *Choice in Currency: A Way to Stop Inflation*, explains why private money such as trade dollars makes sense for electronic commerce. "There is no reason whatever why people should not be free to make contracts, including ordinary purchases and sales, in any kind of money they choose, or why they should be obligated to sell against any particular kind of money. There should be no more effective check against the abuse of money by government than if people were free to refuse any money they distrusted and to prefer money in which they had confidence."

Paul Suplizio, CEO of the International Reciprocal Trade Association (IRTA), in his paper "Commercial Barter Exchanges in Society," wrote: "Modern commercial barter is a system of trade and payments that is emerging alongside the monetary system of trade and payments. Its instrument of payment, the trade dollar or trade credit, is the best illustration today of the privatization of money that Professor Hayek has called for and which Professor Milton Friedman approves."

The trade dollar has all the basic elements of money, as well as some unique characteristics that could make it an excellent choice as a supplemental or alternative electronic currency. Trade dollars fulfill the essential definition of a currency because they can serve widely as a medium of exchange, as a standard of exchange value, as well as a store of exchange value. They have greater potential as an electronic currency than the U.S. dollar because trade dollars can at least be redeemed for goods and services. For every trade dollar in circulation in a trade exchange, there must be an offsetting debit in another participating business owner's trade account. Trade dollars are, in effect, credit lines.

For example, if there were 100 trading business owners in a trade exchange network and each were granted a $10,000 credit line, there could never be more than $990,000 in circulation at any time. Suppose that 99 trade members all drew against their credit line and spent their entire $10,000 at one company. That would mean the creation of $990,000 in new trade dollars. Each exchange member is bound by trading rules to make immediately available their respective goods and services for 100 percent trade dollars to repay their debt to the system. This means that the trade dollars in circulation are backed by the goods and services of the exchange's indebted membership.

Is this a backed currency? Absolutely! In fact, the authors cannot think of a better form of currency backing. If all 99 debtors were to repay their obligation through the sale of their goods on trade, the trade dollars in circulation would fall to zero until another credit-worthy exchange member once again accesses the credit line for buying and thereby expands the money supply.

Trade dollars are among the most credible electronic currencies for doing business on the Internet because the supply of trade dollars expands with legitimate business demands and contracts as demand diminishes.

The balance of this book is devoted to explaining trade dollars, the modern trade exchange industry and its role in the future of money.

SECTION

# The New Barter

THREE

# 13

# Introduction to the Barter Industry

*"Money doesn't always bring happiness. People with ten million dollars are no happier than people with nine million dollars."*
Hobart Brown

The name of John Hancock's uncle escapes Paul Suplizio, but the anecdote about him does not. Suplizio, who is CEO of the International Reciprocal Trade Association (IRTA), which represents barter companies in 31 countries, said from his suburban Washington, D.C., office: "John Hancock's uncle used to ship furniture from New England to Ohio and he took wheat and pork in exchange. He kept records of those deals by hand."

Some things have to change for other things to stay the same. Barter is even bigger business today, but the quill pen had to give way to the Personal Computer for it to become that large. In fact, the ancient practice of barter is experiencing an explosion of growth, thanks to PCs and the other high-tech devices that comprise the Electronic Revolution.

Barter is a dynamic growth industry, an industry as old as man, as modern as the information highway. Over the last decades of the 20th century, the barter industry's growth has been nothing short of phenomenal. The Department of Commerce says that barter in its various forms accounts for about 30 percent of the world's total business. Plus, the International Reciprocal Trade Association announced that U.S. barter transacted through commercial barter brokers exceeds $8.5 billion annually. An IRTA Fact Sheet claims that more than 400,000 U.S. businesses actively use organized barter.

There are many good reasons why more businesses worldwide are bartering their products and services; underlying them all, however, is one fundamental motivation: profit.

Today's Barter Industry operates on three distinct levels:

1. **Retail Trade Exchange:** This is an association of merchants and professionals who come together to barter their surplus goods and services. The trade exchange serves as the clearinghouse for these surpluses. Barter transactions are accounted for through the use of "trade dollars," which is a ledger entry by which goods and services can be bought and sold. As with a bank account, trade dollars are credited and debited to each business' trade account. Exchange clientele are serviced by trade brokers who play a role similar to that of a stock broker. Only rarely do these brokers function as principals in barter transactions. Exchanges are third-party recordkeepers under U.S. law. The majority of transactions consummated through a trade exchange are made on a 100 percent trade basis.
2. **Corporate Barter:** Manufacturers, wholesalers and distributors frequently trade excess inventory for "purchase credits" rather than taking losses on cash sales or dealing with liquidation situations. In addition, these larger companies may have surplus production capacity that can be exchanged for needed items. Corporate barter companies act as finders, buyers and sellers rather than as brokers. The vast majority of purchase credits are used by corporate clients to pay for a portion of their future advertising budgets, travel expenses and equipment needs. There is generally a variable cash component required as a part of the spend-down plan of corporate purchase credits.
3. **International Barter:** This is comprised of two separate elements: countertrade and international reciprocal trading. Countertrade constitutes large single transactions between governments or multinational corporations—or where government approval or assistance will be generally required. International reciprocal trading can occur when trade exchanges and/or corporate barter companies have formed trading partnerships abroad.

### *The Benefits*

The barter industry's growing appeal among businesses is related to the benefits a barter company provides:

- **Retail Trade Exchange**
  New sales/new customers
  Increase in buying power
  Conservation of cash
  Alternative financing
- **Corporate Barter**
  Conversion of slow-moving inventory into current receivables
  Utilization of surplus production capacity
  Increase in market share with low cash investment
  New distribution outlets
- **International Countertrade**
  Preservation of hard currency
  Expansion of production for export
  Access to new markets
  Upgrading of manufacturing capabilities
  Maintenance of prices of export goods

### *Is Barter Commerce or Finance?*

There are many different actual—and potential—"niche" markets within the barter industry. And some barter companies are so attuned to one particular aspect of their business that they almost become that business. Some barter companies, for example, are so closely aligned with the media industry that they might better be described as a media company utilizing barter as a marketing or financial tool, rather than as a barter company specializing in media.

We view the barter industry as an alternative, or adjunct, to commerce coupled with creative finance. The financial industry seems to be driven by three huge economic engines: 1) the securities industry; 2) banking, in all of its forms, including thrift and central banking, and 3) insurance. These three industries are all huge facilitators of business. Each has developed, in addition, its own specialized marketplaces. The barter industry as we know it, although separate and distinct from securities, banking and insurance, is largely of the same ilk; all of these act in the capacity of business facilitators.

In many respects trade exchanges closely resemble the securities business in that they have merged the trading equivalent of a stock exchange (the marketplace, or clearinghouse), with a brokerage operation. Also noteworthy is the fact that corporate barter companies frequently resemble (both in form and function), what stock brokers refer to as market makers and/or investment bankers. This is because corporate barter companies take positions in the deals they construct rather than act simply as brokers. Furthermore, it is curious to note that both trade exchanges and corporate trading companies generally grant lines of credit. Put another way, they allow their clients to buy on margin.

Working from the premise that modern commercial barter has much in common with the securities industry, we might look to the latter's development as a lens through which to view the evolving commercial barter industry. It seems quite apparent, for example, that the trade exchange as it now exists will continue to move toward becoming a true electronic marketplace where the real time execution of orders will facilitate a huge increase in transactions.

One of the more fascinating aspects of the exchange business is that, in one sense, the trade exchange actually provides greater security to its customers than any of the other three engines of commerce. How so? Simply because an exchange operating in compliance with IRTA's model contract conducts business through the use of trade dollars backed by the real goods and services of its indebted membership. The formula

**Currency in Circulation = In-Use Credit Lines**

explains the method by which trade dollars are created within the closed economy we refer to as a trade exchange. Hence every trade dollar in circulation within a balanced exchange is backed by real products.

The U.S. dollar, on the other hand, could be reasonably defined as an unsecured claim on an overdraft government. Clearly this is not a definition well understood or easily accepted by the majority of U.S. citizens, but it is, nonetheless, accurate.

Today's barter industry can be seen as a pyramid formed of the three distinct levels set forth above. The trade exchange segment of the barter industry comprises the foundation tier of the structure. Corporate barter and international countertrade form the second and third tiers. These last two barter industry segments are the subjects of later chapters.

### *The Trade Exchange*

Modern barter is a highly organized, high-tech, communications-driven industry. At its heart is the trade exchange, which is an association, or network, of business owners and professionals comprising a marketplace in which they may barter goods and services. The exchange acts as a barter clearinghouse for its members' trading activities. Transactions cleared through an exchange are accomplished through the medium of the "trade dollar," which represents credit to the seller's account for goods and services sold "on trade."

"Trade exchanges were initially known as barter clubs, when the concept was introduced 30 years ago," according to Bob Meyer, publisher of *Barter News* magazine. "Under the Tax Equity & Fiscal Responsibility Act of 1982 (TEFRA Act), trade exchanges are classified as third-party record-keepers, having the same fiduciary obligations as bankers and stock brokers. For tax purposes trade dollars are taxable in the year they are earned and reported as such on 1099-B forms to the IRS."

Although estimates vary somewhat, there appear to be about 500 retail trade companies in this country. This number includes the two national organizations' independent broker offices that together total about half that number. Another 250 retail trade operations conduct business without access to an organized central system. Most of these latter firms confine themselves to doing business within one particular city. Collectively the two national firms, however, coupled with the other independent trade exchanges, process trades for an estimated 400,000 U.S. businesses. Trade exchange clientele focus on small- to medium-size business owners and professionals. [In the U.S. a small business is defined as one with 500 or fewer employees if a manufacturing concern, 100 or fewer employees for service businesses. Another criterion is gross sales, where $10 million or less is considered "small business." In the U.S. 96 percent of the 17 million nonagricultural businesses fall into the small business category.]

The primary reasons business owners and professionals barter are to increase sales and gain new customers, and to conserve cash. Ask almost any business owner if he or she would like to increase sales while decreasing cash outflow; the response, invariably, will be a resounding "Absolutely!" A good barter broker working in conjunction with a well-established trade exchange can perform both of these services for their business owner clients again and again. Through association with a trade exchange, member businesses find new customers and earn trade dollars selling their surplus, which they can then spend with other members for products and services.

Generally speaking, most barter brokers earn their living by helping their clients make money. It works like this: Effective brokers think in terms of bringing new customers and new sales to their clients. They usually charge a commission for this service. Their next responsibility is to help clients conserve cash by finding them things to buy with their newly earned trade dollars. And again, they expect to earn a fee for professional delivery of this service. While varying somewhat, fee structures typically range between 10 percent and 15 percent overall. The more progressive exchanges break this fee down into two parts and assess half the amount as they complete their first job of bringing a client new business, and the other half as they help that client conserve cash by completing purchases with trade dollars.

The opportunity to wheel and deal increases exponentially as creative minds find ways to use new technologies to buy and sell goods and services around the world through a trade exchange. The BarterWire, an electronic network linking member-traders in one of the larger exchanges, has made it possible for a breeder of miniature horses in Colorado, for example, to use trade dollars she earned for selling surplus colts to someone in Michigan, to buy a vacation in Mexico, to swap with her contractor to have a barn built.

Vacation spots and hotels also find that trade dollars are better than vacant rooms, especially when they can use trade dollars to buy advertising to gain cash customers. Each barter system has its own inventory of vacation and travel offerings, and many independent exchanges trade with each other through reciprocal networks.

### *The Barter Economy*

What is an economy? A nonacademic definition might be a human system through which value is stored and exchanged, whose outward method of storage and transfer has generally been cash. Cash, however, seldom has any true, inherent value. Those who saved their Confederate dollars may have ended up with valuable collectors' items, but the economic system of which they were the instruments has ceased to exist. You can trade them or sell them, but they can't be used for their intended purpose—they can't be spent.

If Confederate currency is cash without an economic system behind it, then the modern barter company is an economic system without cash. Barter networks are an economic system in every sense that the U.S. economy is one, yet, in some ways, more advanced. The barter world is a miniature cashless society. In a sense, "barter" is a misnomer. In modern barter companies, goods are seldom exchanged directly for other goods. Instead, there is an arrangement in which goods and services are exchanged with nothing more than an accounting system recording the transactions. Such dealings render cash obsolete and practically a nuisance. After all, cash can be lost or stolen. With a trade account, there is no wad of bills, no automatic teller machine, no one with a knife or gun who can relieve you of your wealth. What has been created is a true electronic currency that is commodity-based.

The barter economy is related to the larger economy in a countercyclical way. When the larger economy is good and there is plenty of money circulating and everyone's plate is full, the trade economy may be slow. When, on the other hand, the general economy is sluggish and money is hard to come by, people look to barter to generate business. The prudent entrepreneur realizes the value of barter at both ends of the business cycle, and keeps a trade dollar balance at all times.

The barter economy is like all others, in that value flows toward a vacuum. Capital tends to flow toward opportunity. Currently in Eastern Europe, where there are assets and skilled laborers but little hard currency, entrepreneurs are flocking to invest. Much of this investment has been in barter. A prime example is the deal Pepsico made with the former Soviet Union. Pepsi wanted to sell product to the Soviet people but didn't want the worthless currency. Instead, they traded their products for Russian vodka, which they sold in the U.S. market for hard currency. This kind of barter transaction is known as "countertrade."

The trade economy is much more exclusive than the general economy. Anyone with a buck in a pocket is part of the general economy. To become part of the trade system, though, there are certain qualifications: One must have something to offer that others in the barter system want. Unlike the general economy, in which consumers receive scores of unsolicited credit cards every year, a trade line of credit is based primarily on capacity to repay, not on credit history.

Lenders typically think in terms of the three C's, which stand for credit, character and capacity. Trade exchanges are very interested in character and capacity but do not always place a great deal of faith in a credit bureau's idea of what constitutes good credit. Trade exchange administrators will usually make up their own minds about creditworthiness predicated on their direct experience with the participating small business owner. A new subscriber to the barter system, to cite the typical case, will usually not be granted much of a credit line until after he or she has earned trade through new sales made to other members of the exchange and spent that trade successfully. Once a barter broker has developed a good working relationship with a new trader, the first steps are taken to explore new and perhaps unique ways this client could incorporate more barter into day-to-day business activities. As a broker discovers ways to reduce the client's cash costs by acquiring items on barter that were formerly paid for with cash, a larger credit line makes good sense, because the business owner is actually saving cash when drawing against the new line of barter credit.

# 14

# Born of Computers

*"Out of intense complexities, intense simplicities emerge."*
Winston Churchill

Paul Suplizio of the IRTA traces the advent of the modern barter company to the birth of the personal computer in the 1970s. "Trade exchanges would never have gotten off the ground without them. You couldn't keep track of all the transactions manually," he said, especially the little deals, such as the guy who buys his wife flowers on barter. The cost of recording such small transactions would be too great if done manually. "Computers are necessary to keep track of transactions, maintain accounts, create bills, compute commissions, issue monthly statements and render account information to the IRS."

It is this last capacity, perhaps more than any other, that has legitimized barter in recent years. It is possible for swaps to be made without paying taxes to the government on the value received. As a matter of fact, it's estimated that personal, unreported barter transactions amount to between $25 billion and $40 billion per year and are a sizeable portion of the "underground economy." Barter companies today, however, are required to transmit to the IRS a magnetic media report of the barter income of their members. A dollar of trade is taxed like a dollar of cash, and we discuss barter and taxation at length in Chapter 17.

Retail exchanges are third-party record keepers for that aspect of their clients' business that is done on barter. The Tax Equity and Fiscal Responsibility Act (TEFRA) recognized trade exchanges, along with banks, credit card issuers and stock brokerage firms, as official record keepers under U.S. law. As a consequence, all of these industries report various information to the U.S. Treasury Department.

The modern barter industry was born in the U.S. and expanded first to the English-speaking world, starting with Canada, Australia, New Zealand, South Africa and the United Kingdom. IRTA also has member companies in such countries as Lebanon, France, Belgium, Turkey, Colombia, Uruguay, Argentina, Peru, Holland and Iceland. American exchanges have opened offices in Budapest, Singapore, Mexico City and Hong Kong, among other places. The European Reciprocal Trade Association has now been launched. A child of IRTA, it was formed in London with member businesses in several European countries. In addition, IRTA Australasia is now a reality and serves exchanges in countries throughout the South Pacific.

Barter grows as the electronic tools it depends on become more user-friendly. Barter Corp., to make the point, offered its members an e-mail system in the 1980s. "But the members weren't ready," conceded Susan Groenwald, president, who founded the 3,000-member regional exchange with headquarters in Chicago and offices in Milwaukee and Cleveland. "We put online computer terminals in clients' offices, but found they didn't use them. It was brand-new, and they preferred to read bulletins and faxes."

What did work for Groenwald, however, was BART, a voice synthesizer that answered the telephone and helped record deals at any hour of the day. Call Barter Corp. now and a computer voice says: "Hello. This is BART." The voice asks clients to enter their account number, translates it digitally into a synthesized voice, and repeats it back for confirmation. BART helps facilitate a lot of barter transactions that would otherwise not have happened.

### *BarterWire*

BarterWire is currently the major electronic network linking the barter industry. With PC and modem, clients and brokers can access the ITEX data bank at any hour of the day or night, from any place in the world where there are telephones. The system is an electronic, international version of the bulletin board planted in front of the old country store, with notices of items for sale and items wanted, of messages and announcements. Members can get instant information on their trade balance and barter activity and can even generate a report showing their total barter business for up to the last 10 years.

The main draw is the ability to buy and sell. There are literally thousands of goods and services available, ranging from production of radio spots to condos in Florida to typewriters in Montana. Horses, collectors' cars, travel coupons, vacant lots from North Carolina to Colorado, computers.... A totally mixed bag of merchandise that can be sorted by category or by time of posting through keyboard commands. There are also menus for posting wants, industry news, chat rooms, a national barter marketplace, user-definable setups and much, much more. If you're on the Internet and access the World Wide Web, you can reach the ITEX BarterWire by simply going to: http://www.itex.net.

### *ITEX Express*

Another first for the barter industry has been the development of ITEX Express, a hybrid credit/debit card. Embossed with a member's name and identification number, it looks like an ordinary plastic credit card. While a number of other barter companies have issued plastic ID cards to their members, the Express card is the first true debit card that is also a "swipe" card; it is also the only barter card that can currently be used nationwide. ITEX has even issued a Gold Card version for preferred members.

ITEX Express works like a debit, or credit, card, depending on the direction in which the member's trade dollar balance lies. Transactions are frequently posted instantly from Point-Of-Sale terminals. The Express card is swiped through the POS terminal, which reads the magnetic code and signals back authorization for the transaction. When used with a splitter device available at most electronics stores, the ITEX POS terminal can be used with the same dedicated line as Master Card or VISA.

The advantage to using the card is that members don't always carry around their account number or have trade drafts (trade checking account) handy when they want to make a transaction. Using the

Express card means the transaction gets recorded electronically, and the seller knows the transaction is approved before the customer walks out the door with the merchandise. Another advantage is that the seller receives credit immediately. David Burstein of Davco, the firm that manufactures the Express cards in their plant in St. Louis, Missouri, claims that ITEX is the only barter exchange whose cards include a magnetic strip that can be read by POS terminals. Burstein said he produced the cards in exchange for trade dollars.

### *Where's It Going?*

With barter becoming more accepted, Suplizio said the industry is experiencing 15 percent annual growth in new membership, and he expects a million barter clients in North America within a decade. The volume of trade business transacted by these companies should reach $6.5 billion by the end of the century. And corporate barter is expected to expand to $20 billion. Predicting that one out of 20 businesses will barter, Suplizio remarked: "If we are reading the data correctly, the nineties will be remembered as an era when the barter industry entered a takeoff phase." And the technology of electronics will be key to making it happen.

Consider the internal press release issued by IRTA in late 1995 that made these predictions: "Based on present trends, 1.6 million businesses will be engaged in barter in North America within a decade. This would be four times the nearly 400,000 firms now engaged in barter. IRTA expects the number of clients of barter companies to double over the next five years, and to double again by the end of a decade, a 15 percent annual growth rate. A total of 1.6 million barter clients out of 6.3 million small businesses who have employees (excluding small businesses with only one employee) amounts to a penetration rate of 25 percent.

Barter growth is burgeoning worldwide as the concept gains acceptance as a business tool at the same time that companies expand in North America and around the globe. Financed internally for years through retained earnings, the barter industry is attracting private investors and is poised for a takeoff stage of growth.

Arrival of the Internet and a global barter marketplace on the World Wide Web will spur this growth.

Overall trade volume surged in North America during the last recession, rising 24 percent over the two years 1989–91 compared to 19 percent during 1987–89. Trade growth for the most recent decade, 1984–94 for which figures are available, averaged 15.3 percent per year.

The North American industry's ability to sustain a 15 percent growth rate is supported by expansion plans of existing trade networks and strong growth in new startups. Independent barter companies account for half the industry's growth, while networks like BXI foresee 200 offices in two years and ITEX, 300 by 1998. If achieved, BXI would be four times larger, and ITEX six times larger than in 1991. ITEX has already gone public, and investment capital appears to be available to support expansion of existing networks.

IRTA also foresees average trade volume per trade exchange client doubling from approximately $3,500 in 1996 to $7,000 by the year 2006. This estimate is in real terms, not considering inflation, which if included would raise trade volume even more. IRTA's forecast is based on the trend to targeting larger-trading clients and servicing them with more trade brokers equipped with the latest technology and access to global availabilities on the World Wide Web. A universal trade dollar tied to the U.S. dollar will facilitate transactions.

All this means that if the number of clients quadruples during the next 10 years, and average trade volume per client doubles, the trade exchange sector in North America will be a $10 billion business—eight times its size in the mid-1990s. Corporate trade will also expand as more corporations turn to barter and as the average size of both domestic and international transactions increases. Corporate trade volume is forecast to triple to $21 billion in the coming decade.

One of the more amazing aspects of the barter industry is how it has accomplished such growth despite the fact that most people have never heard of corporate barter and/or trade exchanges. Many on Wall Street and others in the investment arena have repeatedly voiced the opinion that it is impossible for an industry of this size to have developed without the investment community having played a major role. Wrong. Not only is it not impossible; it has already happened.

Organized barter has come a long way toward becoming a legitimate mechanism for developing industry, commerce and wealth. Like so many other emerging industries, though, it has had its trial by fire, a story told in the next chapter.

# 15

# Out of Chaos

*"Actually, I have no regard for money. Aside from its purchasing power, it's completely useless as far as I'm concerned."*
Alfred Hitchcock

Barter companies create their own accounting units called "trade dollars." With no actual currency changing hands, though, this is merely a bookkeeping system through which a barter company manages the transactions of its members. Simply by being accepted in exchange for goods or services, trade dollars are valued in the same way any other monetary unit is. Trade dollars, therefore, are as valuable as their spending power; unfortunately, they can also be abused. Those issuing the trade dollars may be tempted to create credit for their own consumption, with nothing there to back it. That's how inflation is created by governments, and that's how it's created in a trade exchange.

## *Trade Dollar Inflation*

In the late 1970's there were more than 1,000 retail trade brokerage operations in the United States, a number that began to shrink rapidly in the early 1980's. Two prime examples of this weeding out process occurred in Nebraska and Nevada. In the 80's there were nine barter companies wheeling and dealing in Nebraska. A decade later, only an ITEX operation prospers.

Martha Heimbuch, who now runs Grand Island ITEX along with Renee Sartin, lived through those frenzied early days of barter, and summed up the root cause of the collapse with plainspoken precision: "Things were priced too high," she said. "Some people charged triple in trade dollars what they would sell things for in cash."

With 40,000 souls located 90 miles across the empty prairie from Lincoln, Nebraska, Grand Island is the state's fourth largest community. With few newcomers to Grand Island, most people know each other pretty well and are relatively slow to accept something new. Now, if things got out of hand in conservative Nebraska, imagine what happened in freewheeling Las Vegas, the capital of the fast buck, where practically everyone is from somewhere else.

"New barter clients would find themselves instantly swamped with customers, buying everything they could get their hands on with trade dollars," recalls David Heller, a Las Vegas barter broker. "The new member thought he or she was getting all kinds of new business, which of course they were, but then reality set in and concern over where to spend those newfound trade dollars became the big question."

The fact that the system broke down in both Nebraska and Nevada says that it isn't local standards or conditions that are at fault, but something deep-seated in human nature, something that can be called "the greed factor." The sad fact is—given an opportunity to get something for nothing—no matter where you are or who lives there, someone is going to try to take advantage of the system ... even if it means the whole thing collapses.

The reason people were overcharging in Nebraska is the same reason people were dumping credits in Nevada: the perception that their trade dollars were worthless. Trade dollars, like any currency, can lose their value as a result of "systemic crimes," such as overprinting the currency, embezzlement, counterfeiting, forgery, fraud, price-gouging and securities swindles. True, no one individual got hurt physically, but everyone who depended on the honest functioning of the economic system was hurt financially.

Heller explained how the barter system was damaged in Las Vegas: "One guy running an exchange was practically printing money. If you came to him with something to sell he would just write you a trade check with nothing to back it up," said Heller. "They created their own inflation by flooding the system with trade currency." But this was only part of the problem.

### *Lack of Honor*

Some intensely competitive traders have thought that the best way for them to get ahead was to destroy the credibility of their competitors by planting rumors about the value of their trade dollars. "Where are you going to spend them?" they would ask, launching into horror stories that were all too often pure fiction to serve their personal agenda. This practice was a much larger problem than that of the dishonest trader intentionally inflating a trade system. "Once someone feels the trade dollars aren't worth anything, they're not," Heller said. "Once people lose trust in the value of the credits, the system tends toward collapse. Rumors can ruin everything."

Heller has uncovered the key to the success of every human organization: trust, the foundation of such relationships as friendship, marriage, business, and government. Take the trust away and, sooner or later, the structure collapses. Stay trustworthy and great things are possible.

Why was a small country like England able to rule one fifth of the earth's land area as well as dominate the high seas while other countries that started exploring the globe earlier fell behind? It was because of the British emphasis on personal character and individual responsibility at a time when many other cultures were mired in bribery, extortion and other forms of corruption. If you can trust a person, you don't have to waste energy and resources making sure they do what they say they're going to do. You can get on with your business. That is how individuals and nations rise, through energy spent productively, rather than negatively on things like police, prisons and lawsuits.

### *Creating Trade Dollars*

When an exchange operates in harmony with IRTA's trade exchange member model contract, the local trading system will be in balance: Everything on the negative side has to be matched by something on the positive side. Assets and liabilities, credits and debits, all should balance to zero.

The U.S. government writes itself a line of credit with every bond it offers. It sells bonds until it raises the amount of money it seeks.

Likewise, a well-run trade exchange does not "print" new money for its own consumption but rather extends credit lines to other worthy exchange members who, in drawing against their line of credit, increase the trade dollars in circulation. This means that trade dollars in circulation are backed by the goods and services of the members who have used their line of credit. Exchange operators are permitted to borrow from the exchange, but not without express permission from the membership to do so; consequently, they are bound by the rules to pay the entire sum back.

The success of the U.S. economy rests in part on controls of the money supply. The way it works is perhaps best described by Paul Suplizio, who, in addition to being the CEO of IRTA, is an economist. In a highly relevant paper on the subject (see appendix "Application of the Quantity Theory of Money to Barter Exchange Management"), he pointed out that if the supply of money is limited, that limited supply is going to have to turn over faster if the volume of trade it represents is to increase. If the supply of goods and services is adequate and they are in demand, it is appropriate to expand the supply of trade dollars within boundaries. The barter company whose responsibility it is to manage the trade exchange is empowered to expand or contract the amount of trade dollars in circulation as needed.

One of the guidelines for the number of trade dollars in circulation within an exchange is a function of frequency of change. Trade dollars should turn over, or change hands, on an average of three times per year. This is called the trade dollar velocity of an exchange and is an indication of what is needed to maintain a healthy economy.

To keep credibility in an exchange, members may not charge more in trade dollars than they would charge for cash. Neither should people paying with trade dollars receive second-class treatment. Each transaction is recorded by computer at the exchange's office where postings between accounts are made. One-sided transactions are not permitted by any legitimate trade exchange.

Throughout the trading process the barter company serves as the structure, the enabler, for the exchange. Clients of the barter company are members of the trade exchange. Everyone has an interest in seeing the system work, simply because of the great value in a correctly functioning barter network. Trading rules are a critical part of exchange membership, and most exchange members value the smoothly functioning system enough to be willing to follow the rules, and to see to it that others do as well (see appendix for sample trading rules).

### Breaking the Rules

In society, people who break the rules are sometimes issued a warning; if they continue to break the rules, they may find themselves separated from those who play fairly. The same is true in a well-run exchange. In a self-policing system, people who commit "systemic crimes" such as those described above are warned and ultimately expelled from the exchange.

One of the first places this happened was in Grand Island, Nebraska, in the mid-1980s. Martha Heimbuch was one of those who had paid $15,000 for an Exchange Enterprises franchise. After a "20/20" television exposé drew attention to the franchisor company's method of operation, it went out of business. Martha, meanwhile, saw no reason why members of her franchise should lose the trade dollars they were holding. She kept her doors open for a year and a half with only 40 trading members. Addressing the main problem inherent in barter head-on, she organized what she called her "board of directors," which acted like barter police. One of the six members of the board was the ethics chairman, who was delegated with the responsibility of rooting out members accused of overcharging. Overcharging was subsequently brought under control. When Heimbuch learned that ITEX operated with a level of integrity she could respect, she joined her company with ITEX to give her members more trading options.

Heller in Las Vegas now gives all his members performance evaluation cards on which they rate others for price and treatment. "We want to know if their barter price is consistent with their cash price. We also want to know if they treat barter customers as they would treat cash customers. If a negative pattern emerges, they're out."

By keeping membership somewhat exclusive, Heller is also able to make membership valuable. "I make it hard to get in," he said. "I have two carpet cleaners who always want more work. If I took in more carpet cleaners, that would just mean dividing the same amount of work among more people." He restricts some business categories to one member and he won't enroll a member for whom he doesn't think he can get new business. "I'm not out for the instant buck," Heller said. "There have to be internal controls in order for the value to remain in the trade dollars."

### *IRTA Takes Action*

By mid-1984, horror stories galore were circulating about barter operators engaging in irresponsible and abusive practices in their businesses. Concerned exchange operators began to voice their frustration with the industry's inability to police itself and drive out these unscrupulous few. A committee of the industry association prepared a draft bill entitled the "Commercial Barter Self-Regulation Act" for introduction to Congress. Divided into three main sections or titles, the purpose of the proposed bill was to: "Promote just and equitable standards and principles of trade, to prevent fraudulent, manipulative or unfair acts and practices of commercial barter or trade exchanges and in general to protect individual members of barter exchanges and the public interest, and to remove impediments to and perfect the mechanism of a free and open national marketplace for the trading of goods and services through commercially organized barter exchanges."

An open letter to the industry by author Terry Neal summed up the problem and provided a call for action. It read:

> Dear Trade Exchange Owners:
>
> Here in Portland the past week's TV programming has been filled with stories of barter scams. First "20/20" aired, then a five-part series about a local exchange's abuses was given extensive coverage. Although our firm was not involved or mentioned, such publicity and derogatory coverage makes it tougher to conduct business. Certainly I'm not alone in recognizing this fact. But I, along with every concerned trade

exchange owner in the business, realize we must put a stop to the negative pall permeating our industry, and we must do it now before it spreads and does irreparable damage. I'm very concerned about the direction we're headed and the public's perception of our industry.

The day of using "bad news" as a self-serving mechanism should cease too, for our own good. Telling the public that everybody, except ourselves, in our industry is to be watched, and not trusted doesn't work; the public's not gullible, nor stupid.

How do we turn things around and create a positive image? Through cooperation and implementation of the far-reaching legislation IRTA has presented us with. Together we can do it. I invite everyone in the industry to accept the responsibility IRTA has given us. We need to work hard and push for the Commercial Barter Self-Regulation Act.

We've already made enormous strides in this direction. Proof of substantial progress is self-evident; since third-party record keeping (1099B reporting) became law, many of the shoddy operators—outright scam artists in some cases—have fled the industry. The first step has been significant. Now's the time to complete the task, getting behind the progressive legislation IRTA has introduced to Congress. I'm tired, as I'm sure you are, of explaining and apologizing for the actions of the errant or inefficient owners.

The future of our industry is truly mind-boggling when you consider the fact that approximately 150,000 businesses are now members of exchanges around the country. Statistically, there's over 14 million non-farm businesses in our nation, businesses that can use our services. There is virtually no limit to our exciting future when you think in this context. Working together through the IRTA we can establish networks that will service our nation's businesses. I can't think of a single industry that offers such challenges and potentially great rewards. I'm excited about the future of this industry and I urge all of my peers to grasp the unique opportunity we've been presented with; one where we can create and mold our own destinies. Together we can establish a climate where the honest, ethical trade exchange owner can thrive and prosper. It's time to do it....."

By March of 1986 Terry had been successful in securing the support of Congressman Jim Bates of California to introduce the Commercial Barter Self-Regulation Act to the floor of the House of Representatives as HR 4201. In his March 13, 1986, letter to Congressional colleagues, Bates argued for bipartisan support as follows:

> A large and growing segment of America's economic transactions now take place through barter exchanges. Last year, barter transactions accounted for over $1 billion of business activity involving over 100,000 businesses. The participants include major corporations, professionals, and small businesses. There are 400 barter exchanges in the United States in major cities such as Los Angeles, Chicago, and Pittsburgh, Houston and New York.
>
> The participants in barter exchanges can effectively increase their productivity by trading the inventory of goods and services, not exhausted by cash sales, with other members of the exchange. Thus, a participant hotelier could let rooms, which would otherwise remain empty, to another participating business in exchange for goods and services at a later date. The barter exchange keeps track of the credits and debits among participants.
>
> Barter transactions are fully taxed. The barter industry worked with the House Ways and Means Committee to devise the barter income tax provisions of the 1982 Tax Equity and Fiscal Responsibility Act. All barter exchanges now submit to the Internal Revenue Service details of the barter sales of their clients.
>
> Unfortunately, the rapid growth of the barter industry and the lack of federal regulation often make the participants in

barter exchanges easy targets for unscrupulous, fraudulent exchange operators. To put the problem in a nutshell, the managers of the exchange have power to create "trade dollars" based on the amount of goods and services an individual business owner can contribute to the system. This power can be abused for the personal enrichment of the exchange owners and operators. The most serious abuse involves depreciating the value of the "trade dollars" by deficit spending. Such abuse can be carried out over a period of years, with the day of reckoning forestalled by signing up new clients for the exchange.

The barter industry now needs the federal authority to operate as a self-regulating organization. The marketplace cannot provide effective regulation because the conditions that indicate fraud do not show up for several years. The barter industry has tried voluntary regulation over the last six years. This proved to be inadequate to protect the public interest.

To promote the continued growth of barter exchanges and to protect against the abuses which can occur in the absence of regulation I have introduced HR 4201, to provide for the self-regulation of the commercial barer industry. The bill establishes a structure similar to that approved by Congress for the regulation of the over-the-counter securities brokers and commodities brokers. HR 4201 requires that all barter exchanges be licensed by the Secretary of Commerce and establishes licensing standards and enforcement regulations. Under HR 4201, the participants in barter exchanges would be protected from fraudulent exchange operators, with minimal involvement by the federal bureaucracy and at the barter industry's expense.

By establishing the self-regulation of the barter industry, HR 4201 will protect the financial stability and orderly functioning of barter exchanges. I hope that you will join me as a cosponsor of this legislation....

Sincerely,
Jim Bates
Member of Congress

In the end, Congress had bigger fish to fry, and the Commercial Barter Self-Regulation Act floundered in the House of Representatives and went nowhere. The fact that the bill was introduced, however, and that it was equipped with real teeth, pretty much scared the scam artists right out of the industry. The process turned out to be valuable even though the act itself was not passed into law.

### *IRTA Safeguards*

To preserve the integrity of trade exchange systems, IRTA's board introduced a number of safeguards during the 10-year period between 1979 and 1989. Some of the accomplishments were:

- Established a Code of Ethics and voluntary self-regulation for the commercial barter industry.
- Secured passage of the Tax Equity and Fiscal Responsibility Act of 1982, recognizing barter exchanges as third-party record keepers.
- Developed a model contract setting forth legal powers and responsibilities of trade exchanges and clients.
- Established a Barter Accounting Standards Board to resolve accounting issues.
- Lobbied Treasury and Congress to eliminate transaction reporting, and moved the industry to magnetic media reporting of information returns to IRS.
- Secured introduction in Congress of HR 4201, the Commercial Barter Self-Regulation Act.
- Curbed trade exchange deficit spending through education and self-regulation.
- Conducted more than 100 investigations of ethics complaints and company failures, resolving disputes through due process and peer reviews; cooperated with state's attorneys to expose scams and get fraudulent operators out of the business.
- Conducted research on legal, accounting, tax and regulatory issues and monitored IRS, SEC, FASB, FTC and court rulings.
- Set up Information Exchange and Expert Advisory Board to advise and assist new startups on prudent operations.

- Established Trade Broker Accreditation Program to enhance competence and professional standards.

In addition there have been a number of IRTA pronouncements that set policy for member trade exchanges. These policies have broken new ground for this burgeoning business activity and set the stage for even greater growth through enhanced trade exchange credibility. These important documents are included in the appendix.

# 16

# Introduction to Corporate Barter

*"Money is just a symbol.*
*We want what the money can buy, not the money itself.*
*Money is just paper and plastic and metal.*
*For the most part, money itself is not very engaging.*
*Some of the pictures on money might be amusing, like the*
*1920's car on the back of the U.S. $20 bill, or the*
*holograms on the credit cards, but that's about it.*
*Even George Washington — whose face is on*
*more money than almost anyone— wrote,*
*'It is not a custom with me to keep money to look at.'"*
John-Roger Peter McWilliams

Corporate barter in the U.S. is big business, accounting for $7 billion of the $8.5 billion in domestic barter. And because of the advantages it offers, it will only grow larger in the future.

***Domestic Corporate Barter***

According to the International Reciprocal Trade Association (IRTA), domestic corporate barter is forecast to triple to $21 billion in the decade following 1996. One IRTA press release points out, "If we are reading the data correctly ... one out of every 4 businesses of significant size will barter, and there will be a psychological breakthrough. Instead of having to painstakingly carry barter's message from business owner to business owner, we will find companies beating a path to our door."

According to Paul Demery, in his article "Bartering Makes It to the Major Leagues" in the December 1995 issue of *Practical Accountant*, "Bartering has become a business tool for thousands of companies, from restaurateurs to multibillion-dollar corporations, who trade their products or services for some other nonmonetary asset. Even accountants themselves do it."

Demery went on to say: "Bartering is an age-old practice that has always been particularly common among businesses in small communities. But it has exploded in recent years into a sophisticated undertaking backed by a huge network of third-party players. Perhaps imbued with the spirit of trade-savvy school kids, business owners and executives have thrust bartering into a multibillion-dollar industry that spans the globe. To its champions, bartering has become a vitally important tool for maximizing a company's return on its assets while building a network of potential cash customers as well as trading partners."

Many companies utilize barter to exchange excess, slow-moving, current, outdated, or even obsolete, inventory for media. Some of the larger corporate barter companies see an average of about 80 percent of their trades involving media. In such trades, the client sells a distressed inventory in exchange for advertising credits. These credits are then used to acquire broadcast time or publication space in accordance with a spending plan developed by the client and its agency.

The barter company, expert in acquiring advertising time and space, places the buy as if it were the media buying department of the agency. Such buys are not placed without client and agency approval, however. Ultimately, the client usually pays up with a mix of cash and credits.

When might barter work for your company? The industry answer is: Most of the time. And, if your company advertises, virtually all of the time.

According to an IRTA brochure targeted to manufacturers with an excess in production capacity or inventory: "You can use barter finance to obtain needed goods and services, thereby reducing cost of capital. You are actually leveraging doubtful assets. You protect your distribution chain, while opening up new channels. You increase your return on investment. You improve cash flow by saving cash expenses. You increase capacity utilization and spread overhead costs. You reduce or eliminate carrying (warehouse) costs. You maintain your present product pricing integrity. You focus your sales and marketing efforts on more profitable objectives."

### *Corporate Barter Versus the Trade Exchange, or, What's the Difference Anyway?*

The main difference between corporate barter companies and retail trade exchange operators is simply that corporate traders act as a principal in a barter transaction. Corporate barter companies are buyers and sellers; only rarely are they brokers. They make money on the resale of the merchandise they acquire on barter.

Barter companies that operate trade exchanges are acting as brokers. They introduce the parties to a barter deal, maintain records of the transaction and charge the parties a commission upon satisfactory completion of the trade.

Trade exchanges typically have between several hundred and several thousand member-clients for whom they are constantly brokering deals. In any given month a local retail trade exchange may process several thousand individual barter transactions for its clientele. The average size of a trade exchange transaction may be as low as $50 or as high as $1,000, depending on the exchange and the clientele's profile.

The size of a single transaction with a corporate barter company, on the other hand, will vary from between $50,000 and $5,000,000. Corporate barter companies do not deal in quantities of routine transactions; they specialize instead in smaller numbers of creative deals of much larger dollar volume. Corporate traders are prepared to custom-make virtually any purchase agreement, whereas the transactions that take place through the trade exchange marketplace are rarely structured differently.

Trade exchanges deal with trade dollars. Corporate barter companies deal with media credits, purchase credits, or cash-equivalent credits, and all of these are essentially the same. There is considerable difference between a trade dollar and a cash credit, however, as we shall see.

### *The Magic of Corporate Barter*

How can you buy for $10, sell for $2 and stay in business? To the uninitiated, it looks like a quick way to go broke, but to the people in corporate barter, it is the path to riches. Corporate barter companies routinely buy surplus inventory or future production capacity from manufacturers at full wholesale prices and sell or remarket the goods away from the manufacturers' primary markets for cash. Corporate barter companies actually specialize in providing solutions for companies with excess inventory.

Corporate barter can be a profitable alternative to traditional markdowns and liquidation activities. When manufacturers consider barter, they are seeking to convert troublesome inventory, or unused capacity, into partial funding of future overhead costs. Corporate barter can be a reasonably safe, sensible and effective marketing strategy. Some of the nation's largest companies, i.e., manufacturers, wholesalers and distributors, along with the larger players in the advertising and hospitality industries, use barter on a routine basis.

Barter is a powerful marketing tool the unenlightened of corporate America ignore to their detriment. Barter solutions can be adapted to a wide array of business situations. It can be used to convert problem loans for greater liquidity and to reduce overall balance sheet liabilities. Barter can provide a solid edge in penetrating new markets. Corporate barter can be used to convert nonperforming assets into immediate working capital and generate real dollar profits through use of surplus production capacity. Corporate barter can be very good for big business.

Clyde Fabretti, past president of IRTA and current chairman of ITEX USA, claims that corporate barter began when an individual in the media business found that he owed money he could not pay; but he also discovered that he could acquire radio spots and newspaper ads for less than his creditors could. The light in his head went on. He told his creditors he wanted to buy their media for them, and the difference between what he could buy it for and what they would normally pay, he wanted applied to his debt.

Today, more than half of all the corporate barter business done in

America is for media. Sharon Gerson, president of Global Marketing Resources, a corporate barter company, said that 95 percent of the goods her firm handles is exchanged for some form of advertising. "We keep a low profile about it," she said. "People prefer to be discreet because they don't want everyone to know they are bartering to liquidate their surplus products."

Barter "unwind" refers to fulfillment of the seller's credit for goods sold. Media and hotel space are prime goods for unwinding barter credits because they are fairly soft and frequently have a lot of spread between the normal market price and what a corporate barter company might pay. Corporate barter and advertising budgets simply work well together. And, as a result, there are some very large corporate barter-media companies in the business. What about businesses with surplus merchandise, or excess capacity, that aren't major buyers of media? Can a corporate barter company help them?

It is the reliance on media for barter unwind that left such an opportunity for Clyde Fabretti and his firm. Fabretti's formula for success is so simple it is hard for some people to understand. He buys goods for full wholesale price, $10 for example, and sells for much less, say $2, and makes a fortune. The way he does it, every dime of "asset recovery" (cash generated from the sale of the merchandise) represents profit to the corporate barter company. It wouldn't matter if he got a nickel on the dollar, he would still be making money. And the exciting thing about the Fabretti technique is that everyone wins. But how does it work?

Fabretti uses the example of a company looking to buy a printing press. The high bid for it was $650,000, the low one, $500,000, which became the benchmark price Fabretti had to meet. His cost for the same product was $375,000. The difference between $500,000 and $375,000 is paid to his barter company in the form of goods; in reality, this is the amount deducted from the client's account in which the client has credit for goods previously sold to the corporate barter company.

### *How It Really Works*

"Say we are offered 10,000 surplus copies of a book," said Paul Shakeshaft, manager of the Corporate Trading Division of a well known barter company. "Let's say they have called a liquidator and the best price they could get was $2.50 per book. The book wholesales for $12 per copy, it cost $6 to produce, and retails for $23.95. "Whatever discount the publisher wouldn't take, we will take. We will pay the full wholesale price, but in credits, not in cash," says Shakeshaft.

Here is where corporate barter gets exciting. The seller of the book gets $12 each, or $120,000 in Cash Equivalent Credits, which is the normally advertised wholesale price. The cash credit, however, is a non-transferrable bookkeeping entry for tracking future discounts for the book publisher. These credits can't be spent anywhere else, but they can be spent like cash under the right circumstances. "The products don't become more valuable as they come into our hands, but the manufacturer gets full wholesale dollar for his goods. The transaction should play out as if he did sell it to his best customer for cash."

That's quite an incentive for a company to do business with corporate barter. The products they liquidate could be outdated, mismatched, damaged, with wrong colors, not selling or otherwise taking up space in the warehouse and remaining on the books. Some companies simply slaughter such merchandise, call the liquidators and take 10 or 15 cents on the dollar, or admit total defeat and call the recyclers. But if they can instead earn a discount on their future purchases of goods and services, and for products that they would have bought for cash anyway, they can come out way ahead.

A well-thought-out corporate barter agreement can keep the financial people happy, especially if the client is a public company. The financial records of the public company may not be forced to reflect a loss or write-down, provided the credits received for sale of the merchandise to a barter company are used within the same fiscal period. Full wholesale price will then have been received. The emphasis is on use of the credits in the same fiscal period, otherwise the publisher should write the value of the book inventory down to what it considers the distressed market value. The value of the cash credits received for the inventory would then be carried at the reduced value of the inventory until the credits have been spent. Assuming the cash credits are used in a subsequent period in conjunction with cash to acquire goods at pre-established benchmark prices, then the publisher would show a gain in the future period equal to the write-down in the prior period. Dumping is a bad move for a public company. One inventory liquidation can eat up profits for an entire year.

IRTA CEO Paul Suplizio said new accounting rules leave it up to corporate controllers and the company's auditors as to whether they want to book such transactions at full dollar value, or to book them conservatively at their written down value. He advises corporate barter clients to have their accounting personnel refer to APB 29 and EITF 93-11 pronouncements from the Financial Accounting Standards Board (FASB) for information prior to deciding how best to book a given transaction.

Bryan Yokley, FASB staff expert on EITF 93-11, said companies should recognize an impairment loss on the nonmonetary asset if the fair value of that asset is less than its book value. He went on to explain that the fair value should not be based on the assumed value of the cash credits to be received. This is because it should be presumed that the fair market value of the nonmonetary assets exchanged is more evident. He advises, however, "if you're converting a nonmonetary asset into credits, and then to cash in the near term, or some equivalent of cash with a quoted market price, then you might be able to use that value," he said.

Once a client has the credits, it's time to spend them. "Let's say the publisher of these books now wants to buy something, such as a $10,000 computer," Shakeshaft said. Utilizing credits earned from turning over inventory is called repatriating the credits, or unwinding. "We will match our client's best cash price, the benchmark price, and he will pay part cash and part of the price will be debited from his barter account." In the example of this $10,000 purchase, our client might wind up paying $7,500 cash, and $2,500 in cash credits he received for the books he sold at full wholesale.

The difference between the corporate barter company's cash cost, available only to them, and the benchmark price, available to the client, is taken in the form of the client's product. "We take our profit from the price we receive for the book," Shakeshaft claims. "Whatever we sell it for is our profit, and everybody is happy."

### *The Recap*

**Step One:** The book publisher sold the surplus, or slow-moving inventory, immediately at standard rates and without discount. He received cash credits, and not cash dollars. So, although he may not have taken an immediate loss by converting the inventory into credits, he must still be concerned about their actual value to his publishing company.

**Step Two:** The publisher has sourced a computer he wants to buy and the best cash price he's been able to find is $10,000. This best cash price is referred to as the benchmark price. Prior to making the acquisition, he submits a simple Purchase Request Memorandum (PRM) to the barter company advising them what he plans to buy and the benchmark price. The barter company matches the item and the benchmark price, and accepts part cash and part cash credits in payment of the purchase.

**The Result:** The publisher is assured that every cash credit spent was equal to $1 U.S. simply because he had, previous to the purchase, already determined the best price available in the cash market for the item he was buying. Assuming he repeats this process until all the cash credits are spent, he will have retained his full margin, thereby making a profit, and will have saved the huge write-off he might otherwise have experienced.

Now, what about the barter company; how did they come out on this deal? Think back to the start of this example, where the publisher had called a liquidator and was offered $2.50 per book. Provided the publisher does not object, the barter company will likely take that deal and be paid $25,000 in cash. Why didn't the publisher simply take that deal? Because the publisher will take an immediate loss for a liquidation such as this, and the loss would be quite real. On the other hand, by accepting cash credits for the full amount rather than cash for the heavily discounted amount, the publisher stands a very good chance of actually making a margin (remember the cost was $6, and they were sold at $12), provided he uses the barter company's "unwind" or "spend down" department to source and match prices on future purchases he will make anyway.

There probably are two more questions: Number one, how does the barter company treat the cash credits on its books, and number two, how can the barter company get better prices than the publisher when making new purchases? Let's treat number two first. The barter company is able to source products at better prices than the publisher because a) that's what it's good at doing; and b) the barter company has multiple vendors for business products who have guaranteed prices that are lower than anyone else can get. But why would vendors give better prices to the barter company than they would to the publisher?

Simply because major manufactures, wholesalers and national distributors are likely to give a large, well-run barter company much lower (in fact, *guarantee the very lowest wholesale*) pricing for their goods, because they understand the barter company will be sourcing them for product for all the companies with whom the barter company is working. In other words, instead of one publisher buying one $10,000 computer, the barter company may well represent the future buying patterns of 400 other companies that may also need computers sometime in the near future.

So ... the barter company came out with all the cash but now must work diligently to unwind the credit for the publisher on a part-cash and part-credit basis. For this reason a number of corporate barter companies insist they receive a cash commission on the spend-down process. They argue that this keeps their motivation high in aggressively seeking opportunities for the client to spend.

Quite often, to protect their own market, the source of goods may insist that the products be sold far from their territory, even out of the country. "In some cases liquidating products could ruin a client's market," said Paul Shakeshaft. "But we can take goods where there is no market. The seller is kept informed as to exactly where it is going."

Cash credits are treated on the barter company's books in a fashion similar to how a grocery store might treat issued discount coupons. They're not a liability and, in fact, they represent probable future business.

### *Spending Plans*

In the example of the publisher above, everyone truly wins. And, as unbelievably good as it may sound, this is exactly how the system is designed to work. Clients can use their credits right away, before the barter company sells or even takes possession of the goods. What happens, though, if the publisher doesn't get around to spending his cash credits?

Returning to Clyde Fabretti, we learn, "Finders are the source of most of our transactions. We teach them right up front that there are three requirements that must be present before we'll pursue a potential deal. Number one, the business must have either a distressed inventory or surplus capacity. Number two, we must be able to talk directly to either the president, CEO or CFO; in other words it must be a decision maker. Number three, the business must have a spending appetite. That means they're regularly out in the marketplace spending large sums in the normal course of operating their business.

"If the target business has a large advertising budget," Fabretti continued, "we know there is a straightforward mechanism for developing a spending plan. If their advertising budget is small, we need to carefully review the kinds of things for which they have a large spending appetite."

According to *A New World of Finance*, published by the corporate trade counsel of the IRTA, "If your company is not a large user of media, you can still benefit from barter. You can have the barter company work with you on a Spending Plan. That's a line-by-line plan of your company's business expense spending categories and the amount you spend on an annual basis. Carefully done, the plan will help you estimate how many credits you are likely able to spend and how long it will take to spend them. Once you know this, you can be more confident in moving ahead with the transaction. You'll know what you'll be receiving, when you'll receive it and how long it will take to acquire it. You can avoid some of the problems that have arisen in the past when company executives made vague or inaccurate estimates on spending potential and trade companies eager to complete the transaction made unrealistic estimates of their client's spending potential. If you avoid that through precision and thoroughness, you will benefit from trading your unmoving inventory for those items you would have normally paid for in cash."

Even with a reasonable spending plan, the corporate culture of many companies is such that they cannot, or will not, make the change to contacting their barter company prior to making new purchases in cash. For those barter companies that specialize in credit unwind through day-to-day overhead expenses rather than through advertising, it is critical that they train their client's buyers.

The primary tool used to facilitate client spending is the Purchase Request Memorandum form. This is a simple one-page faxable sheet designed for use by the client company in making requests on the barter company for spending. All that's really needed is that the client company indicate in writing: 1) what they're going to buy; 2) who they're ready to buy it from; 3) what they're going to pay; and 4) their target delivery date. Armed with this information, a corporate barter company can quickly search its data base of existing vendors who might service this request. If one does not exist and the initial deal is large enough, the barter company will likely begin calling new prospective vendors.

Corporate barter companies are experts at buying right. Eight out of 10 requested items can be bought at a discount, Fabretti says, if there is the promise of volume. "If I get a look at someone's best price, I'm ninety percent of the way there," said Shakeshaft. "The vendor knows we have a real deal, that we aren't fishing." Having an order in hand and the promise of more to come gives the barter company's buying consortium enormous leverage in getting the best price. "It's based on hope. We get significant vendor discounts because they understand we're in a position to bring them more business than they already have."

What this all means is that credit spend-down is feasible; it also means that once a company has exchanged its inventory problem for credits, it will be able to use them. It is essential that the holders of cash credits be diligent in interaction with their barter company. The best way to do this is by completing a PRM and faxing it on to the barter company prior to making any purchase larger than $10,000. A corporate barter company will normally respond within 48 hours on items less than $50,000, and within one week for larger purchases.

### *State-of-the-Art Barter*

Paul Suplizio summed up the current status of the corporate element of the barter industry when he said, "The significance of this takeoff stage of growth is that the industry will be generating the retained earnings, and attracting the outside capital needed to organize, train and deploy the people and technology needed to service a growing number of global clients linked together in the emerging multimedia marketplace. It will add a significant new dimension to the financial and commercial worlds."

# 17

# Barter and Taxes

*"There are a variety of different taxes—
income taxes, sales taxes, corporate profit taxes,
property taxes, and so forth.
All of them have one thing in common.
They take spending away from those taxed."*
Roger N. Waud

All trade dollars from a bona fide barter company credited to a member account will be reported to the IRS. That was the deal the industry made with the government and that is why buying and selling with trade dollars is strictly above board and legitimate. It was not always thus. On October 1, 1979, the IRS initiated a Barter Project to audit the returns of all barter exchanges and a sample of their members. After enactment of the Tax Equity and Fiscal Responsibility Act of 1982, which established a 1099-B reporting system whereby trade exchanges reported the barter sales of their clients annually to IRS, the Barter Project was formally terminated by IRS on June 30, 1983. Since that time, barter participants have not been singled out by IRS for special scrutiny. Members of a trade exchange have the same chance as any other taxpayer to be selected for audit. No longer does belonging to an exchange increase the chance of an IRS audit.

Speaking of IRS audits, the following tidbit taken from the May 22, 1996, issue of the *Wall Street Journal*, is too incredible not to include:

> The General Accounting Office (GAO) is likely to release preliminary findings tomorrow of its annual financial audit of the IRS. For three years in a row, the Congressional watchdog agency has found such big problems that it couldn't even express an opinion on the reliability of IRS financial statements.

Once the report was issued, things really hit the fan. John Cunniff of the Associated Press reported: "If your household financial records were in the same shape as those of the IRS, you couldn't survive an audit. The IRS itself cannot." (July 30, 1996)

The AP report said the GAO had been "unable to express an opinion on the reliability" of the IRS financial statements because of gross errors and omissions in accounting. According to the AP, the GAO reported that uncertifiable records at the IRS are almost routine, and problems remain uncorrected year after year.

Commented Dan Pilla, a tax litigation consultant to attorneys and accountants and the author of eight books: "The IRS demands the average citizen keep accurate records when the trained accountants and financial investigators of the IRS have no clue how to keep track of their own income and expenses."

Added the AP's Cunniff: "Anyone who has been audited by the IRS isn't likely to forget the financial specifics he must produce to justify a few dollars of deductions. But the IRS cannot do that for tens upon tens of millions of dollars."

Each of us, and our respective companies, is required by IRS rulings (which have the effect of law) to maintain careful books and records that may withstand IRS examination. If our records are incomplete, or are not in good order, the IRS may make additional tax assessments that in its opinion may be justified—and it is up to us to prove differently. The very government agency that holds us audit-responsible, however, can itself not withstand the same level of examination. Seem right to you?

The International Reciprocal Trade Association (IRTA) obtained from the IRS, under the Freedom of Information Act, the results of the four-year Barter Project discussed above, and compared the results to other audit projects of average taxpayers. Included in the IRTA Fact Sheet entitled "Tax Compliance Record of the Barter Industry" is the following:

- "In sum, Barter Project audits over four years yielded $2,013 in additional taxes and penalties per return, while the average audit of comparable returns for the public at large yielded $5,332 over the same period."
- "These results demonstrate that, as a group, barterers who buy and sell through organized trade exchanges have a better-than-average record of tax compliance. . . ."
- "These results definitively refute the notion that organized trade exchanges are, in some sense, part of an underground economy. Rather, organized barter is an integral component of the general economy."
- "The fact that IRS has a 1099-B reporting system, that barter exchanges are recognized as third-party record keepers in the Internal Revenue Code, that IRS forms and publications contain information on barter, that tax regulations cover the method of valuing trade dollars, and that Revenue Ruling 80-52 spells out clear and succinct rules concerning the taxation of barter transactions, is due directly to the efforts of IRTA, whose representatives worked with Congress, Treasury, and IRS during 1979–1983 to achieve a consensus on barter provisions of the Tax Equity and Fiscal Responsibility Act of 1982. The industry's tax problems with the Service have been minimal."

The Internal Revenue Service views trade dollars the same as cash, at least when it comes time to pay taxes. Because a participant in a trade exchange can't go to just any store and buy with trade dollars, though, let alone pay the taxing authorities, the question arises: What is the worth of these extra sales and new income that have been paid for with trade dollars, especially if an exchange member must pay cash taxes on it?

### *What's It Worth?*

Think in terms of a foreign currency. If you were in the country of origin of a foreign currency, you could buy anything with it. Try to spend it elsewhere, though, and it isn't accepted.

To use a foreign currency in another country, money changers will usually charge a discount. People from Canada who write checks in the U.S. see those checks discounted to U.S. value. Their currency has worth, but it's worth less outside their own country. The relative value of trade dollars follows the same pattern. Generally speaking, the larger the trading membership of a given exchange, the more valuable the trade dollars. This is true simply because there are more places to spend them.

Trade dollars may also have a higher value when the barter company that manages the exchange is a member of a central clearing network that promotes trading amongst various other exchanges. If a member wants something not available with the local exchange, the possibility of finding it elsewhere is greatly improved.

If a business owner or professional has earned new sales through barter, that represents extra income he or she would likely never have had; the real question about worth, therefore, is how important is this extra business? Provided this same business owner eventually spends these newly earned trade dollars on either business expenses or personal items on which he or she would normally have spent cash, then the issue of paying taxes on the new income with cash is moot. Why? Simply because the trade dollars have been converted into an equal amount of cash savings and therefore a cash surplus has been generated from which to pay the corresponding taxes that may be due.

The bottom line to all of this is that when a business owner generates new profits, be they from cash or trade sales, they cannot escape the taxing authorities. The key to the worth of trade sales is usually an effect of what the trade dollars are ultimately used to buy.

### *Tax Reporting*

Trade dollar sales are reported to both the IRS and the exchange member on Form 1099-B, "Proceeds from Broker and Barter Transactions." Actually, in the case of the IRS, the exchange is required to report the information via electronic media or by modem transfer. This information is reported for a calendar year even though a business may keep its records on a fiscal-year basis. Some business owners and professionals are members of a trade exchange that pays interest on positive account balances above a certain threshold amount. Trade interest earnings are also reported as income.

From a brochure provided by the IRTA entitled "What You Should Know About Barter and Federal Income Taxes" comes this information:

**Question: Are there any tax advantages or disadvantages to barter?**

**Answer:** Barter income should be viewed as you would your cash income. There are no inherent tax advantages or disadvantages just because you use a barter exchange. Barter is a marketing tool, not a tax tool. Generally speaking, as with cash income, barter purchases that are business-related are deductible, and conversely, barter purchases that are made for personal use are not deductible. Naturally, your barter income (sales) and business deductions (purchases) should be accounted for separately on your tax return.

**Question: What constitutes income in barter transactions?**

**Answer:** Barter income accrues to a client of a barter exchange when trade dollars are posted to your account, property or services are received, cash is received, or scrip is issued to you as part of a barter transaction.

**Question: In what year are trade dollars taxable?**

**Answer:** IRS has ruled that trade dollars earned from your barter sales should be included in income for the tax year in which they are credited to your account.

There are inherent problems with the way the IRS requires barter companies to report on the sales of trading members. The IRS requires that a 1099-B must include all of the deposits made to a trade account based on the assumption that a deposit is equal to a new sale. What if the deposit was *not* the consequence of a sale, however? What if the deposit were the result of a third-party loan or if it were a qualifying gift from a parent's trading account to that of a grown son or daughter? What if you've made a loan to a third party and they're now paying you back? Are these new sales? Certainly not; under the reporting rules of the exchange, however, these deposits must be included as if they were sales. It's probably not right, but that's the way it is. This does not mean, though, that the taxpayer must pay taxes on all trade deposits. What it does mean is that the member must keep careful records and be able to document discrepancies between his or her personal tax return and what the exchange reports.

### *Tax Strategies*

A number of barter companies recommend that exchange members who are worried about tax consequences from extra barter sales spend their trade balance by year's end. It is wise to spend down the trade balance on deductible expenses before the end of the year because, although trade dollars are taxed as cash, the IRS does not accept them as payment. Participating traders accept them in lieu of cash, of course, and those expenditures can potentially be deducted from taxes, just as if they were cash costs.

In fact, for year-end planning, some barter members may be better off spending themselves into debt. Responsible, seasoned exchange members will typically have credit lines valued in the thousands of trade dollars available to them. As a tax strategy, such members might make deductible purchases on credit before the end of the year and deduct those expenses, even though they haven't repaid their credit line. In effect, their "loan" from the barter company saves them cash in taxes.

### *Trade and Retirement*

Trade dollars occasionally may be used in retirement plans, some of which allow contributions of art and similar collectibles. Trade dollars might be loaned at a reasonable interest rate, with repayment in cash or trade, and the promissory note could be put into the plan. A person might buy $10,000 worth of advertising on trade for another person, for example, with the promise that it will be repaid in cash.

From time to time, there are stocks, bonds and debentures available for trade dollars that might be contributed to a retirement plan. In such cases, the contributions may be tax-deductible.

Fees paid in relation to barter accounts are legitimate business expenses and can be deducted just as deductions are taken for fees on credit card and association memberships.

### *The Danger*

Business expenses are deductible, but personal expenses are not. Many exchange members find it easy to buy vacations and other personal, fun items, only to realize at tax time that they still have to pay the piper. If structured in such a way as to qualify as a business expense, however, these seemingly nonbusiness purchases may be deductible after all. Restaurant scrip, a massage or a manicure in the form of gift certificates given away to promote a business, for instance, might better be described as a legitimate business expense of "advertising and promotion."

The key, though, is that it has to be justifiable to the IRS. A trading client might have trouble justifying a hot air balloon ride with her husband, but she might use the hot air balloon tickets in a raffle giveaway or as a charitable donation.

Although a business cannot pay the IRS with trade dollars, the IRS can prevent companies or individuals from spending their positive trade balance if taxes are not paid. If that were the case, the IRS has the right to freeze a trade account. The reality is, though, that out of the thousands of trade accounts of which the authors are directly familiar, less than a half dozen have actually been frozen by the IRS.

### *"It Is More Blessed to Give. . . ."*

"Charitable contributions with trade dollars can not only help worthwhile causes, they can put trade dollars to work as a tax deduction," says Kevin R. Andersen, a partner in the Salt Lake City accountancy firm of Andersen, Andersen & Strong. "Contributions of trade dollars can be deductible the same as cash." Most barter companies have in hand lists of charitable institutions anxious to receive donations in trade dollars. Even if a person's favorite charity is not an exchange member, buying supplies or services for the organization with trade and deducting the equivalent value remains a legitimate contribution.

Exchange members have given thousands of trade dollars to the Brass Ring Society, for example. "We fulfill dreams of terminally ill children," according to Ray Esposito, the charity's director and founder. He said his group deals with 100 to 200 youngsters a year, and uses trade dollar contributions to pay for hotel space in Florida.

"Most of the children we deal with want to go to Disney World. That's why we relocated from Tulsa to Orlando," he said.

There are many charitable groups that take trade dollar contributions directly and these are often listed by barter companies. Although the joy of giving comes from a sincere desire to help others, it is quite true that a gift can sometimes also be helpful to the giver's financial picture. If the basis in a trade dollar is relatively low, such as from selling surplus services or goods, and a gift giver deducts that trade dollar as a cash dollar, it is actually possible to come out ahead.

Certainly, there is no lack of need for trade dollars. Esposito, for one, said he can use all he gets. If he could count on a steady supply, he would set up a beach facility for families that have lost a child so they have a place to go to get away and grieve together.

### *Manna From Barter*

Although many of us would like to give more to charitable causes, we worry about keeping bread on our table and a roof over our own heads. Walter Roob of Milwaukee is using his trade dollars for bread and a roof, but not for himself.

"I wondered where I could do some good," said Roob, who holds a master's degree in photography and is the recipient of more than 600 photography awards in Wisconsin. Every month now, for more than a year, he has arranged for several hundred dollars' worth of bread and cookies to be delivered from Chicago to the St. Catherine's meal program for schoolchildren in Milwaukee.

He has found giving so gratifying that he recently had a $10,000 trade dollar roof put on a monastery. Roob, whose profession has trained his eye to behold beauty, has versed his heart to ascertain a need. Such donations may be 100 percent tax-deductible, yielding a tax savings while helping others.

### *Mitzvot*

Trade dollars have provided a way for one individual to practice the essence of his Jewish faith: the "Mitzvah" or good deed. He is using restaurant scrip to feed the poor.

"People tell me, 'You schmuck! Don't you know you can convert that restaurant scrip to cash? Why are you giving it away?' I tell them, 'You should only be a schmuck like me and have the feeling I have in my heart.'" Thus spake Scott Ebberbach, ITEX broker in Fort Lauderdale, Florida, about his innovative program of using trade dollars to help those in need.

"A light hit me in the face," Ebberbach explained. While contemplating the thousands of dollars of restaurant scrip he had in his possession, he realized, "This is food, and there are families out there who are hungry. I am eating, my family is eating, but there are people who are not." Although Ebberbach does not claim to be particularly religious, his Jewish ethics compelled him to act. "I'm sitting on thousands of dollars' worth of food and it's a sin. In God's eyes, maybe the reason he let me become a barter broker is not to create an income for myself, but to find a way to help people."

Restaurants that have issued scrip (dollar denominated prepaid meal vouchers) have already received payment for their food by the barter company. Consequently, the food represented by the scrip belongs to whoever possesses the scrip. But rather than send poor families into fine restaurants and run the risk of embarrassing everyone when it comes time to pay a tip, Ebberbach decided to seek unused space in a strip mall to distribute the food. "That way the landlord also gets a write-off for the contribution," he said.

Working with nonprofit organizations to find the people needing help, Ebberbach also challenges restaurants to match him dollar for dollar in the amount of food given. "If I give back $1,000 in scrip, I ask them to match me with $1,000 in food." So far, several local restaurants have signed on and more are interested. "It's taken on a life of its own," he said.

Ebberbach noted how easily the barter system, which works on the surpluses of the economy, can be used to perform good deeds. He said that if he had to shell out thousands of dollars of cash to do this, he probably would not, while barter lets him feed a lot of people without a lot of money. "I love barter for what it is. I want to see what good I can do with it beyond padding my pocket."

### *Trading for Taxes*

Trade dollars can work wonders. Exchange members can have the goods and services they want and need, while the trade network helps them build new business. Unfortunately, trade members must pay taxes with cash; the government simply won't take trade.

That doesn't mean trade dollars can't become an important component in any tax posture. The key concept here is creativity, flexibility and finding opportunities—the same qualities that assure business success in the first place.

This takes being resourceful enough to substitute trade dollars for cash whenever possible for deductible expenses. And it is much more possible than one might think. Let's say, for example, that someone participates in a "cafeteria" program, one made possible through the C-125 section of the IRS codes. These programs permit payment of FICA, FUTA, SUTA, Workers Compensation and medical benefits for individuals and employees with pretax dollars. In other words, those expenses are off the top; being calculated before tax liability time, they effectively lower taxable income.

Employers can increase workers' compensation equivalent to the amount withheld for the "cafeteria" medical benefits and pay that increase in trade dollars. In effect, a formerly taxable benefit now becomes funded with trade dollars.

Bill Schroeder, chief financial officer of the New London Group in Decatur, Georgia, which administers such plans, said there are a few caveats. For one, once the plan is put into effect, it cannot be changed for at least 12 months, unless there is a change in employment or in marital or family status, such as a divorce, death or birth. Another acceptable reason to change is if the company elects to switch insurance carriers or to make changes to existing coverage, such as adding a dental plan.

There is a medical system hospital in Atlanta, Schroeder reports, that will take trade dollars. Many dentists, optometrists, therapists, naturopathic and chiropractic physicians and others take them as well. Using trade dollars for payments for employee medical benefits makes those trade dollars deductible.

The savings employees realize through the "cafeteria" plan would be wisely invested in their own 401K plan toward retirement. This creates a free savings account for employees and another federal and possible state tax deduction. It also allows employers to shelter up to $9,127 for their own retirement. The average $30,000 employee can save $3,500 a year in tax breaks and 401K savings, and the employer can save about $1,850 in matching benefits.

Another opportunity to use trade dollars for a tax advantage might be to make a tax-deductible contribution to a profit-sharing plan. Let's say a company has free and clear hard assets, such as vehicles, computers or office equipment. The profit-sharing plan could potentially purchase those assets from the company and lease them back to the business with the trade dollars that were contributed—thus making those trade dollars deductible. It's not a good idea to simply give the property, because then there is exposure to gift tax. It would also be possible to pay the lease on the assets to the profit-sharing plan with trade dollars, thereby making them potentially deductible.

Using trade dollars to one's advantage is a prudent investment of resources. Sometimes it is difficult to find the cash to fully fund employee retirement or health care accounts. Trade dollars can generate value from excess capacity, though, and can do so without interrupting cash flow.

These ideas are strictly hypothetical and are not intended to substitute for professional advice. The authors suggest that the reader consult an attorney or tax adviser before implementing any of the theoretical concepts reviewed here.

# 18

# The Future & Money

*"Money, which represents the prose of life,*
*and which is hardly spoken of in parlors without an apology,*
*is, in its effects and laws, as beautiful as roses."*
Ralph Waldo Emerson

And so, we come to the end of our story about money. We have considered barter, commodity currency, coins, paper money, electronic currency and trade dollars. We have seen money transformed by changes in technology. Cashless society? Ever since late in the 19th century when philosopher Edward Bellamy predicted a utopian world where money would be replaced by credits earned by workers with their labor, there have been forecasters predicting a "cashless society." We don't believe it will ever get here, though. Granted, the technology exists, as we saw in the chapters on Smart Cards and electronic currency. But those who believe "cash is dying" understand technology better than they do human nature. Remember the college kids pulling the security threads out of their cash? Remember the people in Russia with $100 bills stuffed under their mattresses? Remember all those people who want to be certain no one can trace their activities?

In our section on the vulnerability of money early in the book, we discussed the ancient Athenians' distrust of their new money. Because of the way they felt, they hoarded the old coins and spent the new ones. It is possible that bad feelings about the new U.S. currency will lead people to hang onto the old cash, perhaps even charge a premium for it. Maybe they will find the modern-day equivalent of the trusted private money of early days.

What we have not seen, so far, is any one monetary system entirely replace a previous one. Each system has survived and continues to operate concurrent with the others. Cash did not eliminate barter. Credit cards did not eliminate cash, and neither will Smart Cards, electronic currency or trade dollars. Which is why when we see headlines that proclaim "Cash Is Dying" (*New York Times*, June 16, 1996), we make no plans to attend the funeral.

### *Possibilities*

Cash will not disappear; each medium of exchange, rather, will be a tool to augment and add to the others, each furthering commerce in its own way. Just as paper money and wire transfers came to prominence to further development of the American frontier, electronic currency in its many forms is emerging for the frontier of the Internet. The Internet, the PC and electronic currency all contribute to making the world a far different place from the one we have known up to now. It's a lot easier to see the impact of one innovation than it is to see the cumulative effect of many. To comprehend the possibilities takes not just technical expertise, but imagination. Understanding how a radio works, which Marconi was able to do, is different from understanding how it can be used.

It took David Sarnoff, an uneducated Russian immigrant to the U.S., to see how the invention could broadcast news and music into every household and eventually every automobile. Sarnoff, for those who don't recognize the name, was the chairman of RCA who led the founding of NBC in order to produce programming for the radios RCA was selling. But even the vision of David Sarnoff was limited to one invention. That's not the kind of vision Bill Gates talks about.

"A hundred years ago, people saw the automobile coming," said Gates in *The Road Ahead*. "It was sure to make fortunes, and also to run over some jobs and industries. But specifics would have been hard to predict. You might have warned your friends at the Acme Buggy Whip company to polish up their resumés, and perhaps learn about engines, but would you have known to invest in real estate for strip malls?"

The Internet, the PC and electronic currency ultimately could have as great an impact as printing, broadcasting and the internal combustion engine combined. No eyes have seen the vast changes this revolution will bring. The transformation is already underway.

### *Industries in Flux*

Communications companies face challenges and opportunities from the Internet. It uses the telephone networks without being controlled by the telephone companies—operating most often on leased lines and out of reach of the phone companies' accounting. And now there are programs available off the shelf that allow people on opposite sides of the globe to talk through their computer over the Internet at virtually no cost. Will telephone companies succeed in having Internet communications regulated, or will they somehow lead this parade?

Broadcasting is another industry that must come to grips with the Internet. George Gilder, futurist and author of 10 books, envisions that the Internet will result in the demise of both television and the telephone. He says the transformation is already under way. The Real Audio program allows transmission of sound over the Internet, radio programs can be received from anywhere in the world. And television may be soon to follow. What we don't know yet, however, is whether this means local broadcasters will go away, or whether they will reinvent themselves as niche broadcasters, such as a stamp collectors' radio station, that is available free to anyone in the world via the Internet.

And anyone can be a publisher and publish anything he or she wants to publish. There is no need for expensive presses, paper, distribution networks or any of the other costs that serve as barriers to entry. It is a treasure trove for readers. Plucky publishers already seem to be on top of this opportunity. *Editor & Publisher* has a Web site (http://www.mediainfo.com/ephome/npaper/nphtm/online.htm) that offers every online newspaper in the world—more than a thousand as of this writing. The site has a world map, and newspapers can be accessed by continent or country. You can actually read newspaper stories from China, Germany and most points in between at the click of the mouse.

Newspapers and magazines were among the first to adopt computers for desktop publishing. As a matter of fact, the history of publishing for the last quarter of a century has been one of assimilating new technologies, from the computer to laser printing and now the Internet. The new technology has brought new competition. "The search engine companies are a major threat to newspapers trying to establish strong online services," according to Steve Outing of *Editor & Publisher*, the organ of the newspaper industry.

Other professionals now must adapt to higher standards. Already, there is almost no such thing as being the only lawyer or accountant in town. Through the Internet, people can do business with the best and brightest anywhere. This creates opportunities for those with real talent to expand their horizons to the extent of their abilities.

### *Decentralization*

Nowhere are the changes wrought by the Electronic Revolution more dramatic than in urban population projections. As recently as 1995, New York was the third largest city in the world, after only Tokyo and São Paulo, Brazil; Los Angeles was the seventh largest. United Nations projections for 20 years hence, however, indicate there will not be a single American city among the world's 10 largest. As a matter of fact, in North America, only Mexico City, ranked fourth largest in 1995, will still be one of the top 10, but only at the bottom of the list.

With the exception of Tokyo, many Americans have never heard of the other exotic cities—all located in poor countries—that will become vast fleshpots of humanity with numbers of people we can scarcely imagine. Bombay in India, for example, will be second only to Tokyo and will swarm with 27.4 million people. Lagos in Nigeria will have 24.4 million; China's Shanghai, 23.4 million and Indonesia's Jakarta, 21.1 million.

People migrate to these cities from the countryside not so much because they want to, but because they can get jobs and food. The tradeoff, unfortunately, is congestion, pollution, poor housing, crime, which few would choose if work were available in the countryside.

Contrast those crowded places with Bill Gates' vision of the future, one made possible by the telephone, fax, computer and the

Internet. "As the information superhighway makes physical proximity to urban services less important, many businesses will decentralize and disperse their activities, and cities, like companies, may be downsized," Gates wrote.

The information superhighway will reduce the downside to living beyond a major population area. Work, entertainment, information, communications will be adequately available anywhere. Says Gates: "There will be significant implications for city planners, real estate developers, and school districts if the opening of the information highway also encourages people to move away from city centers."

### *Redundant Property*

Among the outcomes of such a trend, if those who move away from cities are the affluent, knowledge workers, would be a reduction in the tax base and even rents. The real financial impact, unfortunately, will be felt by those who own immovable assets within cities.

In the mid-1980s, the world's 10 tallest buildings were in three U.S. cities. By the end of that decade there were six proposals to build still taller buildings in America, but none of them were ever built. Five years later, only 10 buildings taller than 20 stories were going up anywhere in the country; by the end of the 20th century six of the world's 10 tallest buildings were to be in Southeast Asia, according to Rick Hampson of the Associated Press (*The Oregonian*, Oct. 29, 1995).

"If the elevator and the steel frame gave birth to the skyscraper, the computer may kill it," he wrote. "The information superhighway will allow more companies to leave the city and decentralize, just as the interstate highways affected society after World War II."

It isn't only telecommunications that reduces the need for office space. Corporations are downsizing, especially in office-intensive middle management. Hundreds of thousands of office workers have lost their jobs in the 1990s, and Manhattan offered fewer jobs in the mid-1990s than in the mid-1980s. By one estimate, Hampson wrote, Fortune 500 layoffs have made available for sublease 250 million square feet of office space, which is the equivalent of 250 Chrysler Buildings.

The result of this movement is that there is so much vacant office space that there will be little need for more until the end of the 20th century. This means that a number of landmark buildings have become white elephants. In the early 1990s, Bertelsmann, a German media conglomerate, bought a mid-Manhattan office tower that had never been occupied for $119 million, a third of what it cost its bankrupt contractor to build.

Sears moved its headquarters from Chicago to a low-rise suburban campus. Its namesake building, which was the world's tallest when built in 1974, was sold half empty in 1994 for half its original cost. The best example of what happens to commercial real estate at a time of flux is downtown Detroit, where about 20 percent of the office buildings are empty or nearly so. After New York and Chicago, Detroit has the nation's largest number of pre-Depression skyscrapers. The *New York Times* news service calls these boarded-up skyscrapers "an embarrassing witness to an era when 'Dynamic Detroit' was among the richest and fastest-growing cities on earth."

These hulks spurred the imagination of Camilio José Vergara, an author and photographer from New York. He said: "I propose that as a tonic for our imagination, as a call for renewal, as a place within our national memory, a dozen city blocks of pre-Depression skyscrapers be stabilized and left standing as ruins: an American Acropolis. We could transform the nearly 100 troubled buildings in a grand national historic park of play and wonder."

These buildings were built to accommodate centralization, when efficiency required people to work in close proximity to one another. The latest advances in communication, though, make it just as productive for a secretary to work in a rural community as in the next office from the boss. And America's skyscrapers will stand as mute monuments to the passing of an era.

### *Are Banks Vulnerable?*

"Banking is essential to the modern economy, but banks are not," according to Richard Fredericks, senior managing director at Montgomery Securities. The Electronic Revolution gives banks great opportunities, but also brings them face to face with decisions they made in the past.

David Chaum of DigiCash said E-cash will be offered by banks and nonbanks alike. DigiCash or CyberCash could work with Microsoft or IBM as well as with Bank of America. Having one of those companies dispensing E-cash directly to consumers could interfere with banks' prime connection with their customers.

Banks sense the heat. "Bankers must move fast to keep up," said Ronald Braco, head of electronic banking at Chemical Bank. He estimates that banks are going to have to come up with a viable E-cash product before the end of the century or lose their market advantage forever.

If banks can keep their credibility, that is what could save them. Some E-cash makers are choosing to partner with banks to capitalize on consumer trust. "We've positioned ourselves to work with the banking industry and make sure that if there are heroes in this, it is the banks," according to William N. Melton, CEO of CyberCash. Had Microsoft succeeded in acquiring Intuit and its Quicken money management program, that could have made them a major player in the electronic transfer of money. And Bill Gates' Microsoft Money program may just do it anyway.

The question is whether banks can maintain their hold on consumer trust in an age of downsizing. Their link to the customer has been the face of the smiling teller, the smiling teller the banks constantly threaten to fire, the smiling teller who, along with her other bank coworkers, could be our daughter or friend or neighbor. Banks have reason to feel vulnerable. They have not exactly played the role of the humanitarian for most of the 1990s. When bank employees hear that their company is going to be bought out by a larger one, they brush up their resumés. They somehow now know that their jobs represent the profits that will be used to fund the purchase.

When Chemical Banking Corp. merged with Chase Manhattan Corp. to form the nation's largest bank, they were able to lay off 10,000 people, according to Farrell Kramer of the Associated Press (Nov. 12, 1995). But Stephen Brobeck, executive director of the Consumer Federation of America, said because of this, "They were somewhat vilified in the country."

This was why First Interstate Bancorp, a large California bank, initially accepted a merger offer for less money than a bid from Wells Fargo & Co., which ultimately wound up buying First Interstate anyway. First Interstate initially resisted the offer because, it was said, that would mean too many layoffs and too much trauma to employees. When Wells Fargo finally took over at First Interstate, heads rolled, just as expected.

Public relations executive Howard J. Rubenstein said: "With a company that might be regulated or involved with the government, they have to be concerned with a public reaction that might backfire politically on them. Second, companies don't want to be portrayed as antipeople."

Banks, unfortunately, often have identical and overlapping management layers, and when they merge, thousands of these positions become redundant. When such jobs are cut and the cash flow remains the same, the difference trickles down to the bottom line. That profit is apparently more appealing than being socially responsible.

Brobeck thinks some companies are waking up to a new atmosphere. "They're now beginning to understand that the public is critical of callous disregard for employees and that they will pay a price later, not only in diminished employee loyalty, but also in the marketplace." By reducing costs through slashing the number of branches, banks destroy their most compelling asset: the personal contact that built customer loyalty. If banks are competing only on price, they will be up against other, hungrier entries into the market, such as Bill Gates' Microsoft, which carry none of the baggage of a distasteful and brutal image from downsizing.

Banks hope that if they can steer consumers toward using their credit cards for purchases on the Internet, bank-controlled E-cash systems can be dovetailed into existing transaction systems and banks will retain their hold on the economy. That sanguine scenario, however, does not count the chickens coming home to roost.

### *Military Power*

The United States remains the world's pre-eminent military power, but it may also be the world's most vulnerable. To attack a potential enemy's ability to communicate, the U. S. has developed "Info War" capabilities. Such tactics, though, are cheap and potentially available to any third-rate power or terrorist group.

"Many senior Pentagon officers fear that an enemy could just as easily develop the same weapons and use them against the U.S.," reported *Time* (Aug. 21, 1995).

"When people talk about the tremendous potential of this warfare, they need to take a bite out of the reality sandwich," remarked Col. Richard Szafranski, an instructor at the U.S. Air Force Air War College who indicated that an Info War arms race could be one the U.S. would lose because it is already so open to such attacks.

Off-the-shelf computers and modems are all that is needed to strike America's electronic infrastructure of commerce and government. All it would take is one disgruntled hacker and one phone call to foul up bank transactions, railroad routing, even airline traffic.

Futurist Alvin Toffler called it "the great equalizer. You don't have to be big and rich to apply the kind of judo you need in information warfare. That's why poor countries are going for this faster than technologically advanced countries."

He's not alone in his warnings. Observed Donald Latham, formerly in charge of Pentagon communications, "A few very smart guys with computer workstations and modems could endanger lives and cause great economic disruption." Powerful, easy-to-use programs are at the disposal of any troublemaker. Intruders don't need to know much about software or computers. "All they need to do is point, click and attack," said Kenneth Van Wyk, a computer expert with the Pentagon.

### *Government Itself*

Private money threatens to wrest from government their monopoly on creation of currency. "Digital cash is a threat to every government on the planet that wants to manage its currency," according to David E. Saxton, executive vice president of Net1, a company dealing with Internet checking.

Electronic currency can easily be sent into and out of a country undetected. That makes it possible to launder crime-originated money. If the government did away with high-denomination currency like $100,000 bills because they made it too easy for criminals to do big, undetected deals, imagine the fits electronic currency must be causing. "Suddenly, someone may come up with a technology that says you can buy your dope and put the money on someone else's card. The government will have no ability to know you bought it," according to Stanley Morris, head of the U.S. Treasury's Financial Crimes Enforcement Network (*Newsweek*, Oct. 30, 1995).

Collecting taxes is another challenge. "One of the hardest questions merchants ask us," said Nathaniel S. Borenstein, one of First Virtual's cofounders, "is when do we owe taxes?" With electronic currency and doing business on the Web, the merchant could be in Poland and the buyer in Guatemala while First Virtual's computers are in Ohio. Whose sales taxes are to be paid? "I tell them (merchants) to consult a lawyer," Borenstein said.

"A government cannot tax what it cannot see," observes John Perry Barlow, cofounder of the Electronic Frontier Foundation. "It may be that because of e-money, income tax will be voluntary, and governments can only collect on tangible goods."

No one is saying government will go away as a result of the changes arising from the Internet and the host of other technological innovations government itself has unleashed. But only a fool would assume it will be business as usual in the capitols of the world in the 21st century.

### *The Future of the Dollar*

The U.S. Dollar occupies an enviable stature among the world's currencies. The questions are, can it stay there and should it? The residents of many countries keep their savings in U.S. dollars, and a large proportion of international trade is conducted in American money. Even though the U.S racks up an astounding trade deficit with other countries year after year, it has so far avoided massive inflation. One reason, as we pointed out earlier, is the large amount of U.S. currency circulating outside the country that has not come back home to bid up prices on goods and services.

One strongly held position is that there are too many dollars in the world, and there does not appear to be any genuine commitment by the U.S. government to stop the growth in the national debt, much less develop a plan for its retirement. The dollar, consequently, is in trouble. At the root of the problem is the democratic process. As in the days of the Free Silver movement at the end of the 19th century, the electorate wants high expansion and low taxes, and they know how to get it.

"Neither a state nor a bank ever have had the unrestricted power of issuing paper money without abusing that power," wrote *London Times* editor William Rees-Moog in 1978. "There never will be a shortage of politicians willing to spend where they have not taxed, nor nowadays is there any shortage of economists wishing to advise them of the wisdom of supporting trade and employment by issuing more money. No money whose issue is controlled by a politician is ever better than the needs of the next election will allow.... To obtain the consent of governments or to obtain the consent of electors requires that same assurance that there will be something in it for them. That something in the case of a currency always involves over-issue."

On the other hand, it could be argued that Americans should stop complaining that the dollar doesn't buy what it used to. If the dollar is now worth a dime, Americans ought to consider it a bargain for what the missing 90 cents bought—defeat of both Fascism and Communism and a chance for international peace and stability.

As we pointed out way back in Chapter 1, ancient Rome paid for its victory over Carthage in the three Punic Wars by reducing the weight of its coins from a pound to half an ounce. If Roman purchasing power were cut by an equivalent amount, their money at the end was worth 1/32 of what it was worth at the beginning. That's why a dollar worth a dime is a good deal by comparison. Complainers could try the alternative to victory, such as burning cash instead of wood the way the Germans did after World War I, or waiting for an airplane to unload foreign currency, the way Russians now wait for dollars.

What would have happened, one may conjecture, if the tables had been turned and the United States had lost the Cold War and the dollar had suffered the fate of the ruble? A retiree with a life savings of $250,000 in U.S. currency would have seen it shrink in purchasing power to $47—enough to buy two of these books.

One of the greatest periods of inflation in modern U.S. history came in the late 1970s, right after the American defeat in Vietnam, while periods of low inflation in modern times have followed military victories. The authors can't help but believe there is a correlation. That's why those who want to pay for social programs by cutting the military would do well to study their history.

### *The Case for Private Money*

No less a light than economist Milton Friedman sees that the threat a democratic society poses to its own currency may be best cured by removing the temptation to over-issue and placing responsibility for money in private hands.

"Increasing interest has been expressed in recent years in proposals to replace governmental issuance of money and control of its quality by private market arrangements," said Friedman. "One set of proposals would end the government monopoly on the issuance of currency and permit its competitive issue. Another would eliminate entirely any issuance of money by government and, instead, restrict the role of government to defining the monetary unit."

Rees-Moog is not the only one calling for private money. *Reader's Digest* senior editor Brian Summers wrote: "In 1864 the private coining of money was banned by an Act of Congress. Today the prohibition against private coinage, the doubtful legality of gold contracts, and legal tender laws assure the Federal government a legal monopoly over money, and prevent buyers and sellers from freely choosing mutually acceptable media of exchange."

Gold, it is often said, is the currency of last resort. Central banks and careful money managers hedge their investments by holding gold as an offset to a devaluing dollar. Gold is not easily counterfeited. It is virtually immune to deterioration. Further, it has the unique distinction of never having become unwanted as a medium of exchange. Over the past 40 years, though, the U.S. government has taken definitive steps to undermine the belief in gold as a currency. Between 1933 and 1975 Americans could not legally own gold. Since 1933 it has been illegal to have a contract payable in gold or indexed to the price of gold. In 1971 the U.S. finally refused to honor any commitments to redeem its paper promises with gold. The precious metal was essentially denounced as a relic of history and declared unsuited for use as money.

The U.S. government wants the dollar to be strong and remain the international unit of exchange while it continues to issue larger numbers of dollars than earned and so operates in a continual and growing overdraft position. Those who deal exclusively in U.S. dollars are tradin' sardines and one day they will find that out.

It is bad enough that the U.S. government is issuing great quantities of dollars with nothing behind them. There are, unfortunately, pirate nations such as North Korea and Iran issuing their own versions of the dollar, not to mention the guy around the corner with a color copier.

This is the crisis in currency—that over-issue and massive counterfeiting will cause people around the world to lose faith in the dollar. What happens when two thirds of the U.S. cash supply suddenly shows up at our doorstep, its Russian and Mexican and Thai owners demanding exchange for some other "real" money? What happens when the world comes to collect their canned sardines and finds that the fish are rotten?

### *In Conclusion*

In the first chapters of this book, we discussed how money has been backed by various commodities, such as tobacco. In theory, any item having some common appeal or widely perceived value could be used as money or to underwrite currency. The two questions we ask about any money are these: What's behind it? and How do people feel about it? The two issues are intimately related. There is no commodity behind the U.S. dollar. The government will not convert it to anything besides another dollar. And yet it remains the most liquid currency in the world because, at this writing, there is no viable alternative. The reality of What's behind it? ultimately must impact the How do people feel about it?

And good feelings are all there is behind U.S. currency. Our monetary system is, at its core, a belief system. Is faith enough, however, to underwrite the expansion of currency needed to facilitate the growth of commerce that will be made possible by the Internet? Or should there be money that can be redeemed for goods and services, a commodity-backed electronic currency?

As we mentioned earlier, the trade dollar is a perfect financial vehicle for doing business on the Internet. It has always been an electronic currency, yet it is backed by the products and the efforts of the thousands of reputable businesses in trade exchanges. So far, each trade exchange has its own currency, and these are traded against one another like foreign money. In order for trade dollars to achieve their potential as a medium of exchange for the Internet, there must be standardization, perhaps one common trade dollar for the entire industry.

Because they are the creation of private enterprise and are constantly reviewed by those participating in barter systems, trade dollars continue to maintain their credibility as a medium of exchange. The members of barter networks can and do have a direct say in how many trade dollars are in circulation and what's behind them.

Trade dollars are like the gold coins minted in antebellum days by Christopher Bechtler. They were not government money and did not claim to be. People trusted Bechtler, though, to mint coins of high-quality gold and of full weight. These coins were accepted everywhere because there was not enough government money to accommodate growth of business. And as we saw in an earlier chapter, because Bechtler's private money was real gold, people insisted on being paid with it when paper money became worthless.

Though not made of gold, trade dollars are a real commodity currency nonetheless; they are backed by the goods and services of thousands of participating businesses that are bound to deliver on demand. Plus, assuming an exchange is operating with an appropriate oversight committee and is supported by the general membership, the integrity of the trade dollar can be assured.

Because of their credibility and inherent worth, trade dollars could assume the role in the general economy that they do among members of trade exchanges: as an expansion currency. Trade exchange members prefer cash, but, when their business is growing, trade dollars help accommodate that growth. They can generate trade dollars with their surplus goods or services, essentially with business they would not have had, and spend the trade dollars to offset expenses for which they otherwise would have paid cash. It is a supplemental money supply that expands and contracts, as we saw, and it can do this as the need dictates.

Trade dollars become perfect expansion currency for Internet commerce because there is already in place an operational barter accounting system that can be backed with substance, and the expansion of this money supply is controlled by businesspeople who do not have to worry about being reelected. It is in the interest of every business owner to have access to an alternative monetary device to take advantage of opportunities. History has shown that cash and conventional credit are not sufficient to meet the needs of an expanding frontier. This is why barter will play a vital role in burgeoning Internet commerce, so businesses can leverage their unused future capacity through the mechanism of trade dollars and grow to their full potential.

Despite the crisis in currency, we remain the optimists. We believe this is simply one more obstacle to overcome. The potential is there for exponential growth: a Golden Age of peace, prosperity and creative achievement surpassing the days of the Pax Romana. To quote John Lennon, you may say that we're dreamers, but we're not the only ones. We are filled with hope for the future, and proud that the barter industry will have a role in shaping it.

# A. Exchange Fundamentals

The material set forth in this section of the appendix represents the framework on which much of the entire trade exchange industry is based and is therefore included for those wanting a more in-depth examination of the trade exchange.

## 1. Barter and the National and International Economy

By increasing demand for final goods and services in an economy, barter generates additional employment, production, and purchasing power. It results in a higher rate of capacity utilization, and enables firms to spread their overhead costs over more units of output, thereby reducing average costs and lessening inflationary pressures. Textbook economics tells us that when an economy is operating at full capacity, costs shoot up dramatically because of resource shortages and bottlenecks. But it is clear that there is a range between capacity utilization (about 80 percent in the U.S.) and capacity within which firms can expand output at constant or even declining cost. It is within this range that commercial barter transactions take place.

The reality is that a modern economy lacks a fully elastic currency, capable of expanding with the growth of production and providing the liquidity needed to clear product and service markets. Because monetary fluctuations have contributed to economic instability in the past, a nation's money supply is not permitted to expand to meet the demand for money to finance an increase in gross domestic product. Instead, the money supply is controlled by monetary authorities who have their eyes fixed on particular economic objectives: curbing inflation, ensuring full employment, protecting the value of the currency in foreign exchange markets, and so on. Balancing between these sometimes conflicting objectives often leads in advanced economies to a policy of monetary restriction. This restrains the flow of spending in the cash economy, limiting demand for output, and creating excess capacity.

Barter and its modern counterpart, the creation of trade credit to finance greater demand for goods and services, helps alleviate monetary stringency, puts unutilized capacity to work, and speeds up the flow of goods and services to their most productive uses. It thus adds an important measure of flexibility to the trade and payments system and market adjustment mechanisms of the domestic and international economies at a period in history when global economic organization is undergoing a dramatic restructuring. Commercial barter should therefore, as a matter of public policy, be encouraged.

*Reprinted by permission of Paul Suplizio*

## 2. Fundamentals of the Trade Exchange

A trade exchange is an association, or network, of business owners and professionals that form a market place to barter goods and services. The exchange acts as a barter clearinghouse for its member's trading activities. Transactions cleared through an exchange are accomplished through the medium of the "trade dollar" which represents credit to the seller's account for goods and services sold "on trade." A trade dollar should not be confused with a "cash equivalent credit," which is the pervasive unit of accounting used by corporate barter companies. Trade dollars and cash equivalent credits have significant differences. The trade exchange deals only with trade dollars, and it is only the trade exchange that is dealt with in this paper.

Trade dollars are valued in accordance with Accounting Pronouncements Bulletin 29, and should be reported in accordance with Emerging Issues Task Force 93-11 pronouncement issued by the Financial Accounting Standards Board.

A typical barter company dealing at the trade exchange level is usually set up such that the barter company and the trade exchange are separate and distinct entities. The barter company is typically empowered to manage a trade exchange which consists of a membership made up of the company's clientele. The association of business owners and professionals that form the marketplace known as the trade exchange is often referred to as a "commercial" or "retail" trade exchange.") Consistent with the TEFRA act passed by Congress in 1982, the exchange and/or the barter management company which operates the exchange, is considered a third party record keeper under US law.

## 3. Accounting Rules for the Exchange

A trade exchange operating in compliance with the International Reciprocal Trade Association's (IRTA) model contract, conducts business through the use of trade dollars which are backed by the real goods and services of its indebted membership. Trade Dollars have value because of the contractual commitment of members to accept them to facilitate commerce. And, because of the contractual obligation of those who have borrowed from the membership through the services of the exchange and have an obligation to repay in goods and services.

The formula

**Credit Lines in Use = Currency in Circulation**

explains the method by which trade dollars are created within the barter network commonly known as a trade exchange.

# 4. Trade Dollars and Trade Dollar Transactions

**General.** A trade dollar is an accounting unit used within the trade exchange to record the value of trades as determined by the buying and selling parties in barter transactions. Trade dollars denote the right to receive goods or services available from other exchange members or the obligation to provide goods or services to other exchange members. Trade dollars may not be redeemed for cash. Trade dollars may be used only in the manner and for the purpose set forth in the rules of the exchange. Trade dollars are not legal tender, securities, or commodities.

**Normal Valuation of Trade Dollars.** Barter companies use the ratio of one trade dollar to one United States dollar in measuring and accounting for purchases and sales, assuming that the barter company is based within the United States. Australia, Canadian, and New Zealand barter companies use a one to one ratio with the dollar of their own countries. Exchanges based in other countries typically use a one to one ratio with the currency of their realm.

Barter companies do not recognize any accounting implications if differences are observed between trade dollars and cash dollar pricing that are within reasonable ranges that might exist between prices of similar cash dollar transactions.

**Abnormal Valuation of Trade Dollars.** For those few significant trade dollar transactions in which fair market values are determined to be materially different from the ratio of $1 to one trade dollar, the fair market values should be used in determining the accounting result of the transaction instead of amounts equal to the number of trade dollars exchanged. This means that the barter company's own purchases or sales would need be adjusted, on an as needed basis, to represent an appropriate reflection of their real dollar value activity.

Abnormal valuations most often occur in certain acquisitions of bulk inventories, such as those entered into by the barter company for it's own principal party trading activities. Members of the exchange experiencing an abnormal valuation of trade dollars have the same responsibility for recording an accounting adjustment to decrease the carrying value of a given inventory or capital asset to fair market value along with a decrease to income for the period. The accounting standard of "cost or market whichever is less" should be the primary barometer for determining whether or not a given acquisition should be adjusted downward. No upward adjustments in the value of trade dollar acquisitions are to be permitted.

**Trade Dollar Valuation in the Statement of Operations.** The ratio of $1 per trade dollar is applicable to revenue and costs and expenses in the statement of operations with the exception of the effects of additional costs and expenses recorded as a result of the circumstances described under the preceding section "Abnormal Valuation of Trade Dollars." It should be noted that to a significant extent, any adjustments to trade dollar revenue would be offset by corresponding adjustments to expenses paid when corresponding trade dollar are spent for goods and services that are charged to costs and expenses.

**Trade Dollar Valuation in the Balance Sheet.** It should be fair to assume that barter company employees are experts in trading. Barter company management generally has developed some form of effective blended cash-trade purchasing program. Barter companies spend trade dollars that have been earned or issued by the company on behalf of the exchange, to pay for goods and services used by the company in its operations.

Any negative trade dollar balance of the company should be shown as a liability in the company's balance sheet. The contractual relationship between the company and members of the exchange typically permits the barter company to borrow credit through the issuance of trade dollars in excess of the amount specifically earned by the company, within certain specified limits.

At each balance sheet date, in accordance with generally accepted accounting principles, any positive trade dollar balance of either a member business or the barter company would be evaluated for net realizable value. The company should adjust the carrying value of the trade dollars if the fair value of the trade dollars is less than the carrying value, or it is probable that not all trade dollars will be used.

Information that would be used to support the net realizable value of a significant positive trade dollar balance at a balance sheet date would include the company's past track record of utilizing trade dollars, evident ability and intent to utilize the trade dollars in a reasonable time, indicated by the quantity of trade dollars relative to the size of the company's procurement budget for items the trade dollars may be used for, and preparation of a trade plan for timely utilization on a $1 per trade dollar basis for goods and services that will be available.

Notwithstanding the method for determining value set forth immediately above, a barter company should consider taking a more conservative approach in recording earned trade dollar surplus at its fiscal year end. There is a conflict of interest between a barter company's inherent responsibility to regulate and administer the total trade dollars in circulation within the exchange it operates, as contrasted with that of it's carrying trade dollars as a company asset on its own balance sheet. The more conservative approach would suggest that a barter company not record any earned trade dollar surplus as an asset on it's balance sheet at year end. Instead, any earned surplus might be used to acquire inventories for principal party trading, (market making activities), where when needed, value is supported by independent outside appraisal. Other options may also exist, such as contributing an earned surplus to the debt reserve of the exchange where justified, and/or returning such surplus to the exchange membership at large.

## 5. Inventory for Principal Party Trading Using Trade Dollars

**Inventory Purchased and Sold for Trade Dollars.** Purchases of inventory for principal party trading paid for in trade dollars are valued at the amount of trade dollars paid unless the circumstances described in the preceding section "Abnormal Valuation of trade dollars" are present. For significant purchases of inventory for principal party trading paid for in trade dollars in which fair market values are determined to be materially different from the ratio of $1 per trade dollar, the fair market values are used in determining the accounting result of the transaction and the carrying value of the inventory, in such situations, an accounting adjustment is recorded to decrease the carrying value of the inventory to fair market value along with a decrease to income for the period.

## 6. Determination and Substantiation of Fair Market Value

Barter companies procedures for inventory for principal party trading should include obtaining appraisals of fair market, comparison to equivalent cash market prices that would be required for similar purchases, or both.

**Revenue Recognition.** Revenue is recognized for sales of inventory for principal party trading when the buyer has made an unconditional commitment to convey the applicable consideration to the company and the company has culminated the earnings process by having shipped the inventory to the buyer or performed such other acts necessary to have completed its required performance pursuant to the applicable transaction. For any transaction resulting in revenue to a barter company, if any material contingencies are present, revenue recognition is delayed until all material contingencies are eliminated. Further, no revenue should be recognized unless collection of the applicable consideration is probable.

## International Reciprocal Trade Association Commercial Barter and Public Policy

To understand the role of commercial barter in the modern world, let us look at barter's role at four distinct levels: the firm, the community, and the national and international economies.

### *Barter and the Firm*

Business people barter because they are able to finance the purchases of things they need out of additional sales of their own product or service. When a merchant buys something using barter credits, he knows that the purchase will be paid for in whole or in part by his sales to other businesses in the barter marketplace.

In a cash situation, the cash spent by a merchant for a purchase would have to come out of existing sales, not new sales. He has no assurance, when he makes a cash purchase, that this will result in additional sales of his own product. His prospects for making added profit increase when he participates in the barter marketplace, because he can make additional sales of his own product or service, and obtain greater value from sales compared to liquidation or costly markdowns. Sellers in the barter marketplace can make additional sales because they have a steady source of demand from buyers looking for opportunities to pay for the things they want with their own unused inventory or spare capacity.

The economic advantages of barter hinge on the fact that barter brings in new business and conserves cash. Barter sales are an increment over and above cash sales, at a price over and above incremental cost. All firms can take advantage of barter to bring in new business. Those firms with spare capacity or excess inventory have strong incentives to do so.

Financing purchases through additional sales of one's own product or service is often the cheapest method of finance available to a business. This is because it is paying for its purchases with the profit margin on its extra sales or unused capacity.

Barter sales yield trade dollars or trade credits which may be spent with the barter company or other members of the barter system. Trade dollars are units of account denominated in dollars representing the right to receive, or the obligation to pay, in goods or services available through the barter system. The cost of one trade dollar is in inventory, labor, or other cost of producing an additional dollar's worth of barter sales. A firm buys with trade dollars which cost it less than the revenue it earns from its sales. In textbook economics, so long as incremental revenue exceeds incremental cost, there will be an economic incentive to make the barter sale.

As an example, take an auto parts supplier who does a good deal of direct mail advertising. He joins a barter exchange and notes that several printers are members. Other things being equal, he has an incentive to buy his printing from the barter printers because (a) he won't have to reduce his cash flow for this business expense, but instead, (b) he can finance this expense out of trade dollars earned from barter sales of his own products and services to other members of the barter system, at a price that exceeds his incremental cost.

Barter aids the business person who has reached a certain level of cash sales and still has the capacity to expand output; or who has excess inventory or unproductive assets. Few and fortunate, indeed, are the business people who, having made an investment in plant and equipment, find themselves operating at full or over-full capacity. For most firms, spare capacity and obsolescent or unused inventory are a normal occurrence, with a powerful economic plus: they permit additional sales at relatively low incremental cost.

Examples are the printer, with large sunk costs in equipment, but relatively low cost of additional output; the hotel with rooms unfilled; the dentist with time to take more patients; the radio or television station with unsold advertising. These firms are foregoing income from their unused capacity. If shown hot to stimulate additional sales through barter, they have a strong incentive to make those sales as long as they can cover their costs. The price at which they can sell on barter will either be the same as the normal cash prince, or as a minimum, a price greater than the cash liquidation value of inventory. Firms with high cash inventory costs will find barter even more advantageous if they are able to receive some cash in the transaction to apply to the cost of their inventory.

Income taxes take away *part* of the extra profit from barter sales. However, even at the highest bracket rate, a firm makes money *after taxes* on its additional sales. While reducing the extra profit, the income tax should not affect a firm's decision to make sales to reap that profit. This applies whether the additional sales are cash sales or barter sales. Since passage of the Tax Equity and Fiscal Responsibility Act of 1982, barter exchanges are required to report the barter income of their clients to IRS on Form 1099-B.

The economic advantages of barter can be seen by comparing a firm's position before and after barter. We see that barter results in additional revenue, hence added profit; barter enables a firm to conserve cash, resulting in better liquidity and a saving equal to the going cost of money. Firms also gain from an intangible web of referrals, advertising, and associations that generate both additional cash and barter business.

The barter company's commission charges must be included in a firm's cost calculation, but these charges are normally not a deterrent to barter. Indeed, the largest cost a firm can experience is the income foregone by *not* selling on barter. In many cases, firms might find it profitable to pay an even higher commission in order to have the opportunity to reap additional profits through barter sales.

### *Barter and the Community*

Barter would benefit an economic community even if the barter system consisted of firms who had previously been each other's cash customers. This is not to say that barter sales should replace cash sales at the same selling price—they should not. But the reality is that cash sales are limited by the cash incomes of firms in the community, resulting in some firms having excess capacity. These firms do more business with each other if they can barter because of their ability to (1) make additional sales out of excess capacity, earning "new" money in the form of trade credits, and (2) paying for what they buy with these additional trade credits whose cost to them is the incremental cost of their own product or service.

Establishing a barter exchange results over-all in new business for the community rather than displacement of pre-existing cash business. This conclusion stems from the existence of surplus inventory or excess capacity in the cash economy, and the ability of firms to make extra sales and earning "new" money in the form of trade credits. The new money supply adds to the cash money supply, and the extra liquidity finances a higher level of real trade.

### *Barter and the National and International Economy*

By increasing demand for final goods and services in an economy, barter generates additional employment, production, and purchasing power. It results in a higher rate of capacity utilization, and enables firms to spread their overhead costs over more units of output, thereby reducing average costs and lessening inflationary pressures. Textbook economics tells us that when an economy is operating at full capacity, costs shoot up dramatically because of resource shortages and bottlenecks. But it is clear that there is a range between *current* capacity utilization (about 80 percent in the U.S.) and *full* capacity within which firms can expand output at constant or even declining cost. It is within this range that commercial barter transactions take place.

The reality is that a modern economy lacks a fully elastic currency, capable of expanding with the growth of production and providing the liquidity needed to clear product and service markets. Because monetary fluctuations have contributed to economic instability in the past, a nation's money supply is not permitted to expand to meet the demand for money to finance an increase in gross domestic product. Instead, the money supply is controlled by monetary authorities who have their eyes fixed on particular economic objectives: curbing inflation, ensuring full employment, protecting the value of the currency in foreign exchange markets, and so on. Balancing between these sometimes conflicting objectives often leads in advanced economies to a policy of monetary restriction. This restrains the flow of spending in the cash economy, limited demand for output, and creating excess capacity.

Barter and its modern counterpart, the creation of trade credit to finance greater demand for goods and services, helps alleviate monetary stringency, puts unutilized capacity to work, and speeds up the flow of goods and services to their most productive uses. It thus adds an important measure of flexibility to the trade and payments system and market adjustment mechanisms of the domestic and international economies at a period in history when global economic organization is undergoing a dramatic restructuring. Commercial barter should therefore, as a matter of public policy, be encouraged.

*Reprinted by permission of Paul Suplizio*

## B. Exchange Consolidations and Reporting

The materials included in this section of the Appendix provide general information and background regarding barter company spending in a trade exchange, exchange consolidations, and an approach to exchange reporting.

### 1. Author's Opinion

At the time of this writing, few exchanges have, as yet, made the commitment to exchange member reporting. The primary reason for this reluctance is the issue surrounding trade system deficits. Exchange operators are reluctant to admit that such deficits were either developed by them, or accrued as a consequence of the conversion of another deficit spent exchange. Further, the few exchanges who have mustered the courage to "show it all" have been aggressively assaulted by their competitors who tend to dramatize the deficits in competitive presentations but do not reveal any similar information about their own networks. In other words, it has simply not been competitively expedient for independent exchanges to comply with a reasonable disclosure dictate.

In the author's opinion, until either government edict, or an industry association directive, absolutely requires the kind of report discussed herein, the current business practice of non disclosure will likely continue. This is unfortunate, but certainly not fatal. Business owners and professionals comprise the clientele of trade exchanges, and by their very nature they are better educated about the risks of doing business in unregulated arenas. Owning and operating a business entails great risk, and virtually every decision made regarding marketing strategies, financing, asset allocations, etc., are a part of the risk-return compendium.

In the final analysis, although membership in a trade exchange does entail risk, the opportunity for continued returns for regular participation in a reasonably well-run barter network far outweigh the downside.

## 2. Barter Company Spending in the Exchange

A barter company manages the trade exchange which is an association or network of business owners who have come together to trade their goods and services in a barter marketplace. Trading rules govern use of member trade exchange accounts. Trading rules set forth the terms under which the operators of an exchange may use the exchange for their own benefit. For example, contained within the recommendations of the International Reciprocal Trade Association's (IRTA) model contract is the following: "Client recognizes and grants to barter company, its shareholders and officers, the right and power to borrow from the exchange, and to spend an aggregate amount not to exceed three (3) years' earnings of trade dollars."

Trading rules should make clear that the barter company manages the exchange, and that notwithstanding this fiduciary responsibility, it is entitled to borrow a line of trade dollars from the exchange. The specific limits to such borrowing must be clearly defined in the trading rules. However, as set forth in Chapter 16 in the section "Trade Dollar Valuation in the Balance Sheet" the fact that the operating company is involved in the creation and control of trade dollars in its management role of the exchange, suggests that it would not normally be permitted by its auditors to carry earned trade dollars as an asset in its own corporate financial reports. Therefore the exchange management company would generally endeavor to bring it's own trade accounts to zero by the close of each annual period.

Although an exchange operator has the right to borrow trade dollars from the system and use them as it sees fit in the operation of the company, just like any other exchange member, it is responsible for repayment of any credit line use.

## 3. Exchange Consolidations

On February 20, 1994, the author submitted a paper to the Board of Directors of the International Reciprocal Trade Association entitled *The Barter Industry: A Brief Overview and Forecast*. Fom this paper the following is quoted:

> Working from the premise that we have much in common with the securities industry, we might look to their evolution as a sort of potential mirror image for examination as we consider our own development. For example, I am convinced that the trade exchange as it now exists, will continue to move towards becoming a true electronic marketplace where the real time execution of orders will facilitate a huge increase in the volume and the size of what we ... refer to as barter transactions....
>
> It is my opinion that the barter industry's future would be best served by consolidation of the many individual exchanges into perhaps five to ten large, well organized, real-time computer clearinghouses. These consolidated trade exchanges would be more akin to the Nasdaq, New York, American, Boston, and Toronto stock clearing marketplaces. .... The financial commitment is large and those that embark upon this course of action will need to be totally committed to the future they see, rather than simply to business as usual.

Trade exchange consolidations are taking place, but how does one exchange merge with another when the debit and credit relationships are out of balance?

# 4. Exchange Conversions—A Historical Perspective

Business Exchange, Inc. formerly known as BX, then BXI, and now most recently BX Trade Exchange, (BXI) began converting various independent trade exchanges into its barter system in approximately 1980. ITEX began the conversion process of non ITEX trade exchanges in late 1982. Barter Exchange, Inc., (BEI) and a barter company originally known as "Internet" also developed national trade networks and in approximately 1984-85 began similar programs to consolidate various independent trade exchanges into single network clearinghouses. In every case the exchange being converted had more trade credits outstanding than they had trade debits to secure them. This problem is pervasive in the exchange industry simply because during its infancy all of the original exchange franchisors with which the author is familiar and with the exception of the original BX, promulgated faulty economic models for exchange operation and management.

In the author's experience and opinion, every single exchange in America, including BXI, harbors a system deficit accumulated early on, or as a result of a conversion of a trade system from an earlier period. It is also the authors opinion that although these deficits exist, they are now largely contained and quantified and most exchange operators have developed plans for their continued containment and/or actual retirement.

The conversion program pursued by a number of the larger exchanges was designed to allow members of the "deficit spent" trade exchanges to redeem their trade credits for BXI, Internet, BEI, or ITEX trade dollars, subject to certain terms and conditions and provided that the operator of the converting exchange was in support of the project. The difference between the trade dollars issued converting clients, and the trade debits assigned from the converting exchange to the surviving exchange for collection, was charged to a credit line granted a conversion fund account. The amount of the negative trade balance in this account represented the total of the trade debt that had been accumulated by the converting exchange during previous years as a result of either a policy of deficit spending or poor credit and collection policies, or both.

It is interesting to note that by 1994 approximately 41.9% of the trade dollars in use throughout the ITEX barter system were a result of the long-term retirement process developed from converting trade exchanges into ITEX. No comparable figure is available from BXI. The Internet exchange changed their name to Primenet when they were purchased by a California law firm. The latter was evidently unable to operate it successfully and eventually it was closed. The BEI exchange was absorbed in 1995 by ITEX.

In the author's experience, personal guarantees were initially required on conversion accounts from the trade exchange operators that were sponsoring the conversion of a specific exchange membership. Originally, conversion loans were made predicated on pay-back analysis, and on an evaluation of the benefits that conversion of a given exchange might provide existing members of the target trading network, such as BXI or ITEX. Revenues developed from the various trade fees assessed exchange clientele were theoretically able to provide the resources from which conversion fund obligations were to be eventually retired.

By assuming the accounting for converting trade exchanges, both BXI ITEX, and others, were able to immediately stop the expansion of unsecured trade credit. Over the years ITEX has performed this service for about eighty deficit spent trade exchanges. BXI does not report on these activities but to the best of the author's knowledge there have been at least twenty such conversions.

Currently there are a number of successful exchanges not referred to above, that are absorbing the membership base, and the debit and credit relationships of other independent trade exchanges.

## 5. Conversion Funds

By the mid 1980's ITEX had assisted a number of its brokers, (previously independent exchange operators), to liquidate conversion obligations ahead of the planned schedule for retirement. This was done where such help did not create an undue tax liability for the affected operator and where a trade surplus was available. However, this action produced the net effect of shrinking the total trade dollars in circulation more rapidly than might have been wise. ITEX trade dollars began to appear stronger because they became harder to obtain. And, although the perception caused by the shrinkage of trade currency had its good points, in the long run, the reduction of trade dollars within the barter system reduced trade volume.

Trade volume is the total of member trade activity and thus reflects the prime reasons business owners join an exchange to begin with, ie: to increase sales and conserve cash. Just like a country's money supply, if there is not enough in the marketplace, commerce will decrease. It is also true, that like a country's money supply, if there are more trade dollars in circulation than is comfortable to the majority of business owners accepting them as payment for the extra sales they represent, then inflation may develop. Managing the money supply, or the trade dollars in circulation, is an important responsibility of an exchange operator.

Section D of the Trading Rules of the ITEX Trade Exchange is entitled *Administration Of The Exchange And Its Trade Dollars*. Contained within this section in paragraph 4b it says:

> Client grants to ITEX and the Exchange the right to extend loans in Trade dollars to trade exchange owner/operators whose exchange systems have become "deficit spent" and who wish to endorse the conversion of their members trade credits into ITEX Trade dollars.

In 4c it goes on to say:

> Client acknowledges that such conversions are designed to improve membership growth while providing a mechanism to increase the available trade dollars in circulation in order to benefit the membership of the Exchange at large and that conversion loans are made, predicated on a pay back analysis only, and not on specific collateral.

In early 1992, acting on behalf of the exchange, ITEX Corporation released a group of individuals from the personal guarantees that were a part of conversion accounts with which they were originally associated. BXI had evidently taken similar steps some time previous, but due to their penchant for secrecy this cannot verified.

By the close of fiscal year 1992–93 ITEX determined that the retirement period for conversion obligations should be extended in order to maintain sufficient trade currency in circulation. As a result several hundred thousand trade dollars earned through trade assessments were bonused equally to the auto-pay members of the ITEX trade exchange rather that simply shrinking the credit in circulation by reduction of the conversion account. This infusion of trade credit back into the system, rather than being applied to conversion fund retirement, helped generate more income for the general membership by providing the resource with which more clients could facilitate more business. The net effect of this action was an increase in the trading activity of the membership at large.

BXI has evidently pursued an alternative mechanism for increasing the supply of trade dollars in their exchange. In one particular example, BXI acquired $2,778,000 in preferred stock with newly created trade dollars. The company selling the preferred shares began immediately to spend the trade dollars in the BXI system thereby increasing the trade dollars in circulation where the preferred shares were presumably held by the exchange as collateral.

## 6. Exchange Reporting

Although most barter companies operating a trade exchange do not yet provide their trading members a routine report on the condition of their respective exchanges, some of the more progressive barter companies have incorporated language in their trading rules similar to that as follows:

> ... will make available on a periodic basis a report on the status of the exchange which sets forth totals of the negative and positive member balances, reserves, inventories and other assets and liabilities of the exchange.

More recent developments that will surely play a major role in the evolution of the trade exchange as a legitimate mechanism for commerce, include the appointing of an oversight committee to report on the condition of an exchange to it's specific membership. For example, an Advisory Board of Governors might be appointed to review the record keeping services of the barter company on behalf of it's exchange. The Board of Governors should claim, as a minimum, advisory responsibilities to both the exchange membership at large, and to the Board of Directors of the barter company managing the effected exchange. The report to the barter company should be performed in the capacity of an "oversight committee" and should include an assessment of the handling by the company's management of the third-party recordkeeping activities they perform.

An Exchange Board of Governors ought provide an annual report to the exchange membership entitled "Exchange Membership Report." The Board should also prepare an "Exchange Trade Dollar Report," "Trade Exchange Statement of Condition," or similar document, that sets forth the total of the trade credit held in member accounts, the trade debits that secure the outstanding credit, and distribute the information to effected parties.

An exchange functioning under IRTA guidelines should operate a "debit-zero" barter accounting system.

This means that for each trade dollar in circulation in the barter system, (positive trade dollar balance in a client account), there must also be a trade debit, (debt owed, or secured by, another client's account.)

The term debit-zero is derived from the requirement that the trade debits in the exchange must offset to zero the outstanding trade dollars, in other words debits and credits need to balance.

A sample Exchange Trade Dollar Report follows:

### ITEX Retail Trade Exchange 1994–95
### Exchange Trade Dollar Report (USA Operations)

Barter is a strategic marketing tool used by business owners worldwide to increase sales and conserve cash. The ITEX barter concept requires that the ITEX "exchange", (which is an association of business owners and professionals that form a market place to barter goods and services), acts as a barter clearinghouse. Transactions cleared through the exchange are accomplished through the medium of the ITEX trade dollar which represents credit to the seller's account for goods and services sold "on trade".

Since 1984, ITEX has encouraged Congress to act on the Commercial Barter Self Regulation Act. Background disclosures, a standardized report on trade credit in circulation, and a ban on Exchange owner's deficit spending are requirements of this Bill.

Responsible legislation will increase confidence and improve propriety by requiring that registered exchange operators routinely disclose the economic status of their trading system. ITEX Corporation is a public company and therefore reports to the Securities Exchange Commission on a quarterly basis its business and financial activities. This information becomes part of the public record and is available to anyone wanting to know more about the Company. ITEX Corporation manages the ITEX exchange, and consistent with the Tax Equity and Fiscal Responsibility Act, is an official third party record-keeper under United States law.

It is important to note that the financial information of ITEX Corporation and that of the ITEX exchange are separate and distinct. As set forth in the ITEX Trading Rules, ITEX Corporation on behalf of the ITEX exchange, agrees to: *"make available on a periodic basis a report on the status of the Exchange which sets forth totals of the negative and positive member balances, reserves, inventories and other assets and liabilities of the exchange."*

The following information on the ITEX exchange is presented in a format consistent with ITEX's recommendations for exchange disclosure presented to the International Reciprocal Trade Association in 1984.

## 7. 1994-95 Exchange Trade Dollar Report

| | |
|---|---|
| **Trade Assets** | |
| Current | |
| Credit Lines in Use | $37,377,588 |
| Notes Receivable | 1,644,538 |
| Traveler's Fund Surplus | 564,157 |
| Total Current | $39,586,283 |
| Non Current | |
| Conversion Fund Receivables | $28,574,583 |
| Total Non Current | $28,574,583 |
| **Total Trade Assets** | **$68,160,866** |
| **Trade Liabilities** | |
| Current | |
| Member Balances Outstanding & Spendable | $57,692,751 |
| Total Current | $57,692,751 |
| Non Current | |
| Member Balances Linked to Overdue Fees | $8,259,420 |
| **Total Trade Liabilities** | **$65,952,171** |
| **Exchange Reserves** | |
| Exchange Reserves | $2,208,695 |
| **Trade Liabilities and Exchange Reserves** | **$68,160,866** |

## 8. Notes to Exchange Trade Dollar Report

1. ITEX Corporation manages and operates the ITEX "Barter System" or the "exchange" which is a trade association of several thousand business owner members who trade their goods and services through the use of trade dollars. In this capacity ITEX Corporation acts as a third-party record keeper of barter transactions among the members of the exchange, which is a network of business owners who have come together to barter surplus goods and services. Members of the exchange are considered clients of the company. The ITEX Trading Rules constitute the contract between ITEX Corporation, its clients, and the Retail Trade Exchange.

2. Trade dollars are an accounting unit used to record the value of bartered transactions as determined by the buying and selling parties. Trade dollars denote the right

to receive goods or services available from other exchange members or the obligation to provide goods or services to other exchange members. Trade dollars may not be redeemed for cash. Trade dollars may be used only in the manner and for the purpose set forth in the trading rules which govern use of an ITEX trade account. Trade dollars are not legal tender, securities, or commodities.

3. Trade dollars are placed in circulation through the extension of lines of credit to members and brokers of the exchange. The in-use portion of these lines of credit represent the total of the trade dollars actually in circulation at any given moment in time. The magnitude of the trade currency represented by these trade dollars can be set forth by the formula: **Currency = In-Use Credit Lines.**

4. ITEX Operates a "debit-zero" barter accounting system for the exchange which means that credits (trade liabilities) are at least equalled by debits (trade assets) accept as it relates to the conversion of previously independent trade exchanges into ITEX who had, prior to their association with ITEX, developed a trade system deficit. The liquidity of the trade dollars in circulation are exclusively the responsibility of the exchange members who owe the barter system.

5. ITEX uses the ratio of one trade dollar to one U.S. dollar in measuring and accounting for purchases and sales. There is no accounting implications recognized for any differences that may exist between trade dollars and cash dollar pricing predicated upon the premise that sample observations of routine trade transactions are within the reasonable ranges that may exist between prices of similar cash dollar transactions.

6. The total trade activity represented by trade dollars for both sales and purchases during 1994-95 was **$215,129,706.**

7. By fiscal year end the total cardholders in the exchange was 22,352. Two events during the 1994-95 fiscal year had significant impact on the number of cardholders. The first was a policy change early in the year which automatically deleted any client with no payment activity for 60 days; the results of this policy enactment reduced the total client count. The second significant change was the acquisition of the active client list of Barter Exchange, Inc., resulting in an increase in total client count. The net effect of these two items was a reduction in the total client count from previous years, but an increase in per client trading activity.

8. At year end there were:
   a. $1.18 in exchange assets for each *spendable* trade dollar on deposit in member accounts.
   b. $1.03 in exchange assets for the *total* trade dollars on deposit in member accounts.
   c. $.65 in current exchange assets for each *spendable* trade dollar on deposit in member accounts.

9. The ultimate security of the exchange is the selling obligation of its membership. Exchange members have agreed to continually accept new barter sales until reaching and maintaining a positive trade balance of $15,000 in their respective accounts. As long as exchange members continue to accept trade dollars in payment of surplus goods and services, trade dollars will continue to have worth.

10. The ITEX exchange has absorbed the memberships of a number of independent barter exchanges whose trade dollar economies were in deficit. The conversion of trade credit from non-ITEX trade exchanges into ITEX trade dollars, for which there were insufficient offsetting trade receivables, have been charged against credit lines assigned to a Conversion Fund (CF) account. Approximately 41.9% of the

trade dollars in circulation within the ITEX exchange is a result of the long-term repayment obligations of non-ITEX exchange operators, and/or ITEX brokers, having initiated the conversion of an independent trade exchange into the ITEX system.

ITEX Corporation, it's management and employees, are not allowed to participate in unsecured deficit spending within the ITEX exchange. Therefore, the total system deficit, or conversion fund receivable, is comprised of either previous exchange owners having deficit spent within their own exchange, or because of uncollectible trade credit lines extended to their exchange members prior to their becoming ITEX, or both. And, where these previously non ITEX trade exchanges were subsequently consolidated into the ITEX exchange thereby accumulating a system deficit.

The conversion fund receivable, or system deficit, is designed to be self liquidating over time as a consequence of trade revenues developed from monthly association dues and other trade charges assessed the general membership. (See the *1994-1995 Exchange Membership Report* for further information on this important subject.)

11. Total trade activity divided by spendable trade dollars at year end reflects trade dollar velocity of 2.68 times per year.
12. The exchange occasionally acts as a principal in barter transactions. Inventory may be held in its name when collateral has been pledged by a member to secure a trade credit line, and where that credit line has defaulted and the exchange has taken temporary possession of the affected collateral until resold.
13. Explanation of Terms

**Credit Lines in Use.** Represents the amount of credit used by Exchange members in good standing from open lines of credit.

**Notes Receivable.** Represents the amount of credit issued to Exchange members and brokers in good standing where a specific promissory note has been obtained.

**Traveler's Fund Surplus.** Constitutes the earned breakage from Traveler's Checks issued but unredeemed by the expiration date.

**Conversion Fund Receivable.** Represents the total of the conversion fund or CF accounts. The total amount of trade dollars set forth in this account is also known as the "system deficit." (See the associated report entitled *The Economics of the ITEX Retail Trade Exchange* for an in depth review of this important information.

**Member Balances Outstanding & Spendable.** The total positive trade dollar balances in member and broker trade accounts where cash fees are current and the balance is available for immediate spending.

**Member Balances Linked to Overdue Fees.** The total positive trade dollar balances in member and broker trade accounts where cash fees are NOT current and the effected trade balance may not be spent.

**Exchange Reserves.** The difference between the total trade assets and the total trade liabilities.

The above reporting format entitled *Exchange Trade Dollar Report* was originally presented as an IRTA model when the author served as the industry Chairman of the Barter Accounting Standards Board. Several years later under the direction of Matthew O'Hayer's leadership, (then president of Barter Exchange, Inc.) an alternative reporting mechanism was presented as an industry standard. Thereafter Matt and I conducted barter accounting workshops together during industry conventions for many years. Matthew O'Hayer's recommended presentation approach follows:

# 9. Statement of Condition Trade Exchange System

This is not a Balance Sheet of (The Company), but of the client/member system

______________(Date)

| | |
|---|---|
| **Assets:** | |
| **Current:** | |
| Total negative member balances or revolving accounts | xxx |
| Less estimated allowance for doubtful accounts (not provided for in Loan Loss account) | <xxx> |
| | XXX |
| Trade dollar loans, current portion | xxx |
| Inventory owned by system | xxx |
| Total Current Assets | XXX |
| **Non-current:** | |
| Trade dollar loans, less current portion | xxx |
| Less estimated allowance for doubtful accounts (not provided for in Loan Loss Accounts) | <xxx> |
| | XXX |
| House accounts with negative balances | XXX |
| **Total Assets** | XXX |
| **Liabilities:** | |
| **Current:** | |
| Total positive member balances | xxx |
| Total positive house accounts | xxx |
| Other system liabilities | xxx |
| Total Current Liabilities | XXX |
| **Non-current:** | |
| Loan Loss Reserve Account | xxx |
| **Total Liabilities** | XXX |
| **System Deficit (surplus)** | XXX |
| **Total Liabilities & System Deficit** | XXX |

# C. IRTA Pronouncements

The materials included in this section are ones that, in the author's opinion, have had far-reaching impact on the development of the commercial barter industry. The following materials are drawn exclusively from the barter industry's oldest and largest trade association, the International Reciprocal Trade Association (IRTA).

These materials are the exclusive property of their respective author's, and/or the IRTA, and may not be reprinted without express permission of the appropriate parties.

### *International Reciprocal Trade Association*

The International Reciprocal Trade Association (IRTA) was founded in 1979 to foster the interests of the commercial barter industry in the United States and worldwide and to uphold high standards of ethical business practice. The Association conducts research into contract, regulatory, and tax laws and accounting principles applicable to barter transactions. It maintains an information clearinghouse and public relations program and it actively represents its members before government agencies.

Membership in IRTA is open to any individual or firm, domestic or foreign, who subscribes to the aims of the Association, provides required background information on business activities, and meets the qualifications for membership.

IRTA administers the Barter Political Action Committee (BARTERPAC) under special authority of the Federal Election Commission. IRTA's programs stress industry self-regulation and upgrading professional standards through education and training. Under IRTA's lead, barter companies in the U.S. and worldwide are constantly in touch with each other and sharing the latest and most successful methods of business practice. IRTA's promotion efforts aim to spur the growth of a young and dynamic industry by reaching out to the media and answering many firm's requests for information about barter.

## 1. Commercial Barter and Public Policy

To understand the role of commercial barter in the modern world, let us look at barter's role at four distinct levels: the firm, the community, and the national and international economies.

### *Barter and the Firm*

Business people barter because they are able to finance the purchases of things they need out of additional sales of their own product or service. When a merchant buys something using barter credits, he knows that the purchase will be paid for in whole or in part by his sales to other businesses in the barter marketplace.

In a cash situation, the cash spent by a merchant for a purchase would have to come out of existing sales, not new sales. He has no assurance, when he makes a cash purchase, that this will result in additional sales of his own product. His prospects for making added profit increase when he participates in the barter marketplace, because he can make additional sales of his own product or service, and obtain greater value from sales compared to liquidation or costly markdowns. Sellers in the barter marketplace can make additional sales because they have a steady source of demand from buyers looking for opportunities to pay for the things they want with their own unused inventory or spare capacity.

The economic advantages of barter hinge on the fact that barter brings in new business and conserves cash. Barter sales are an increment over and above cash sales, at a price over and above incremental cost. All firms can take advantage of barter to bring in new business. Those firms with spare capacity or excess inventory have strong incentives to do so.

Financing purchases through additional sales of one's own product or service is often the cheapest method of finance available to a business. This is because it is paying for its purchases with the profit margin on its extra sales or unused capacity.

Barter sales yield trade dollars or trade credits which may be spent with the barter company or other members of the barter system. Trade dollars are units of account denominated in dollars representing the right to receive, or the obligation to pay, in goods or services available through the barter system. The cost of one trade dollar is in inventory, labor, or other cost of producing an additional dollar's worth of barter sales. A firm buys with trade dollars which cost it less than the revenue it earns from its sales. In textbook economics, so long as incremental revenue exceeds incremental cost, there will be an economic incentive to make the barter sale.

As an example, take an auto parts supplier who does a good deal of direct mail advertising. He joins a barter exchange and notes that several printers are members. Other things being equal, he has an incentive to buy his printing from the barter printers because (a) he won't have to reduce his cash flow for this business expense, but instead, (b) he can finance this expense out of trade dollars earned from barter sales of his own products and services to other members of the barter system, at a price that exceeds his incremental cost.

Barter aids the businessman who has reached a certain level of cash sales and still has the capacity to expand output; or who has excess inventory or unproductive assets. Few and fortunate, indeed, are the business people who, having made an investment in plant and equipment, find themselves operating at full or over-full capacity. For most firms, spare capacity and obsolescent or unused inventory are a normal occurrence, with a powerful economic plus: they permit additional sales at relatively low incremental cost.

Examples are the printer, with large sunk costs in equipment, but relatively low cost of additional output; the hotel with rooms unfilled; the dentist with time to take more patients; the radio or television station with unsold advertising. These firms are foregoing income from their unused capacity. If shown hot to stimulate additional sales through barter, they have a strong incentive to make those sales as long as they can cover their costs. The price at which they can sell on barter will either be the same as the normal cash prince, or as a minimum, a price greater than the cash liquidation value of inventory. Firms with high cash inventory costs will find barter even more advantageous if they are able to receive some cash in the transaction to apply to the cost of their inventory.

Income taxes take away part of the extra profit from barter sales. However, even at the highest bracket rate, a firm makes money after taxes on its additional sales. While reducing the extra profit, the income tax should not affect a firm's decision to make sales to reap that profit. This applies whether the additional sales are cash sales or barter sales. Since passage of the Tax Equity and Fiscal Responsibility Act of 1982, barter exchanges are required to report the barter income of their clients to IRS on Form 1099-B.

The economic advantages of barter can be seen by comparing a firm's position before and after barter. We see that barter results in additional revenue, hence added profit; barter enables a firm to conserve cash, resulting in better liquidity and a saving equal to the going cost of money. Firms also gain from an intangible web of referrals, advertising, and associations that generate both additional cash and barter business.

The barter company's commission charges must be included in a firm's cost calculation, but these charges are normally not a deterrent to barter. Indeed, the largest cost a firm can experience is the income foregone by not selling on barter. In many cases, firms might find it profitable to pay an even higher commission in order to have the opportunity to reap additional profits through barter sales.

### *Barter and the Community*

Barter would benefit an economic community even if the barter system consisted of firms who had previously been each other's cash customers. This is not to say that barter sales should replace cash sales at the same selling price—they should not. But the reality is that cash sales are limited by the cash incomes of firms in the community, resulting in some firms having excess capacity. These firms do *more* business with each other if they can barter because of their ability to (1) make additional sales out of excess capacity, earning "new" money in the form of trade credits, and (2) paying for what they buy with these additional trade credits whose cost to them is the incremental cost of their own product or service.

Establishing a barter exchange results over-all in new business for the community rather than displacement of pre-existing cash business. This conclusion stems from the existence of surplus inventory or excess capacity in the cash economy, and the ability of firms to make extra sales and earning "new" money in the form of trade credits. The new money supply adds to the cash money supply, and the extra liquidity finances a higher level of real trade.

### *Barter and the National and International Economy*

By increasing demand for final goods and services in an economy, barter generates additional employment, production, and purchasing power. It results in a higher rate of capacity utilization, and enables firms to spread their overhead costs over more units of output, thereby reducing average costs and lessening inflationary pressures. Textbook economics tells us that when an economy is operating at full capacity, costs shoot up dramatically because of resource shortages and bottlenecks. But it is clear that there is a range between current capacity utilization (about 80 percent in the U.S.) and full capacity within which firms can expand output at constant or even declining cost. It is within this range that commercial barter transactions take place.

The reality is that a modern economy lacks a fully elastic currency, capable of expanding with the growth of production and providing the liquidity needed to clear product and service markets. Because monetary fluctuations have contributed to economic instability in the past, a nation's money supply is not permitted to expand to meet the demand for money to finance an increase in gross domestic product. Instead, the money supply is controlled by monetary authorities who have their eyes fixed on particular economic objectives: curbing inflation, ensuring full employment, protecting the value of the currency in foreign exchange markets, and so on. Balancing between these sometimes conflicting objectives often leads in advanced economies to a policy of monetary restriction. This restrains the flow of spending in the cash economy, limited demand for output, and creating excess capacity.

Barter and its modern counterpart, the creation of trade credit to finance greater demand for goods and services, helps alleviate monetary stringency, puts unutilized capacity to work, and speeds up the flow of goods and services to their most productive uses. It thus adds an important measure of flexibility to the trade and payments system and market adjustment mechanisms of the domestic and international economies at a period in history when global economic organization is undergoing a dramatic restructuring. Commercial barter should therefore, as a matter of public policy, be encouraged.

## 2. Commercial Barter Exchanges in Society

Address presented by Paul E. Suplizio, IRTA,
to the Chicago Association of Commerce and Industry
Chicago, IL, September 18, 1985

Ladies and Gentlemen:

One can hardly come to Chicago to speak on an economic subject without reference to Henry Simon or Milton Friedman. A quotation from Milton Friedman happened to be at hand and I would like to share it with you:

> Increasing interest has been expressed in recent years in proposals to replace governmental issuance of money and control of its quality by private market arrangements. One set of proposals would end the government monopoly on the issuance of currency and permit its competitive issue. Another would eliminate entirely any issuance of money by government, and, instead, restrict the role of government to defining a monetary unit.

The former set of proposals derives largely from a pamphlet by F.A. Hayek entitled *Choice in Currency: A Way to Stop Inflation.* Hayek proposed that all special privileges (such as "legal tender" quality) attached to government-issued currency be removed, and that financial institutions be permitted to issue currency or deposit obligations on whatever terms were mutually acceptable to the issuer and the holder of the liabilities. He envisaged a system in which institutions would in fact issue obligations expressed in terms of purchasing power either of specific commodities, such as gold or silver, or of commodities in general through linkage to a price index. In his opinion, constant-purchasing-power monies would come to dominate the market and largely replace obligations denominated in dollars or pounds or other similar units and in specific commodities..."

Modern commercial barter is a system of trade and payments that is emerging alongside the monetary system of trade and payments. Its instrument of payment — the trade dollar or trade credit — is the best illustration today of the privatization of money that Professor Hayek has called for and which Professor Friedman approves. As Hayek has put the case:

> There is no reason whatever why people should not be free to make contracts, including ordinary purchases and sales, in any kind of money they choose, or why they should be obliged to sell against any particular kind of money. There could be no more effective check against the abuse of money by government than if people were free to refuse any money they distrusted and to prefer money in which they had confidence.

You are all aware of the proliferation of monetary instruments as financial institutions have been progressively deregulated during the past decade—money market funds, NOW accounts, credit and debit cards, to mention just a few. But all are tied to the existing monetary framework, wherein the Federal Reserve has exclusive power to issue non-interest bearing notes which comprise the monetary base. No other bank, no other financial institution has the power—or has dared in recent memory to assume the power—of issuing its own notes for circulation.

But, as we shall see, a barter exchange has the power to do just that. It issues trade dollars by making loans to members of the exchange. Its power to do so is based upon contract between the members and the exchange, and as such has the strongest possible support under our legal system.

The barter exchange maintains a record of the trade dollar balances of its clients. These are nothing more than the liabilities of those clients with negative balances, that is, who owe the system. The exchange acts as a clearinghouse, shifting balances among members' accounts to effect payment.

Recent Internal Revenue Service regulations recognize that trade dollars are a form of currency, and empower the barter exchange to establish the exchange ratio between trade dollars and cash for tax purposes. The Tax Equity and Fiscal Responsibility Act of 1982, the "Magna Carta" of the barter industry, recognizes the contractual basis of the barter system and places barter exchanges alongside commercial banks, credit card companies, and other institutions as third-party record-keepers. Under the Code, third-party record-keepers maintain financial records of taxpayers, and are accorded certain legal protections in the event the IRS should seek to review such records.

### *Legal Structure of Barter Exchanges*

The typical barter exchange is a corporation that has a proprietary interest in the fees and commissions it collects for the services it renders. These services include making a market for buyers and sellers, advertising the availability of products and services, processing sales vouchers, record keeping, and so on. Businesses who contract with a trade exchange are entitled to sell to other businesses, receiving payment in trade dollars. They are also entitled to use trade dollars, either earned or borrowed, to make purchases from other members of the barter system.

However, the right to buy and sell through the exchange is not an unconditional one; it is conditioned by the terms of the exchange contract. The first condition that may be mentioned is that the exchange assumes a "best efforts" obligation to broker trade dollars into the products and services sought by the client. The range of products and services available for purchase is limited to those offered by members of the exchange, though of course most effective exchanges are working assiduously to expand the range of products and services available. If products and services acceptable to the owner of the trade dollars are not available despite the best efforts of the exchange, obviously a waiting time occurs during which trade dollars must be held until buying opportunities materialize.

At the present stage of development of commercial barter, trade dollars have obvious disadvantages as a form of wealth holding, namely, waiting time, depreciation where waiting occurs, and inconvertibility to cash. But these disadvantages are offset by the fact that trade dollars represent value attained that would otherwise be foregone, for barter sales are incremental business that would not otherwise exist.

Obviously, the more widespread barter becomes in the economy, the more the risks of waiting for buying opportunities to materialize will lessen. The present trend toward inter-city networking of barter exchanges has led to a significant amount of procurement of goods and services outside of local market areas, and may culminate some day in an electronically connected national market system for barter transactions.

Another contractual condition imposed on buying and selling is the power of the exchange to ration high-demand items. Most exchange contracts provide for rationing of commodities which are not available in sufficient supply to satisfy prevailing demand. To this the International Reciprocal Trade Association adds an ethical standard, that such practice be carried out in a fair and equitable manner.

A further condition is the regulation of borrowing by clients. The power to make trade dollar loans to clients, and to establish the terms and conditions of such loans, is vested in the exchange by most barter contracts. As such loans represent additional purchasing power, in the form of an increase in the supply of trade dollars in circulation, they must be carefully regulated for the obvious reason of preventing depreciation of the barter currency.

Trade dollar loans represent a claim upon the products and services of the clients of the barter system. Such loans must be repaid with trade dollars earned through sales to these same clients. It goes without saying that trade dollar loans must be made as a strictly commercial proposition, to keep losses within prudent levels and to avoid serious imbalance between the supply of trade dollars and the supply of goods available for purchase.

A final condition of barter contracts relating to buying and selling is the proviso for suspending the trading of any client who is in arrears in payment of service fees, commissions, or other charges.

### *Trade Dollars and the Security Laws*

As defined in the model statute of the International Reciprocal Trade Association, a trade dollar is a unit of account denoting the right to receive, or the obligation to pay, in acceptable and available goods or services. By "acceptable" we mean products or services acceptable to the holder of trade dollars. Obviously, no one is obligated to receive products or services, in exchange for trade dollars, that he does not want. By "available" we mean products or services available from clients of the barter system.

Dollar prices prevailing in the monetary economy are the pricing standard for barter transactions. Thus a trade dollar, as a unit of account, is equal to one nominal U.S. Dollar. In a barter transaction, 100 trade dollars should ordinarily purchase $100 worth of goods or services available through the exchange.

Trade dollars are not a commodity currency. To be such, they would have to be defined in terms of a fixed physical quantity of some commodity or commodities, and be regularly exchangeable for that quantity.

It may be possible in the future for holdings of trade dollars to be adjusted to provide protection against inflation. Including an inflation component in the interest rate charged on a barter loan would make such a loan a "price-level adjusted note" or PLAN. For instance, if 6 percent was the going interest cost of borrowed trade dollars, and the inflation rate in the economy was 5 percent, then 11 percent would be charged on a"price-level-adjusted" loan. Holdings of trade dollars could also be adjusted by an amount equal to the inflation rate, making them a "price-level adjusted deposit", or PLAD. The terms "PLAN" and "PLAD" are those of Professor Milton Friedman.

There is some interest in whether a universal trade credit is feasible for the barter industry. It is certainly feasible, but such a credit will only evolve when competition forces individual exchanges to accept each other's credit. Right now, no exchange is in a position to accept another exchange's credits, beyond certain narrow limits, because of the fear that those credits may not be redeemed in goods. This condition parallels very closely the early evolution of banking, where notes of some banks gained only limited acceptance because of the fear they could not be redeemed for specie. However, this condition did not last. As Lawrence H. White has described the evolution of the Scottish banking system,

> Competition had led all issuers to accept one another's notes at par and to join in a single note-exchange (clearinghouse) system. Notes issued by Bank A in a loan would, after being spent by the borrower, soon come into the possession of individuals who deposited them with Banks B through Z; these banks would return the notes to Bank A through the note-exchange system and demand redemption of them. No individual bank could overissue without rapidly being disciplined by adverse clearing balances. The case of the Ayr Bank, discussed at length by Adam Smith, bears witness to the efficacy of the note-exchange mechanism.

As the barter industry develops, we may see the emergence of a system for clearing the credits of different trade exchanges, which would lay the foundation for a common currency. Eventually, as Professor White explains, a single currency should predominate:

> ...there is an inherent tendency for traders in an economy to converge on a single good (or a very small number of goods) as outside money. Carl Menger long ago explained why: Each individual in pursuit of the easiest way of completing his desired trades finds it advantageous to accept and hold an inventory of the good or goods that other individuals will most readily accept.

A trade dollar may represent debt and credit in the barter exchange system. Under the Securities Exchange Act of 1933, only debt instruments having a maturity of more than one year are considered securities under Federal law. The trade dollar, which has no specified maturity and is not in itself a debt instrument, thus does not fall within the scope of Federal regulation.

However, as an "evidence of indebtedness," trade dollars may be considered securities under State law. One state—Oklahoma—has ruled that a particular barter exchange (which is now defunct) had engaged in the sale of securities and was required to register with the State Securities Commission. The Commission found that this particular exchange, which was inadequately capitalized, had engaged in the sale of "investment contracts" because the membership fees it collected were the principal source of operating capital, and the members expected the exchange to profit through the efforts of a third party — the exchange. Under the securities law of Oklahoma, both the membership contract and the trade dollar of this particular exchange were deemed to be securities.

The commercial barter industry has disagreed strongly with the view of the Oklahoma Securities Commission as a general rule to be applied to barter exchanges. It is the industry's view that fees paid to an exchange are fees for services rendered and are not investment capital. It is also the industry's view that trade dollars are a unit of account, and are not an evidence of indebtedness in the same sense as a promissory note or a dollar bill. Since the Oklahoma ruling in 1981, no other state has moved to declare barter contracts or trade dollars to be securities.

### *Anti-Trust Aspects of Reciprocal Trade*

IRTA has received frequent inquiries as to whether barter and reciprocal trade violate the anti-trust laws. It is the Association's view that barter and reciprocal trade per se are not antitrust violations. Thus, barter transactions through trade exchanges, and reciprocal trades resulting from an arms-length negotiation, would not normally be viewed as objectionable forms of competition. Barter usually comprises only a small percentage of a particular firm's business, so it is difficult to see how bartering alone could result in restraint of trade. One would have to look at the total impact of all the firm's selling practices — not just the barter/reciprocal trade part, which is relatively minor — to determine if there were any lessening of competition in the marketplace. In sum, barter and reciprocal trade are not per se antitrust, and do not appear to constitute restraint of trade.

### *Taxation of Barter Transactions*

The Tax Equity and Fiscal Responsibility Act of 1982 defined barter exchanges in the Internal Revenue Code, and imposed on each exchange the obligation of reporting annually the barter sales of its clients. The report is submitted to IRS on Form 1099-B. A copy of the information submitted to IRS must be provided to each client of the exchange.

When IRS receives form 1099-B showing barter sales income, it will enter this information into its computers for the client concerned. To do so, an accurate taxpayer identification number for the client must be shown on Form 1099-B. Congress has made it a legal obligation for taxpayers to furnish their TIN to the barter exchanges they do business with. Failure to do so could result in mandatory backup withholding of 20 percent of the proceeds of each barter transaction.

IRS intends to match in its computers the amount of barter income reported by the taxpayer on his return with the amount reported by the exchange on Form 1099-B. For this reason, the taxpayer should always use in his tax return the figure reported by the exchange for barter income. Failure to do so may result in a document mismatch, and a computer-generated inquiry may be sent to the taxpayer asking for an explanation of the discrepancy.

Each barter taxpayer must include in gross income the amount of his barter income. However, the taxpayer is entitled to include barter purchases made for business purposes with his cash deductions for business expenses.

IRS regulations require each barter exchange to establish the average value of its trade dollar in terms of cash, for tax purposes. This value is then used in making the report to IRS on Form 1099-B, and the same value should be used in figuring the deduction for barter business expenses. Normally, it would not be proper for each taxpayer to figure his own trade dollar value, because IRS regulations require and average value to be computed by the exchange for all its clients. The exchange's computation of this value is subject to review by IRS, and could be changed if not considered accurate.

For corporations and partnerships, IRS regulations require only aggregate barter sales for the calendar year to be reported by the exchange on Form 1099-B. However, for individual taxpayers IRS requires each separate transaction to be reported. The barter industry considers this latter requirement to be needless and burdensome, and has been seeking the elimination of transactions reporting by the Congress.

In its rulings on the taxation of barter, especially Revenue Ruling 80-52, IRS has held that a trade dollar is a thing of value. Consistent with this opinion, IRS has ruled that trade dollars must be recognized as income in the taxable year in which they are credited to the taxpayer's account — *not* in the year in which they are spent. This means that all trade dollars earned from barter sales during the calendar year will be reported to IRS on Form 1099-B, and must be included in gross income by the taxpayer.

With respect to trade dollars acquired through trade dollar loans, it is IRTA's position that such loans will be repaid out of future earnings which will be taxed; therefore, loan proceeds should not be included in gross barter income for tax purposes.

### *Regulation of Commercial Barter*

It is evident that commercial barter has strong underpinnings in the nation's legal system, in the Federal tax code, and in basic legislation establishing the right of exchanges to exist alongside commercial banks and other financial institutions. Given the role that barter can play in the nation's economy, as high interest rates have repressed demand and lowered the rate of capacity utilization, it is little wonder that many business firms are using barter as an important marketing technique. In addition, barter entrepreneurs have been overcoming capital limitations by linking up with venture capital firms, private placements, and public offerings of stock. Recently, another barter company completed the process of going public, bringing to a total of four the number of such companies that are publicly owned.

Aside from tax regulations, the barter industry is presently unregulated by Federal or state law. There are no minimum capital requirements, no financial oversight, and no assurance of protection of the public in operation of the exchange. While this has stimulated innovation, it has its downside in the ease with which incompetent owners and crooks can get a foothold in this young industry. As a result, the past six years have witnessed significant failure rates among exchanges and too many scandals bordering on outright fraud.

Obviously, barter exchanges are different from an ordinary business in this respect: when an ordinary business fails, only the owners and creditors get hurt; when a barter exchange fails, not only the owners and creditors but all businesses in the community who belonged to the exchange suffer losses. In an effort to cope with this situation, the International Reciprocal Trade Association upholds a strong Code of Ethics and a body of regulations for the barter industry. But compliance with these regulations is voluntary, and the association lacks adequate investigation and enforcement powers.

If the problems of this young and growing industry were limited to fraud and mismanagement, one could argue that in time the marketplace itself would sort out the winners from the losers. But there is another paramount reason why some form of self-regulation established by law is necessary. That is, there are no restraints (other than the voluntary ones now imposed on its members by IRTA) on deficit spending by the exchange itself. The temptation for the owners to borrow from the exchange and spend far more than its earnings, for both business and personal use, is simply too great for many persons. Such deficit spending results in the over-issue of trade dollars; and with everyone in the system holding large balances, trading abruptly halts because no one wishes to accumulate trade dollars further. As it may take 4 or 5 years for an excessive exchange deficit to build up, business firms have no way of knowing that the exchange is at risk until it closes its doors. Then it is too late.

Reviewing the development of the industry over the past decade, and perceiving the need to enhance public confidence and ensure financially viable trade exchanges, the International Reciprocal Trade Association 2 years ago unanimously adopted a resolution to seek legislation from Congress to establish a statutory framework for self-regulation of the barter industry by its own duly constituted bodies. Such a statute has been drafted and reviewed by legislative counsel, and upon introduction in the House and Senate will be referred to the Commerce Committees of these bodies. The barter industry is kicking off this month a lobbying campaign for the passage of this legislation.

As next year is an election year, we expect to again assist our friends in Congress with their election campaigns. Three years ago, IRTA formed the Barter Political Action Committee, or BARTERPAC, and obtained permission from the Federal Election Commission to receive political contributions in trade dollars and to make in-kind contributions to Federal candidates. This is a further recognition of barter by government that you may not be aware of.

The commercial barter self-regulation bill, or Barter Bill of Rights, is patterned after a scheme of regulation adopted by the National Association of Securities Dealers and the National Futures Association, the latter of which is located in your home town of Chicago. We have consulted with both those associations in drawing the statute, which provides for licensing of barter exchanges, minimum financial and competency standards, and the establishment of a registered national barter association to administer the self-regulatory scheme. IRTA will seek to become so registered.

#### *The Industry's Future*

Looking to the future, the industry trends we have identified include a greater flow of capital into the industry and more public offerings, more intensive marketing and advertising by barter companies, more specialized services such as barter of real estate, insurance, and travel, the offer of additional financial services to holders of barter cards, rapid growth of inter-exchange and inter-city trading, and, of course, the gradual evolution of an electronically-interconnected national barter marketplace.

If these visions are realized, it will be due to the efforts of pioneering entrepreneurs like those assembled in this room. Market competition is a *discovery process.* In the unique vision of Professor Hayek,

> Its results are different than anyone could predict or deliberately bring about, and therein lies its virtue: Its unpredictability is owing to its aptitude for discovering that goods and ways of providing goods not previously known, or at least not previously known to be profitable, are in fact profitable. This is true of competition in the provision of outside money as in the provision of any good. Only through the competitive process can we discover what sorts of outside money, and what ways of supplying it, are best suited to consumer preferences.

It is an exciting industry, and we welcome you as a part of it. Are there any questions?

## 3. Character, Use and Valuation of Trade Dollars

This statement expresses IRTA's position on the character, use, and valuation of trade dollars for accounting purposes. Here we consider only the trade dollars of a barter exchange, not "purchase credits" or "cash-equivalent credits" which have a different contractual basis and require separate treatment. This statement is based upon the practice of the commercial barter industry in the U.S. for more than two decades, that is, since the issuance of APB 29 in 1972 by the predecessor to the Financial Accounting Standards Board. Industry practice has naturally been shaped to a significant degree by professional accounting advice and opinion. This statement presupposes knowledge of the basic structure of the modern commercial barter exchange. It should be read in conjunction with the following IRTA Fact Sheets:

"Why Business People Barter"
"The Modern Commercial Barter Exchange"
"Borrowing and Lending in a Trade Exchange"
"Legal Liability for Trade Dollars in a Barter Exchange"
"Commercial Barter and Public Policy"

The subject of barter accounting is comparatively new and raises novel issues. The principle guidepost is Opinion Number 29, "Accounting for Non-Monetary Transactions," issued by the Accounting Principles Board. It seems clear that, in calling for gain or loss to be recognized in an exchange of non-monetary assets, the Board was saying that in general such exchange would be considered the culmination of an earnings process. Recent work by the Financial Accounting Standards Board (EITF 86-29 and 87-10) leaves unclear where the boundary lies between asset exchanges that do or do not culminate an earnings process. However, none of this work has been issued as an opinion, so APB 29 stands as the principal authority at this time.

RTA believes that barter transactions have financial consequences, and that in general such consequences should not be ignored in the preparation of financial statements. This applies with particular force to the financial statements of a barter company, which may engage in a large number of barter transactions that, taken together, would be material to an accurate portrayal of the financial position of the company.

Under APB 29, the financial consequences of a contract for non-monetary exchange of assets generally should be reported for the accounting period during which the transaction occurred. We believe the authors of the Opinion recognized that, as a general rule, deferring recognition to a later period when the asset acquired has been exchanged for cash or a financial instrument, may result in an inaccurate picture of the firm's assets, liabilities, and value for the current accounting period.

### *Character and Use of Trade Dollars*

Trade dollars arise in the course of barter trade between buyers and sellers who are organized into a network of trading partners by means of written agreement with a company known as a barter exchange. Section 6045 of the Internal Revenue Code defines the term "barter exchange" as follows:

> The term 'barter exchange' means any person with members of clients that contract either with each other or with such person to trade or barter property or services either directly or through such person."

The contract that organizes the barter network and establishes the terms and conditions of trade is executed by each client with the barter exchange. Under the terms of a typical contract, the client agrees to make available a certain dollar amount of goods or services for barter trade with other clients and with the exchange. In so doing, they agree to accept a specified minimum amount of barter business by selling goods or services in return for payment received in the form of trade dollars.

As defined by the International Reciprocal Trade Association, a trade dollar is a unit of account that denotes the right to receive, or the obligation to pay, one U.S. dollar's worth of goods or services available within a barter system. (The terms "barter network" and "barter system" are identical). The Treasury Department has recognized the existence of trade dollars in Treasury Regulations T.D. 7873 (26 CFR Part 1) issued March 11, 1983: "Property or services are exchanged through a barter exchange if payment for property or services is made by means of a credit on the books of the barter exchange or scrip issued by the barter exchange or if the barter exchange arranges a direct exchange or property or services among its members or clients or exchanges property or services with a member or client." The fact that a credit on the books of the exchange is linked in the same sentence with a direct exchange of property or services indicates the essential equivalence of the two transactions in the eyes of this authority. Where credit is given on the books of the exchange, payment is to be made by delivery of goods or services in the future, rather than in the present as occurs in a direct exchange.

In the cash economy, when a sale is made and payment is deferred, there is an extension of credit from seller to buyer. In a barter network, when a sale is made and payment (in goods and services) is deferred, there is likewise an extension of credit by the seller. Under the exchange agreement, sellers accept trade dollars as payment and look to the other participants in the barter network *collectively* to fulfill their trade dollars.

At any point in time within a barter network, some participants will be net creditors, that is, holders of trade dollars. They have given up greater value than they have received in goods and services, and so they hold the balance as an asset or claim on goods or services available from the system. They are said to be in a positive or surplus position in their account. Other participants will be net debtors, that is, they will have spent more than their earnings and will owe trade dollars. They are said to be in a negative or deficit position.

Trade dollar assets are the liabilities of debtor members collectively, that is they are liabilities of those members who owe the system. It is axiomatic that barter assets and liabilities should always balance, that is, for every trade dollar outstanding there is a contractual obligation imposed on debtor members of the network to make available a U.S. dollar's worth of fulfillment goods and services.

The Internal Revenue Service has analyzed barter exchanges to determine whether trade dollars received in payment constitute income. In Revenue Ruling 80-52, IRS promulgated the "valuable right" doctrine. Under this doctrine, trade dollars are a "valuable right" and receipt of trade dollars as payment constitutes receipt of income. Promulgation of the "valuable right" doctrine supports IRTA's view that trade dollars constitute real claims upon valuable goods and services available from the members of the barter system. This capability is underpinned by the exchange agreement and by the debtor-creditor relationship established among the members, and between the exchange and its members, in the course of executing numerous barter transactions daily. Trade dollar assets are offset by an equal number of trade dollar liabilities, that is, an unqualified obligation of debtors within the exchange network to pay in goods and services an amount certain (valued in U.S. dollars) by a date certain.

Writing in Minnesota Law Review, Vol. 67:441, 1982, Professor Robert I. Keller states in "The Taxation of Barter Transactions":

> Trade units, however, represent more than the mere promise of the individual member for whom the taxpayer performed services or to whom he or she sold goods. Rather, each trade unit represents the promise of the entire exchange membership, as a group, to allow the recipient of the unit to use it to acquire the goods and services offered by the membership. Moreover, at least in the case of the established exchanges, these promises represented by trade units, are readily assignable or transferable to other members of the trade exchange. (p.494).

Concerning the exchange's own use of trade dollars, Professor Keller writes:

> It is in its capacity as broker that the Exchange receives commission from members. Any commissions the Exchange receives in trade units it can use in the same manner as any member to acquire goods and services within the system. The Exchange may use the goods and services it acquires from its members for its own business purposes or may transfer them to the individual shareholders, proprietors, or partners of the Exchange to be used by them for personal purposes. Frequently, however, Exchanges use their trade units to acquire merchandise which is maintained in the showrooms and warehouses of the Exchange for

retrade to members. This results in the Exchange's second role as a trader of goods.

To the extent the Exchange sells the acquired merchandise for the same number of trade units it paid for them, it simpley acts as a clearing house for members' goods. Nevertheless, the Exchange clearly benefits from this activity. Most importantly, by acquiring members' goods for trade units, the Exchange keeps units circulating and thereby maintains an active barter economy. Also, to the extent the Exchange succeeds in retrading the acquired goods to members, the Exchange earns additional commissions.

As a participant in the barter system, the exchange earns trade dollars through commissions and profits on sale of goods and services to the other participants. Clearly, the trade dollars earned by the exchange represent a valuable claim on the goods and services of other members of the barter system. These members may be those seeking to earn trade dollars to repay their debt, or those seeking additional sales to increase their stock of trade dollars. *In preparing the exchange's financial statements, it would seem inappropriate, even irresponsible, to fail to account for the exchange's trade dollar assets, liabilities, receipts, and expenditures.*

### Valuation and Accounting for Trade Dollars

The U.S. Government, in Treasury Regulation T.D. 7873 cited above, addresses the question of trade dollar valuation as follows:

> The amount received by a member or client in an exchange includes cash received, the fair market value of any property or services received, and the fair market value of any credits to the account of the member or client on the books of the barter exchange or scrip issued to the member or client by the barter exchange, but does not include any amount received by the member or client in a subsequent exchange of credits or scrip. For purposes of this section, the fair market value of a credit or scrip is the value assigned to such credit or scrip by the issuing barter exchange for the purpose of exchanges unless the Commissioner requires the use of a different value that the Commissioner determines more accurately reflects fair market value.

In requiring trade exchanges to set the value of their trade dollar for all participants in the barter system, and to set that value at the amount (in dollars) used "for purpose of exchanges," Treasury was following an approach recommended by Professor Keller. Professor Keller called his method of valuation the "medium of exchange" approach and describes it as follows:

> The value of a trade unit should be determined by what it can buy within the exchange, and not the cash price for which it can be purchased or sold. By analogy, if a U.S. taxpayer receives foreign currency, usable within the foreign country to acquire goods and services, but not readily convertible into U.S. dollars, an informal market often develops, in which the taxpayer can sell the foreign currency to U.S. citizens wishing to invest or spend the currency in the foreign country. In such circumstances, it would be clearly improper to value the currency at the dollar amount realizable in the United States, since "the dollar amount realizable in the United States might be but a fraction of the dollar value of the property...which the foreign income would buy in the foreign country." Since trade units are the equivalent of a foreign currency, they too should be valued by their "purchasing power" within the trade exchange, and not by what they would bring in a cash sale....
>
> The more appropriate approach, both as a matter of substantive law and from the viewpoint of administrative convenience, would be one that treats trade

> units, when used to acquire goods and services, as a medium of exchange. Under this approach, the goods and services acquired would be conclusively assumed to be equal in value to that of the trade units used to acquire them. Good deals and bad deals would simply be ignored. The taxpayer would, in effect, be treated as receiving the average value of the goods and services a trade unit could buy, which, absent exchange fluctuation, would be the same amount the taxpayer took into income on receipt of the unit. Assuming that there is indeed no change in the value of the trade unit itself from the time of acquisition to the time of disposition, this approach would result in no gain or loss to the taxpayer on the disposition of trade units, and produce tax deductions, if deductible business goods and services were acquired, equal to the value of the units used."

The basic doctrine for barter exchanges is set forth in Accounting Principles Board Opinion Number 29, "Accounting for Non-Monetary Transactions." This document was issued in 1972 by the predecessor to the current Financial Accounting Standards Board. It is an authoritative pronouncement of the accounting profession.

Bost and Yeakel (*Management Accounting*, December 1992) summarize the basic tenets of APB 29 as follows:

> APB Opinion No. 29. Accounting for Nonmonetary Transactions, defines nonmonetary assets and liabilities as those which are not fixed in terms of units of currency by contract or otherwise. With these transactions, questions may arise due to the subjectivity in valuation of an asset received or resulting liability, or the recognition of any gain or loss on the transaction. The Opinion states that the cost of a nonmonetary asset should be recorded at the fair value of the asset surrendered to obtain it. Any difference in fair value and book value given is recognized as a gain or loss. If fair value of the asset received is clearer than that of the asset given, the former should be used in valuation. Fair value should equal estimated realizable value for cash transactions involving same or similar assets, quoted market prices, independent appraisal, estimated fair value of merchandise or service received in exchange, or other available evidence. No gains should be recognized if fair value is not determinable within reasonable limits or if an exchange is not the culmination of an earnings process, such as exchanges of similar productive assets. Disclosures are required on the nature of the transaction, the basis of accounting, and any gains or losses recognized.

It should be stressed that *"Fair value should equal estimated realizable value for cash transactions involving same or similar assets, quoted market prices, independent appraisal, estimated fair value of merchandise or services received in exchange, or other available evidence."*

In light of the foregoing authorities, the sole issue is the validity of the International Reciprocal Trade Association's position, which expresses the view of the leading members of the commercial barter industry, that the value of a trade dollar in an operating commercial barter exchange (one that executes above 1,000 transactions per year) is, on average, equal to one U.S. dollar. IRTA's position asserts that one trade dollar equals one U.S. dollar not because the barter industry has arbitrarily assigned this value, set it for administrative convenience or simplicity, or established it for tax compliance purposes, but that the value of a trade dollar is in fact one U.S. dollar, on average over a broad range of transactions executed through a commercial barter exchange.

The key to this proposition is that, while trade dollars are indeed a unit of account and a medium of exchange within a barter system, the *prices* of goods and services bought and sold and denominated entirely in U.S. dollars. This means the trade dollar is a unit of account, but not a standard of value. A trade dollar has meaning in value terms only by reference to the U.S. dollar prices of the goods and services it can purchase. U.S. dollar prices are the same for the barter system as for the cash system under the terms of the contract between the exchange and its clients, and in actual practice for the vast bulk of trades. In algebraic terms, the larger the number of transactions considered, the more the value of the trade dollar will approach one U.S. dollar as a limit.

The trade dollar is a unit that has no intrinsic value, because prices set in trade dollars would be meaningless and, in fact, are non-existent. Prices are set only in U.S. dollars, and the number of trade dollars given or received is determined entirely by U.S. dollar prices and quantity. Put another way, a trade dollar is a financial unit of identical value to a cash dollar, except that a trade dollar is redeemable only by a dollar's worth of goods and services and not by cash.

The crucial role of U.S. dollar prices as the standard of value in the barter economy means that, on average, across thousands of transactions, the value of trade dollars spent within the barter system is one U.S. dollar. While in particular cases there can be a variance between cash and trade dollar prices, in the vast majority of transactions these prices are the same.

To properly depict the financial results of barter transactions in financial statements, IRTA is persuaded that the trade dollar should be valued as a *medium of exchange* rather than looking at its value in discrete transactions. The latter approach would considerably magnify and complicate the accounting process, with little attendant benefit. It can be demonstrated empirically that the value of a trade dollar as a medium of exchange (the average value for a large number of transactions) is one U.S. dollar.

### *Trade Dollars Are Money*

The medium of exchange for barter transactions is no more nor less in value than the U.S. dollar. But this is not to say that the two currencies are of equal utility for commerce. The supply of one is controlled by government, the other is privately-created and capable of expanding with trade. The value of one erodes steadily with inflation, but the trade dollar can realize constant-purchasing power by means of an annual price level adjustment applied to each deposit. The trade dollars required to pay for this adjustment can be obtained by transfer from debtors, or by a small levy on the gains from trade.

Trade dollars are a medium of exchange or currency within the barter system, not within the U.S. economy. They represent a claim on an ascertainable stock of assets held by participants in the barter system, who are obligated by contract to make a specified portion of that stock available for trade upon demand, and who willingly accept trade dollars and seek to acquire them to finance their purchases.

True, unlike lawful currency, trade dollars are not claims on the gross national product. But a trade dollar nonetheless represents a legal claim for a U.S. dollar's worth of real goods and services. The fact that the claim is on a specific subset of firms in the economy, and not on the economy at large, has little relevance. All that matters is that the owners of trade dollars hold legally binding claims against others—not just a single firm but the entire group of firms who comprise the barter network. This lends solidity to the contractual promise to provide goods and services to the holders of trade dollars on demand.

Trade dollars are a form of privately-created money based upon contract. They are not lawful currency of the United States, but this does not mean that their financial consequences can be ignored in the preparation of financial statements. Under APB 29, as a general rule the financial consequences of a contract for non-monetary exchange can and should be valued. The IRS holds that only in rare and exceptional cases can a non-monetary transaction not be valued for tax purposes.

Under APB 29, in general an exchange of non-monetary assets is assumed to culminate an earnings process, so that gain, loss, and income should be currently recognized. Deferring recognition to a later period could significantly distort the financial picture, especially for a company that engages in a large number of transactions on a daily basis.

Comments on this statement by members of the accounting profession and the barter industry should be submitted to Paul Suplizio, Chief Executive Officer, IRTA, 6305 Hawaii Court, Alexandria, VA 22312.

## 4. Borrowing and Lending in a Trade Exchange

Without the use of trade credits as an accounting unit to denote barter receivables and payables, modern commercial barter which permits multilateral trade among many participants would not be possible. To illustrate, A, a carpet distributor, sells $1,000 worth of carpet to B, a restaurant owner. A does not have a simultaneous need for $1,000 worth of B's meals. Therefore, A has extended credit because the barter is incomplete and A has not been aid. The evidence of this transaction is a bookkeeping entry in the records of the exchange denoting that A has a receivable due in goods and services. Under terms of the exchange agreement, the receivable is not due from the particular restaurant B, but from all member of the barter system collectively. We refer to this collectivity as the network of exchange members, or barter system. The accounting unit, known as a trade credit, trade unit, trade dollar or similar term is fulfilled when member or services to A in return for payment in trade dollars. The crediting of 1,000 trade dollars to A's account means that A has a receivable in the amount of $1,000 worth of goods or services due from other members of the exchange.

Similarly, if B had been providing meals to members of the exchange, extending credit to them and earning trade dollars in the process, he could at the time of purchase of the carpet have 1,000 trade dollars in his account, indicating a receivable due him from the members. In simplest terms, he will use his trade dollars to pay for the carpet. We see from this example that credit is extended by sellers to the exchange members that they sell to. Sellers extend credit when they accept trade dollars as a means of payment. Credit is extended to members as a group because sellers are obliged to sell to all members who tender trade dollars as payment and must look to members as a group to fulfill their trade dollars. The receivable in goods and services denoted by trade dollars is due not from any particular member but from the members as a whole. Trade dollars may be spent with any member in accordance with the exchange agreement.

Under the rules of a typical exchange, members initially contract to make available a certain dollar amount of their inventory for barter purposes. In doing so, they agree to accept a minimum amount of barter business by selling goods or services in return for payment received in the form of trade dollars. trade dollars have value because of the willingness and obligation of members to accept them as a means of payment and hold trade dollar balances. Members consent to accept and hold trade dollars because of their confidence that they are exchangeable for goods and services.

A member may borrow trade dollars or use a pre-arranged line of credit to make purchases. The commercial barter exchange does not extend such credit, rather, the mutual association of members does. This is because it is the members who extend credit when they accept trade dollars as a means of payment. Such borrowing is administered and regulated by the exchange on behalf of the members collectively. In determining the amount of credit that a member may be allowed, an exchange considers the normal criteria of creditworthiness, personal and business financial position, and so forth In addition, most exchanges lay emphasis on having a period of experience with the member's trading, so as to estimate the amount of barter sales the member is likely to make in a year. Many exchanges use a rule of thumb that credit extended to a member should not exceed the amount of barter sales to be made by the member in a year. In this way, a member's borrowing is tied to his ability to repay from trade dollars earned through barter sales to members.

In its administration of the lending power on behalf of the members, the exchange regulates the extension of credit in the interest of the barter system as a whole. To illustrate, if B wishes to purchase $10,000 worth of carpet from A, but was providing meals to members at the rate of only $100 a month or $1,200 a year, the exchange might prohibit the transaction even though A himself was personally willing to extend credit to B. The reason is that, if the transaction were permitted, A's 10,000 trade credits would have to be made good by other member of the exchange (through sales to A) who were themselves not receiving commensurately from B. This would be unfair to the other members, because the credit they extended B would not be repaid through B's sales of goods and services to them in a reasonable time. It could also impair the operation of the exchange if A's expenditures caused some members to stop trading or go on standby. (standby occurs when a member accumulates trade credits beyond a level he considers desirable; he is then allowed to restrict his trading in conformance with his exchange agreement.)

It can be seen from this example that an exchange is involved in credit regulation not only to prevent a member's excessive indebtedness, but to avoid creation of excessive barter buying power relative to the supply of goods services, which is self-defeating in the operation of the exchange. It is important to note that the trade exchange itself does not extend credit. Credit is extended, or rather credit sales are permitted, by the exchange members. The exchange management performs an administrative function by regulating member s' borrowing in the interest of the entire barter system. The exchange s own borrowing is limited by the members through a provision in the client agreement.

At any point in time, some members of the barter network will be net creditors, that is, holders of trade dollars. They are said to be in a positive or surplus position in their account. Other members will be net debtors, that is, they will owe trade dollars. They are said to be in a negative or deficit position. Trade dollar assets are collectively the liabilities of those members who owe the system. Holders of trade dollar assets (creditors) are collectively owed by members who have borrowed (debtors).

Members' holdings of trade dollars comprise the money supply of the barter system. One of the great advantages of this privately created money is that the supply of trade dollars expands and contracts with the needs of trade. As trade expands, members' total borrowing increases to finance their larger purchases. Increased borrowing leads to increased supply of trade dollars, while repayment of loans leads to reduction in the supply of trade dollars. In a soundly managed exchange, the number of trade dollars in circulation is a function of the total dollar value of goods and services traded on the exchange. Expanding trade leads to increased supply of trade dollars through increased credit extension. This accommodates the increased demand for trade dollars to finance a growing trade volume. A study available from IRTA, "Trade Exchange Monetary Management", expands on this point.

## 5. Due Bills and Scrip

This responds to an inquiry concerning ethical obligations in the use of due bills or scrip.

Due bills were more in use in the 70's and 80's than they are today. Today, the common practice is for the issuer of credit to set up a master account for the barter company or other beneficiary in his computer. This is evidenced by a letter that states to the effect that, "We have opened an account in your favor for a specific number of dollars worth of our products or services." The letter states the terms or conditions on which the product or services may be acquired against the credit of the due bill.

When formal due bills are used today, the front page states what products or services it is for, the amount, and the terms and conditions. Usually, the amount is divisible, so that products or services may be obtained as required on the faith of the single due bill, rather than all at once. When a divisible due bill is used in this manner, it may have a form printed on the reverse which the parties endorse each time a draw is made against the due bill. The due bill is sent back and forth between the parties until its face amount is exhausted. Such due bills differ in form depending on whether they are for media, hard goods, or services.

Scrip is a form of due bill issued in monetary denominations for goods or services available from the issuing establishment. Terms and conditions are usually printed on the reverse. When a barter company has a contract with a client, such as a hotel chain, for a certain dollar amount of goods and services, the barter company may itself print and issue scrip of various denominations to permit convenient marketing of the product or service in divisible amounts to end users.

Who actually prints the scrip and controls the amount of its issue is important. If a barter company has a $2 million contract with a hotel, and has the right to print and issue scrip for the hotel's services, it may issue more than $2 million to allow for "breakage", that is, scrip which is sold but not redeemed. Since scrip is extensively traded, the barter industry has an interest in ethical standards to prevent over-issue. In general, the amount of scrip issued should not exceed the contract amount plus a reasonable allowance for breakage.

A further issue is whether a barter company or any other industry seller of scrip has an ethical obligation to tell a prospective buyer what it knows about risks surrounding performance of the scrip by the vendor. Should it learn that the vendor who made the original contract may default, is it ethically obliged to disclose this information to scrip purchasers? Recognizing that ordinary business risks arc implicit in scrip deals, if the deal appeared sound at the time it was concluded a requirement to disclose any ordinary business risk would not make sense because we are all business people and we accept ordinary risks. The problem arises when an issuer becomes an above-normal risk.

Suppose a seller of scrip has information that there is a good chance the scrip might become worthless. Re would then owe an ethical obligation to inform any buyer. At law, there is a point where failure to disclose a material fact makes a sale fraudulent. IRTA might reasonably set an ethical standard that would require a seller of scrip to disclose to a potential buyer information in his/her possession that the scrip issuer was an above-normal business risk or that redemption of ~he scrip was an above-normal business risk.

For example, if a vendor was in serious financial straits and had filed for bankruptcy or such filing was imminent, this information should be disclosed. Whether or not prior purchases should be refunded would depend on the specific circumstances of each case.

To the list of disclaimers printed on the scrip an issuer should consider adding words to the effect that: "Holder acknowledges that acquisition of scrip entails ordinary business and that such acquisition is entirely at one's own risk."

Whether one is an owner and re-seller of the scrip (having purchased it from the vendor) or a broker of the scrip (which makes a person the vendor's agent) should also be clarified by the disclaimers printed on the scrip. Ill law, a broker is an agent of either the buyer or seller and has legal obligations to the buyer or seller that he must faithfully perform. (When we use the term "broker" in the barter industry, as in "trade broker", we don't mean "broker" in the legal sense at all, for by no means is a trade broker an agent of the buyer or seller, nor should he be. Rather, when we say "broker" we mean "market-maker", one who brings buyers and sellers together to facilitate the marketplace.)

So when one says they are a broker of scrip, do they mean this in the sense that they are a "market-maker," or are they saying that they are the vendor's agent? If a barter company were the vendor's for the sale of scrip, and not simply a middleman who bought and sold scrip, it is possible the law of agency may allow it to be sued for the vendor's default. If one means to say that the barter company is a "middleman" or "market-maker" then we suggest (if your counsel agrees) that you stop using the term "broker" in relation to scrip.

In conclusion, since scrip is so widely traded, it is commercially important that market players have confidence they arc assuming no more than ordinary business risk when they buy and sell scrip. They should have confidence that scrip will not be over-issued; and that facts tending to create an above-normal risk of fulfillment will be fully disclosed.

# 6. Abandonment or Forfeiture of Trade Dollars

It is standard industry practice to regulate the forfeiture and abandonment of trade dollars in the contract between a barter company and its clients. Forfeiture and abandonment provisions are included in virtually all industry contracts, with the essential idea being that abandoned or forfeited trade dollars inure to the benefit of the barter company that has contracted with the defaulting client. The rationale is to compensate the costs and liquidate the damages incurred by the company as a result of the default.

A contract is a mutual exchange of promises to perform. If one of the parties defaults by failing to perform as promised, the defaulting party incurs a legal liability for costs and damages incurred by the other party resulting from the default. The abandonment and forfeiture provisions of barter contracts ensure that the party to the contract who incurs costs and damages from the default of the other is appropriately compensated. This is normally done by transferring ownership of trade dollars in a defaulting client's account to the barter company.

**Abandonment** of trade dollar balances occurs when a client ceases participation in the barter system due to bankruptcy, relocation (often not leaving a forwarding address), cessation of business, and so forth. In the typical case, the client's mail is returned, his phone is disconnected, and he is not heard from again. The client thus defaults on his barter contract, and the barter company incurs costs associated with unpaid fees, deprivation of services, attempts to locate the client, and efforts to recruit a replacement. Sometimes the barter company, to preserve good will, finds it necessary to compensate other clients who have suffered losses on goods or services not delivered by the defaulting client. While unanticipated departures from a barter system are a fact of life for any firm that deals mainly with small businesses, significant costs are incurred by the barter company as a result of those departures, and the company is entitled to damages from the defaulting party.

**Forfeiture** of trade dollar balances occurs when a barter contract provides for forfeiture as a penalty for failure to liquidate the account within a reasonable time after notice of termination is given under the contract for any reason. A termination notice may be given by either party. Termination notices may be given by the company for a number of reasons, but the bulk of such notices stem from failure to abide by the trading rules or meet the contractual obligation to keep one's account current by paying fees when due. Thus, most termination notices issued by a barter company are due to a prior default by a client. In most contracts in use in the barter industry, forfeiture is the final action in a series of steps providing for orderly liquidation of a client's balance after notice of termination. These steps are fully disclosed in the client agreement. They provide an opportunity to spend down the balance in the account to zero, at which point the client's participation in the exchange ceases. If full spend-down is not achieved in the manner specified in the agreement, the client forfeits the remaining balance to the barter company under the contract. The company incurs costs in providing the spend-down opportunity to a defaulting client, and is entitled to damages stemming from the client's default for and failure to pay fees or abide by the trading rules.

**Transfer** of ownership of positive trade dollar balances in a client's account to the barter company when abandonment or forfeiture occurs is a way of compensation the costs and liquidating the damages stemming from the default. is an openly disclosed provision of the client agreement. Its practical effect is to relieve the defaulting party of any further legal liability to the company, and to relieve the company of the need to pursue the defaulting party for costs and damages. It is an efficient and effective business practice. This *is* the common practice in the industry today, and in IRTA's view the practice is fully proper when provided in the written agreement and thus consented to by the client.

The important point to remember is that it is the barter company and the client who are parties to the contract. When a client defaults, it is the company that incurs costs and has the legal right to damages. When positive account balances are abandoned or forfeited, ownership of the balances always transfers to the company as a means of compensating the costs and liquidating the damages in an efficient and effective manner. Once ownership transfers, the company may utilize the balances as it sees fit.

## 7. Legal Liability for Trade Dollars in a Barter Exchange

Trade dollars arc defined by modern commercial barter exchanges as "a unit of account denoting the right to receive, or the obligation to pay, in goods or services available within a barter system" This "valuable right" is founded on the contract between a trade exchange and its clients whereby clients agree to accept trade dollars in payment for goods and services. In the U.S., written pronouncements of the highest accounting and tax authorities have likewise held that trade dollars are a "valuable right." Therefore, trade dollars are assets to their owners.

If trade dollars are assets, they must be the liability of someone. Many people unfamiliar with the barter industry, including some traders, believe trade dollar are the liability of the barter exchange which manages the barter system. That this notion is erroneous can be readily demonstrated.

A barter system is a network of reciprocal trading partners. This network is established by written contract between the barter exchange and its members This written agreement establishes, among other things, the terms and procedures whereby members make purchases and sales to and from each other. When sellers accept dollars in payment, they are extending credit to the other members of the network. The other members collectively have the obligation to fulfill the trade dollars of any member by selling goods and services to the member.

If businessperson A goes to businessperson B and purchases the product or service of B "on account, B has extended credit to A. in commercial law this is known as "open book credit." B simply records on his books a receivable due from A.

A commercial barter exchange is based on the same idea, except that, rather than B's doing the bookkeeping the barter exchange acts as a third-party recordkeeper for all parties who join the barter system. The barter exchange keeps the books which reflects the purchases and sales of the members. The advantage of this system is that it enables multilateral trade to take place, therefore overcoming the disadvantages of conventional two-party barter.

In a barter exchange, A purchases from B, paying with trade dollars. B has extended credit to the members collectively, because the barter is incomplete and B has not yet been paid in goods and services. B may spend his trade dollars with anyone, looking to members as a group to provide him with fulfillment goods and services.

In sum, members who hold trade dollars (have net positive balances) are collectively owed goods and services by those who have borrowed from the system (have net negative balances). The legal liability to fulfill trade dollars rests on the members collectively who owe the system. Trade dollars are not the liability of the exchange, but of all members (including, perhaps, the exchange) who have spent more trade dollars than they have earned, and have thus borrowed from the system.

As trade dollars circulate throughout the system, and the debtor or creditor status of the membership continually changes, no single debtor (including the barter exchange) can be singled out as the liable party for any particular trade dollars. All that can be said is that the debtor members collectively owe the creditor members collectively.

Thus, legal liability for the fulfillment of trade dollars lies with the network of member, specifically with those who are in deficit in their account and owe goods and services to others in the barter system. The soundness of the trade economy depend on the creditworthiness of the debtor members and their contractual obligation to repay. It is expected that they repay their borrowing by making sales of their product or service to other members, thereby earning trade dollars and liquidating their indebtedness. If they fail to repay, loan losses must be absorbed by the entire barter network. This is done by charging a loan loss reserve account, which is owned not by the barter exchange but by the members of the barter network collectively. Loan losses reduce the supply of goods and services available within the trade system, and must be controlled through prudent credit extension.

Trade dollars have value because of the willingness and obligation of the members of the barter network to accept them as a means of payment and hold trade dollar balances. Members consent to accept and hold trade dollars because of their confidence that they are exchangeable for goods and services. Trade dollars are "backed" by (1) the goods and services of members of the barter network who have a contractual obligation to accept them as payment up to a prescribed limit, and (2) the obligation of members who owe trade dollars to repay their debt.

Over time, some members may increase their borrowing to finance larger purchases. In this way, the number of trade dollars in circulation expands to finance a larger volume of trade.The legal liability to fulfill the outstanding trade dollars rests, as always, with the debtor members of the system. The loan loss reserve established by the exchange, through deduction from each member's account, ensures there are at all times sufficient trade dollars to pay the indebtedness of doubtful accounts.

A barter exchange is not like a commercial bank, which makes commercial loans and is liable for all demand deposits. A barter exchange does not extend credit, the members who accept trade dollars do. A barter exchange, as one of the members of the barter system, is liable only for its own borrowing (if any) and not for all the trade dollars in the system The amount of borrowing by a barter exchange is limited by the members through the contracts in use in the barter industry.

In sum, legal liability for redemption in goods and services of trade dollar in a barter system lies with the debtor members collectively. A barter exchange may or may not be a debtor member, and is liable only to the extent of its own borrowing. A barter exchange does not extend credit, only the members of the network collectively do. The exchange has a managerial role in the extension of credit among members, verifying creditworthiness, collecting delinquencies, etc., but has no credit-extending power of its own.

# 8. Trade Exchange Contracts and the Securities Laws

SECTION I.

A. **Purpose.** The purpose of this regulation is to promulgate actions required by IRTA members to minimize the possibility that their member contracts, franchise contracts, and/or trade credits may be construed as securities by State or Federal regulatory bodies.

B. **Applicability.** This regulation is binding upon all members of IRTA who have clients in the United States. Canadian members of IRTA will use this regulation as a guide in conjunction with applicable Canadian law.

C. **Effective Date.** This regulation became effective on May 16, 1983, upon its ratification by the Annual Meeting of Members.

**SECTION II. Actions Required**

A. Members of IRTA will not include in their contract provisions a guarantee or undertaking that the trade exchange will bring in a stipulated amount of business to the client.

B. Members of IRTA will not offer lifetime memberships to their clients.

C. Members of IRTA may not make a grant of trade credits equal to, greater, or less than the enrollment fee paid by new clients, as such fees are ordinarily absorbed by the exchange's cost of servicing its clients and this practice may result in the creation of an unsecured trade deficit.

D. Before members of IRTA will include offers to sell trade credits for cash in their exchange contracts, the member shall seek and obtain a written advisory from either a state securities commission (or similar body), or a qualified securities attorney affirming that in the opinion of the same such program does not violate any securities laws.

E. Members of IRTA will not give preferential treatment to any account, especially the accounts of exchange owners and other principals, staff, families, and so forth, except as disclosed in the exchange contract and/or rules and regulations.

F. Trade exchange contracts with clients will specify that client fees are received in payment for services rendered in processing clients into the exchange system (opening an account, providing forms, membership cards, monthly statements, and newsletters, etc.), maintaining records, and facilitating the client's use of the exchange.

G. Members of IRTA who engage in the practice of blocking the accounts of clients who are in arrears in their fees or commission payments, or who violate the provisions of their contract with the exchange including the rules of trading, will ensure that the contract agreed to by the client specifically concedes this power to the exchange and states that the determinations of exchange management in exercising this power shall be deemed final and conclusive.

H. IRTA members shall include in all contracts with their clients a statement to the effect that the client recognizes and grants to the exchange, first, the power to regulate and control the quantity of trade credits outstanding in the exchange system, in order to facilitate trading among the clients; and second, the power of those who have an ownership interest in the exchange, to borrow from the exchange and spend within the exchange system, an amount which in the aggregate does not exceed two years earnings of the exchange.

**SECTION III. Administrative Provisions**

A. Members of IRTA will ensure that a written contract is on file for each client doing business with the exchange, in which the client agrees to the contract provisions and to the exchange's rules and regulations. Such contract will be dated and signed by the client.

B. Members of IRTA are advised to seek the advice of local counsel in drafting contract language because the securities laws differ among states.

C. Members will keep IRTA informed of developments in their states with regard to the construction of barter contracts by the courts or regulatory authorities.

## 9. Allocation of High-Demand Items

1. **Background:** IRTA recognizes that when demand exceeds supply for an item that becomes available through a barter company, some form of rationing, i.e., decision

as to who gets the item, must inevitably take place. Clients may find fault with whatever system is used, and in order to minimize client complaints this policy statement is being used.

2. **Policy:** Association policy is that whatever system is used to allocate high- demand items shall be transparent, that is, fully disclosed to the clients and regularly brought to their attention. Acceptable systems currently in use include, but are not limited to: (1) establishing a client wait list on a first-come, first-served basis; (2) auctioning the item among all interested clients; (3) offering the item to the client with the highest trade balance; (4) offering the item to the client having the largest trade balance over $3,000 for the longest time; (5) offering the item to the client who has traded the largest amount over $3,000 in the last 3 months. Whatever system is used shall give preference to clients over the barter company, its owners, and employees.
3. **Applicability:** This policy statement shall be adhered to by all IRTA members.
4. **Effective Date:** This policy statement shall be effective immediately upon approval by the Board of Directors.
5. **Membership Review:** This policy statement may be reviewed and amended by the membership at the next annual meeting. Any member wishing to amend this document at the annual meeting shall obtain a seconder for his amendment and notify the Executive Director so the matter may be placed on the agenda for the business meeting.

# 10. Application of the Quantity Theory of Money to Barter Exchange Management

by Paul E. Suplizio

The purpose of this paper is to present a concept that may assist trade exchanges to determine the proper amount of trade dollars in their system to finance a given volume of trade. It may also be useful for judging the effectiveness of trade broker operations, and improving the quality of clients by enhancing their propensity to trade.

### *Quantity Theory of Money*

In monetary economics, the expression MV=PQ is a formula of major significance. The formula has enjoyed widespread acceptance for 200 years and is still taught in economics courses today.

The formula states the truism that the volume of trade, PQ (price times quantity, measured in dollars per year or some other unit of time) is equal to the money supply (M) times its velocity of turnover (V). V is the number of times a unit of M must turn over during the year in order to finance the volume of trade, PQ.

In the formula

M = money supply
V = velocity of turnover, i.e., the number of times M turns over during a year in order to finance a given volume of trade.
P = average price of goods and services
Q = number of units (physical quantity) of goods and services sold

Applied to the national economy, PQ is another way of expressing GNP, the total volume of all final goods and services produced and sold during the year; M is what the Federal Reserve calls M1, the amount of currency in circulation plus demand deposits of commercial banks; and V is the velocity of circulation of M1, a variable that is regularly measured by the Federal Reserve.

Applied to a barter economy,

M = number of trade dollars in circulation, i.e., the total amount of positive balances in clients' accounts and any house accounts used regularly in trading.

V = velocity of turnover of trade dollars, a figure that depends on the clients' propensity to trade, and how effective trade brokers are in stimulating trades.

PQ = total volume of trade per time period, measured as total sales or total purchases on the exchange, not the sum of total sales and purchases.

For example, say the total volume of trade for a barter exchange was $6 million in 1984. The exchange measures its money supply, M, as the average amount of positive balances in the hands of its members and in the exchange's house accounts used regularly in trading during 1984, and finds this amount to be $2 million trade dollars. Then the formula tells us that the velocity of circulation (V) for this exchange, is 3, i.e., each trade dollar turned over an average of 3 times during the year.

Suppose the same trade exchange sets $9 million as its trading goal for 1985, a 50 percent increase over 1984. Knowing that its velocity of circulation is 3, and anticipating no significant change in velocity due to increase in the number or skill of trade brokers, or increase in the clients' propensity to trade, it knows that the number of trade dollars in circulation should increase to $3 million ($9 million divided by 3) in 1985. Given a velocity of 3, the only way a trade volume of $9 million per year can be achieved is with a money supply equal to $3 million.

### *Money Expansion and Trade Growth*

The process by which trade volume grows in a barter system starts with the growing needs of buyers. Clients who want to increase their purchases of things they need will seek ways of acquiring additional trade dollars. The demand for trade dollars to finance larger purchases results in clients' seeking additional sales and/or additional credit.

As buyers seek to acquire more trade dollars to fulfill their needs, much of the increased demand for trade dollars will be satisfied by credit expansion, which puts additional trade dollars (M) into circulation. Credit expansion in the barter economy is the vehicle by which buyers obtain additional trade dollars to make their demand effective. Trade volume will then rise as buyers increase their spending to satisfy their growing needs.

In sum, the money supply in a barter system increases through credit expansion in response to buyers' growing demand for trade dollars to spend. More total spending causes trade volume to rise. As total trade grows, the money supply in the system rises to finance the increased trade volume. Increased money supply (M) is a consequence of growing trade volume and not the other way around.

The principal way of stimulating trade growth is by stimulating buyers' needs. It is buyers' needs that increase the demand for trade dollars and cause M to expand through expansion of credit.

To illustrate, the barter exchange in our example expects to increase its total trade volume by 50 percent, from $6 to $9 million, between 1984 and 1985. Assume for purposes of discussion that each client desires to increase its total spending by 50 percent. Further that during 1984 Client A made $50,000 in trade sales (which are the purchases of others) and $50,000 in trade sales (which are the sales of others) in the system. (We count A's trade volume as $50,000 in 1984, not $100,000 as is sometimes done, in order not to double-count transactions.)

Let us assume that Client A intends to raise its total purchases to $75,000 in 1985. Where will it get the trade dollars to finance these purchases if M remains constant? First, it can increase its sales to other clients. But with a fixed supply of trade dollars, the other clients will have fewer trade dollars with which to increase their spending. The only thing that will allow total trade volume to grow, if M is fixed, is for A to spend its trade dollars faster, thus putting trade dollars back in the hands of other clients who are just as eager as A to raise their sales and spending. Faster spending means increased velocity of circulation.

The formula MV = PQ confirms this result, for it tell us that, if M remains constant, the only way that trade volume PQ will rise by 50 percent is if velocity (V) rises by 50 percent.

There is another way that total trade volume can rise: M can expand while V remains constant. If A wishes to make $75,000 in purchases, it can expand its sales to $75,000, or failing that, it can borrow the difference. If A succeeds in raising its sales to $75,000, others will be short the trade dollars required to expand their own purchases, and they will have to borrow. Such borrowing by A and other clients increases M, the supply of trade dollars in the system, by the full amount of the borrowing. Thus, the demand for trade dollars by clients to finance their growing purchases leads to expansion of M through the lending power of the members who comprise the exchange, and the larger M finances a larger volume of trade.

If velocity of circulation (V) is essentially stable, since it depends on the number of quality of trade brokers and the clients' propensity to trade, normally M should expand if trade volume is to rise. Holding M constant could frustrate the desire of buyers as a group to increase their total spending, for whereas a few clients may be able to increase their spending through greater sales to others, all buyers collectively will be unable to do so, since they cannot obtain the trade dollars needed to increase their spending.

In theory, because the lending power of a barter system is based upon contract (clients grant administration of their lending power to the exchange and limit any borrowing by the exchange itself), the supply of credit to the exchange's clients is capable of expanding to fully satisfy the demand of whatever interest rate is set. In practice, however, the supply of credit must be governed by the normal canons of credit worthiness, or else an excessive number of problem loans to the clients will endanger the health of the system. (If too many clients borrow from the exchange and then go bankrupt, they leave the system with a large unsecured deficit; remaining clients hold positive balances with reduced opportunities for exchanging them, and trade may consequently fail or stop altogether.) The prudent administration of the lending power is one of the strictest duties of management.

Credit expansion in the barter system does not require that loans be increased to each and every client. It requires only that additional credit be extended to the most credit worthy clients. The spending of these clients will put trade dollars into the hands of other clients, thereby increasing the total supply of trade dollars (M) in circulation.

### *Pump Priming and Deficit Spending*

There is another way of increasing M, the number of trade dollars in circulation, and that is by the exchange's making a loan to itself (or to its owners or principals) rather than to its clients. Unlimited access to the credit window by the exchange is a source of abuse that can destroy a bartering system.

In principal, just as many additional trade dollars are put in circulation if the exchange purchases a certain amount of Client A's products instead of loaning A the same amount. Where does the exchange get the trade dollars to spend? One of its options is to create them by lending to itself. It is true that all trade exchanges have significant trade dollar earnings, but they also have significant trade dollar expenses; the result is that unless management exercises prudence and maintains strict budgetary controls, more trade dollars will be spent than are earned. That is, the exchange or its owners will have recourse to the credit window.

When a client requires a loan, he must apply to the exchange for approval, hence his access to credit is limited. When the exchange requires a loan it applies, as it were, to itself, hence its access to credit is restrained by no effective power other than stipulations of the client agreement, the laws governing fraud, regulations of the International Reciprocal Trade Association, or moral self-restraint.

IRTA regulations require a provision to be inserted in each client contract obligating an exchange to keep its borrowing within prudent limits. Kept within prudent limits, which IRTA defines as no more than two years gross income of the exchange (not gross trade volume), and fully or partly collateralized, an exchange's deficit spending can be exercised to benefit, rather than cause damage to the barter system.

As with loans to clients, the exchange's own borrowing and spending adds new trade dollars to the quantity in circulation. To prevent excessive supply of trade dollars, the exchange's deficit spending must be rigorously controlled. As with other loans, the exchange's borrowing must be repaid.

The theory of pump-priming holds that, in order to stimulate a growing volume of trade, M should be expanded through deficit spending by the exchange (or by its owners or principals). The idea is that placing more trade dollars in the hands of the members will encourage them to spend and trade volume will grow. This sometimes works at first, but it quickly leads the unwary exchange manager down the path of excessive deficit spending and oversupply of money to the system. This eventually causes trade volume to decline, because once their need for liquid balances is satisfied, members will accept no further trade business until they can first spend the balances they have accumulated. This is when all members of the system hold excess balances, no one will sell and trade volume falls to zero.

It should also be noted that excessive deficit spending normally consists of uncollateralized borrowing by the exchange, so the trade dollars in the hands of members are doubly worthless: they have no transaction value, and the exchange has no assets with which to redeem them.

The pump-priming theory places the cart before the horse. The idea is that if you expand M, trade volume growth will follow. It fails to recognize that M will expand to meet the demand for trade dollars by buyers, and not the other way around. If you put more trade dollars in the hands of buyers, there is no certainty they will spend. The path to more trade volume is by stimulating buyers' needs and increasing their propensity to trade. They will then seek to acquire the trade dollars needed to fulfill their purchase objectives, and as they do so, M will expand.

The pump-priming theory has been responsible for excessive deficit spending by some barter exchanges, resulting in large trade dollar balances held by clients. Instead of stimulating trade, this situation has resulted in rapidly declining trade and eventual trade gridlock; that is, existing clients unwilling to accept further trade dollar balances. This results in cessation of trading, the collapse of the exchange and total loss of the value of balances held by clients.

The proper way to stimulate trade is through advertising and marketing of products available on trade, and an effective cadre of trade brokers. Placing more trade dollars, M, in the hands of clients, is not the answer. There must be opportunities for increased sales of the products and services they have, and opportunities for increased purchases of the products and services they need.

### *Application of the Quantity Theory to Barter Exchange Management*

The quantity theory of money not only brings valuable insight to the ebb and flow of trade in the barter economy, but it also has valuable management uses. These applications may be described under two general headings: monetary management and velocity management.

Monetary management helps the barter exchange to answer the question: "What is the optimum supply of trade dollars I should have in the system to finance the trade volume I expect?" In order to answer this question, the exchange should study its trading records and make the best possible estimates, based on past experience, of the velocity of circulation, V. (The methods of estimating and projecting V are discussed below.) Since expected trade volume PQ is known, and V is known, the optimum M can then be computed by the formula:

$$M = PQ/V$$

This M is the required average amount of trade dollars to be in circulation over a year's time. In practice it cannot be expected to remain constant over the entire year, or be subject to precise control. Volumes have been written about the Federal Reserve's inability to precisely control M1, the money supply of the national economy.

To approximate the optimum M in the barter economy, the trade exchange should average the M for the beginning of the year with the M for the end of the year. Thus,

$$\frac{\text{M Optimum} = \text{M Begin} + \text{M End}}{2}$$

Because M optimum and M begin are known, the target M for the end of the year can be computed. The exchange should use this target M for the year-end as a guide to control the supply of credit to clients during the year. Any increase or decrease in the supply of credit will change M by the same amount. That is,

$$\wedge C = \wedge M$$

where C is the total volume of outstanding loans to the exchange and its clients.

Most credit extension in a barter system occurs by allowing clients to "spend into the negative" (that is, their accounts will show negative balances) against a pre-established line of credit. This client deficit spending adds to the supply of trade dollars in circulation. *A basic principle is that credit extension increases the supply of money, and loan repayments reduce the supply of money, in the barter economy.*

Thus, by regulating the amount of credit extended during any time period, the total number of trade dollars in circulation by the end of the time period, i.e., the target M, can be approximated.

Trade exchanges may also compare their M and V with the corresponding figures for other exchanges having approximately the same trade volume, or with an industry average, and in this way gain insight as to whether their money and credit policies are overly lenient or overly restrictive.

Velocity management helps the trade exchange answer the question, "Are my trade broker operations efficiently moving the supply of trade dollars to finance a growing trade volume through spending down the high-balance accounts, bringing the deficit accounts back to surplus, and similar trade management policies?"

Sound velocity management is a precondition to sound management of the trade dollar money supply, as an accurate estimate of V is essential before the optimum M can be calculated. Even when historical V is accurately computed, what V will be in the year ahead in light of the projected number, training, skill, and experience of the trade broker staff, and in light of the trading propensities of the clients, should be projected as realistically as possible in management's best judgement.

To compute the average velocity (V) for any time period, the trade volume (PQ) for the period should first be determined. The average number of trade dollars in circulation, M (positive balances in clients' accounts and house accounts used regularly in trading) should then be estimated, either at a single point during the period or as the average of the money supply for the beginning and the ending dates of the period, that is:

$$\frac{\text{M Average} = \text{M Begin} + \text{M End}}{2}$$

The average velocity during the period should then be computed using the following formula:

$$\frac{V = PQ}{M}$$

It is desirable to make several estimates of V over different time periods to gain an idea of the variance of this factor. This will assist in arriving at the best possible estimate of V. The exchange's estimate of its own particular velocity of circulation is one of the most important estimates it can arrive at, as the figure can be used as a guide to expanding the volume of trade by improving trade floor operations and increasing clients' propensities to trade. It is also crucial for accurately estimating the optimum supply of trade dollars (M) for the exchange, which serves as a guide for the exchange's credit policies.

Once a historical estimate of V is made, the caliber of trade floor operations and the average propensity to trade of the clients during that period should be considered. As previously mentioned, trade floor operations can be evaluated in terms of the number, training, and experience of trade brokers. Client propensities to trade can be evaluated by a simple scaling technique, by having trade brokers rate clients on their trading initiative on a scale from one to ten. The average trading propensity for all clients can then be computed. Some exchanges periodically purge their client lists, dropping from membership those that show low trading volume or low inclination to trade. Such exercises generally serve to raise the propensity to trade in the system.

The *marginal propensity to trade* is a measure of the clients' tendency to spend trade dollars, rather than maintain trade dollar reserves and idle balances. Trade dollars have value principally as a medium of exchange; they have limited use as a store of value. Nevertheless, either from lack of opportunity to obtain what is needed, or from lack of initiative, idle balances are carried while time is spent waiting to consummate trades. This obviously reduces velocity of circulation and trade volume.

If average idle balances and waiting time can be measured, these factors can be taken into account in estimating the velocity of circulation. The *marginal propensity to trade* is defined as the fraction of each new trade dollar that is spent within some time period, say 3,6,9 or 12 months. The more time that elapses, the larger the fraction that will be spent. MPT's can be estimated for individual clients and for the exchange as a whole. The average propensity to trade is the fraction of total trade dollars in one's account that will be spent in a given time period. APT's may also be computed for both individual clients and the exchange as a whole.

Management actions to raise the average and marginal propensity to trade of each client will increase V and stimulate greater trade volume and profits for the exchange. Other things being equal, clients with high MPT's are good candidates for trade credit loans and for referral of new business. Clients with low MPT's should be worked with, educated, and provided more trading opportunities to meet their needs and raise their propensity to trade.

A higher velocity also reduces loan exposure, as a small amount of lending is required to achieve the optimum money supply. A high velocity (V) should be adjusted judgementally to take into account any significant changes in trade floor operations and/or trading propensities anticipated in the next time period. If no significant changes are anticipated, the historical figure for average velocity should be used.

Once V is estimated, the question for management is whether it is "right" for the exchange. The best way to determine this is to compare the figure with the V's for other exchanges. If Trade Exchange A is financing \$5 million annually in trade with M of \$5 million, and Trade Exchange B is financing the same trade volume with an M of \$1 million, A's velocity is 1 and B's is 5. A could well question why its velocity is so low, and its loan exposure so high. If industry averages were available, analysis could further pinpoint why differences in velocity occur and what management actions are dictated.

In sum, the quantity theory of money helps exchanges to better understand and manage their trade operations. It generalizes into a single formula the myriad trading activity that goes on in an exchange, and identifies relationships that might otherwise be obscured. The variables have important management applications when measured on a systematic basis and compared to similar data for other exchanges or to industry-wide averages.

# 11. Position Paper on Accounting for Trade Credits

by Joseph Morris, CPA

The International Reciprocal Trade Association ("IRTA") was established in 1979 to foster common interests of the commercial barter industry in the United States and worldwide and to develop and uphold high standards of ethical business practice in the commercial barter industry. The commercial barter industry consists of approximately 600 barter companies that serve all parts of the United States and also overseas markets. Approximately 500 of the barter companies operate as clearing houses for the exchange of products and services between "members" or "clients" of the exchanges. Approximately 100 of the barter companies operate as corporate barter companies, engaging in exchanging trade credits for companies' assets and selling goods and services to the companies for payments partly in cash and partly in trade credits. There is some overlap among the barter companies in these two basic techniques of bartering.

The commercial barter industry is approximately 20 years old. Members of the industry have formed IRTA, the leading industry association. IRTA worked with the U.S. Congress in developing the barter tax compliance provisions of the Tax Equity and Fiscal Responsibility Act of 1982, which recognized barter exchanges on par with banks and credit card companies as third party recordkeepers, and also requires that barter exchanges provide an annual Form 1099-B for each client's barter revenue to the Internal Revenue Service.

IRTA conducts research about contract, securities, and tax law, and also accounting principles and procedures applicable to barter transactions. IRTA maintains information sharing and public relations programs and actively represents the commercial barter industry and barter companies before government, regulatory, and standard-setting organizations.

At present, IRTA has 168 members including the leading U.S. barter companies and several affiliations with foreign barter companies. IRTA is governed by a 16-member Board of Directors, which meets quarterly. An annual meeting of members is held each year and one or more training conferences are held to educate and improve professional competence of those serving in the industry. An industry accreditation program allows qualified persons to attain certification in a specialty or specialties. An information exchange and expert advisory board assist new start-ups in the barter industry.

IRTA administers various community service programs and also the Barter Political Action Committee (BARTERPAC), under a special Federal Election Commission ruling that approved trade credit and in-kind contributions to candidates for federal office by stockholders, executives, and administrative personnel of barter companies. Trade credits are recognized by the FEC on the basis of one trade credit equals one dollar.

IRTA was responsible in 1980 for a Civil Aeronautics Board ruling allowing unrestricted barter of air transportation. The CAB later issued rules to the airlines on accounting for barter transactions, and copies are available from IRTA. IRTA cooperates with the Better Business Bureau and American Institute of Certified Public Accountants on matters of mutual interest. IRTA works with the Federal Trade Commission to keep franchisers and licensors apprised of federal and state franchising regulations. IRTA has assisted tax and securities authorities, other regulatory bodies, and state attorney generals in New York, Ohio, Oklahoma, Missouri, Texas, Florida, and California with expert advice on the barter industry. IRTA lobbied successfully to defeat proposed adverse legislation in California and Iowa, and helped protect the public by exposing a fraudulent barter operation in California.

IRTA's programs stress industry self-regulation and upgrading of professional standards through education and training. IRTA's action programs include member services, business leads, media relations, speaker's bureau, government affairs, education and training, conventions and meetings, technical consulting, supporting international members, assisting new start-ups, eliminating restrictive government regulations, industry surveys, and publications.

The Corporation Trade Council ("CTC") is a self-governing arm of IRTA. The CTC mission is to promote corporate trade domestically and internationally and to uphold the CTC Code of Ethics, which was adopted in 1990. A copy of the IRTA and CTC Codes of Ethics are attached as Exhibit A.

### Background on the Commercial Barter Industry

Commercial barter has become a prominent way to transact business in the United States. IRTA estimates that over $6 billion in barter transactions are presently occurring each year, with an estimated rate of increase of 8% per year. IRTA estimates that over 250,000 business firms, including both small businesses and a growing number of well-known larger companies, are presently engaging in commercial barter.

Business firms enter into barter transactions to generate incremental sales, to conserve cash for essential expenditures, to exchange unproductive or unwanted inventories and unused capacity. Barter enables firms to operate profitably at their incremental cost of production—as long as the incremental benefits available from barter exceed the related incremental cost, it is usually in the best interest of a firm to barter.

The exchange of unwanted assets or excess inventory for needed goods and services enables firms to realize higher values for them than available from selling the unwanted assets or excess inventories by lowering the cash price or selling on a liquidation basis through normal liquidation channels.

Barter is sometimes accomplished by direct trade. However, the barter process has evolved to enable trading without the need for a direct trade with another party. Two predominant forms of non-direct bartering have evolved.

### Barter Exchanges

Organized barter exchanges act as clearing houses for many firms that engage in barter. The clients of the exchange provide goods and services to other clients and receive trade credits (which are sometimes referred to by other names, such as "trade dollars" or "trade units"), which are used by clients in purchasing and sales activities on the basis of $1 of purchasing power per trade credit. The trade credit is essentially used as a private currency and medium of exchange within the closed economy of the barter exchange. Because dollar prices are used to value the commodities being bought and sold, it can be demonstrated empirically that on average the value of a trade credit equals one dollar. The barter exchanges maintain client accounts in which trade credits earned, spent, and available, are accumulated for each client. The barter exchanges' primary function is to act as record keepers and brokers for their clients, and less frequently as buyers and sellers for their own account. The clients normally pay membership fees and commissions to the barter exchange. Clients of barter exchanges are of all sizes, from small retain operations and individual professionals to medium and large companies and they engage in numerous transactions of all sizes. A typical trade transaction in a barter exchange would be less that $1,000 and a typical client of a barter exchange might have a trade credit balance of $2,000 to $3,000.

### Corporate Barter Companies

Corporate barter companies generally specialize in client relationships with medium and large companies and larger but fewer transactions. These transactions can be in the $1,000,000 range and even higher, and consequently clients of corporate barter companies can have trade credit balances much greater than the balances typically held by clients of barter exchanges. Corporate barter companies function almost exclusively as buyers and sellers of goods and services. In a typical transaction, a corporate barter company will acquire unwanted assets or excess inventories from a client in exchange for trade credits valued at $1 per trade credit. The trade credits issued by corporate barter companies are sometimes called "purchase credits" or "AR" (accounts receivable) credits. These trade credits may be used by client companies to purchase goods or services from the corporate barter company. The corporate barter company enters into an agreement to supply to the client goods and services that the client may pay for partly in cash and partly in trade credits, with $1 of purchasing power attributed to each trade credit. Here again, the prices of commodities being bought and sold are denominated in dollars, and trade credits are used as a medium of exchange. In order for this arrangement to make economic sense for the client, the total of cash and trade credits paid for the goods and services is generally equal to or less than the amounts for which the client can obtain the same goods and services by paying cash elsewhere. Of them, the economics of the transaction are demonstrated by comparison to prices previously paid by the client for comparable goods and services, or prices the client would currently have to pay.

In both of the predominant forms of commercial barter today, trade credits are a form of privately created money, originating in the contract between a barter company and its client. Like money, trade credits serve as a medium of exchange and a unit of account, but their *standard of value* is the dollar because dollar prices are used to record exchanges where trade credits are used as a means of payment.

In the barter industry, trade credits serve as a medium of exchange and are valued like any currency. Their value is not determined in particular transactions, but as an average over a range of exchanges. This is the conclusion arrived at by Professor Robert I. Keller and adopted by the Internal Revenue Service when they reviewed the subject of trade credits. (See Robert I. Keller, "The Taxation of Barter Transactions," *Minnesota Law Review*, Vol. 67, No. 2, December 1982, pp. 441-511.) Following Dr. Keller, the Internal Revenue Service's information reporting regulations for barter exchanges (T.D. 7873, 26 CFR Part 1, issued March 11, 1983) adopt the view that trade credits should be valued as a currency. The regulations state: "For purposes of this section, the fair market value of a credit or scrip is the value assigned to such credit or scrip by the issuing barter exchange for the purpose of exchanges..." The Keller article and Treasury regulations are attached as enclosures B and C.

### The Real Issue: When Should Trade Credit Transactions Be Recognized and How Should They Be Measured?

The issue presented above describes the basic accounting questions related to barter transactions denominated in trade credits. The two aspects of the question, when to recognize and how to measure, are interrelated in that the criteria for recognition include having the ability to measure.

### Trade Credits Are Assets

As a threshold point, it should be established that a trade credit meets the definition of an asset and has the three essential characteristics of an asset as provided in the FASB's conceptual framework.

Assets are probable future economic benefits obtained or controlled by a particular entity as a result of past transactions or events (FASB Concepts Statement No. 6, paragraph 25).

An asset has three essential characteristics: (a) it embodies a probable future benefit that involves a capacity, singly or in combination with other assets, to contribute directly or indirectly to future net cash inflows, (b) a particular entity can obtain the benefit and control other's access to it, and (c) the transaction or other event giving rise to the entity's right to or control of the benefit has already occurred. Assets have other features that help identify them—for example, assets may be acquired at a cost and they may be tangible, exchangeable, or legally enforceable (FASB Concepts Statement No. 6, paragraph 26).

The kinds of items that qualify as assets under the definition in paragraph 25 are also commonly called economic resources. They are the scarce means that are useful for carrying out economic activities, such as consumption, production, and exchange (emphasis added) (FASB Concepts Statement No. 6, paragraph 27).

The common characteristic possessed by all assets (economic resources) is "service potential" or "future economic benefit", the scarce capacity to provide services or benefits to the entities that use them. In a business enterprise, that service potential or future economic benefit eventually result in net cash inflows to the enterprise...The relationship between service potential or future economic benefit of its assets and net cash inflows to an entity is often indirect...(FASB Concepts Statement No. 6, paragraph 28)

*Assets other than cash benefit an entity by being exchanged for cash or other goods or services* (emphasis added), by being used to produce goods or services or otherwise increase the value or other assets, or being used to settle liabilities(FASB Concepts Statement No. 6, paragraph 30).

Trade credits are a form of privately-created money. Trade credits are not lawful currency of the United States, but the ownership of trade credits results in similar financial consequences to the ownership of United States currency—the ability to acquire goods and services.

> Money (cash, including deposits in banks) is valuable because of what it can buy. It can be exchanged for virtually any good or service that is available or it can be saved and exchanged for them in the future. Money's "command over resources"—its purchasing power —is the basis of its value and future economic benefits (FASB Concepts Statement No. 6, paragraph 29).

Trade credits do not have the same commercial utility as money because the economic transactions in which they can be spent relate only to subsets of firms, products, and services. However, as demonstrated by the huge volume of barter transactions in which trade credits are spent, ownership of trade credits constitute a probable future economic benefit—albeit not the same universal claim on goods and services available from cash.

### Trade Credit Transactions Meet the Criteria for Recognition

Most barter transactions involving the exchange of trade credits meet the criteria for recognition in financial statements.

An item and information about it should meet four fundamental recognition criteria to be recognized and should be recognized when the criteria are met, subject to a cost-benefit constraint and a materiality threshold. Those criteria are:

> **Definitions.** The item meets the definition of an element of financial statements.
> **Measurability.** It has a relevant attribute measurable with sufficient reliability.
> **Relevance.** The information about it is capable of making a difference in user decisions.
> **Reliability.** The information is representationally faithful, verifiable, and neutral... (FASB Concepts Statement No.5, paragraph 63)

The following sections discuss IRTA's views about how trade credits generally meet the criteria for recognition in financial statements.

### Trade Credits Meet the Definition of an Element of Financial Statements

As discussed in the previous section, "Trade Credits are Assets," trade credits meet the definition of an asset, one of the elements of financial statements.

### Trade Credits are Measurable

In order to be measurable, an asset must have one of the five measurement "attributes" described in FASB Concepts Statement No. 5, paragraph 67.

> (Measurability means) (t)he asset, liability, or change in equity must have a relevant attribute that can be quantified in monetary units with sufficient reliability. Measurability must be considered together with both relevance and reliabilit. (FASB Concepts Statement No. 5, paragraph 65).

Of the five attributes in paragraph 67, trade credits have the attribute of "net realizable (settlement) value."

> d. Net realizable (settlement) value. Short-term receivables and some inventories are reported at their net realizable value, which is the nondiscounted amount of cash, or its equivalent, into which an asset is expected to be converted in due course of business less direct costs, if any, necessary to make that conversion (FASB Concepts Statement No. 5, paragraph 67).

In this respect, trade credits are most similar to short-term receivables. The value expected to be realized from a receivable is established in an exchange which, in the case of a revenue producing transaction, may result in the recording of income or a gain because the value of the receivable acquired is greater than the carrying value of the assets surrendered in exchange for the receivable. The trade credits are convertible into cash or its equivalent because they can be used to pay for goods and services that would otherwise be paid for in cash.

The valuation of trade credits in accordance with net realizable (settlement) value is consistent with the notion of reflecting elements of financial statements at value established at the time of exchange.

> Historical exchange price" is more descriptive of the quantity most generally reflected in financial statements in present practice (and "transaction-based system" would be a better description of the present accounting model than "historical cost system") (FASB Concepts Statement No. 5, paragraph 69).

### *Ownership of Trade Credits is Relevant Information*

> (Relevance) is a primary qualitative characteristic. To be relevant, information about an item must have feedback value or predictive value (or both) for users and must be timely. Information is relevant if it has the capacity to make a difference in investors', creditors', or other users' decisions. To be recognized, the information conveyed by including an asset, liability, or change therein in the financial statements must be relevant. (FASB Concepts Statement No. 5, paragraph 73)

> The relevance of particular information about an item being considered for recognition cannot be determined in isolation. Relevance should be evaluated in the context of the principle objective of financial report- ing: providing information that is useful in making rational investment, credit, and similar decisions. Relevance should also be evaluated in the context of the full set of financial statements—with consideration of how recognition of a particular item contributes to the aggregate decision usefulness. (FASB Concepts Statement No. 5, paragraph 74)

The ownership of trade credits results in financial consequences and the future benefits purchasable with them are important to an accurate portrayal of the firm's financial position. To omit trade credits from a firm's balance sheet would be similar to omitting a bonafide receivable or, to an extent, omitting cash.

### *Trade Credits Meet the Criterion of Reliability*

Reliability is the other primary qualitative characteristic. To be reliable, information about an item must be representationally faithful, verifiable, and neutral. To be reliable, information must be sufficiently faithful in its representation of the underlying resource, obligation, or effect of events and sufficiently free of error and bias to be useful to investors, creditors, and others in making decisions. To be recognized, information about the existence and amount of an asset, liability, or change therein must be reliable (FASB Concepts Statement No. 5, paragraph 75).

> Representational faithfulness...refers to the correspondence or agreement between the accounting numbers and the resources or events those numbers purport to represent (FASB Concepts Statement No. 4, Summary of Conclusions).

> Verifiability is a quality that may be demonstrated by securing a high degree on consensus among independent measures using the same measurement methods (FASB Concepts Statement No. 4, Summary of Conclusions).

> Neutrality means that, in formulating or implementing standards, the primary concern should be the relevance and reliability of the information that results, not the effect that the new rule may have on a particular interest (FASB Concepts Statement No. 4, Summary of Conclusions).

A trade credit is a unit of account that denotes the right to receive, or the obligation to pay, one U.S. dollar's worth of goods and services available within a barter system. While trade credits are indeed a unit of account and a medium of exchange, the prices of goods and services bought and sold are denominated entirely in u.S. dollars. The trade credit has meaning in terms of value only be reference to the U.S. dollar prices of the goods and services it can purchase—U.S. dollar prices are the same for goods and services purchased for trade credits as on a cash basis of exchange.

The crucial role of U.S. dollar prices as the standard of value in the organized barter industry means that, on average, across a range of many transactions, the value of a trade credit is $1. That is the basis on which value is negotiated in barter transactions and the economic basis on which firms decide whether to enter into a particular barter transaction. That is the basis on which fulfillment goods and services are provided when trade credits are subsequently exchanged. Since fulfillment goods and services are commonly available items with quoted market prices (media, printing, hotels, etc.) denoting trade credits on financial statements as a medium of exchange representing so many dollars worth of fulfillment goods and services would have a high degree or reliability.

While in specific cases there can be variances between identified trade credit and cash prices, there can as well be variances between cash prices for identical goods or services. Indeed, many factors influence the price of any individual transaction, whether denominated in trade credits or cash. When comparing trade credit and cash prices for fulfillment goods and services, the relevant cash price is the price capable of being commanded by the firm if it had to pay cash for the fulfillment goods and services.

### *Recognition of Gains on Trade Credit Transactions*

The conceptual framework seems to place a higher threshold on recognition of transactions in amounts that result in gains. The notions underlying this are important to considering the recognition of gains on trade credit transactions and also to the recognition of trade credit assets, even when gains are not recorded.

> (E)arnings measures the extent to which asset inflows (revenues and gains) associated with substantially completed cash-to-cash cycles exceed asset outflows (expenses and losses) associated, directly or indirectly, with the same cycles. Guidance for recognizing components of earnings is concerned with identifying which cycles are substantially complete and with associating particular rev-

enues, gains, expenses, and losses with those cycles (FASB Concepts Statement No. 5, paragraph 80).

The acquisition of trade credits represents a substantially completed cash-to-cash cycles between an asset is acquired and a cost is incurred to acquire that asset. It is only in a subsequent and entirely separate cash-to-cash cycle that trade credits may be utilized for acquisition of goods or services or payment of a liability that would otherwise be paid for with cash.

The sections of FASB Concepts Statement No. 5 that discuss revenues and gains and also recognition of changes in assets and liabilities include the following:

> Revenues and gains of an enterprise during a period are generally measured by the exchange values of the assets (goods or services) or liabilities involved (FASB Concepts Statement No. 5, paragraph 83).
>
> Initial recognition of assets acquired and liabilities incurred generally involves measurement based on current exchange prices at the date of recognition (FASB Concepts Statement No. 5, paragraph 88).

Because trade credits are assets and their exchange is denominated based on $1 per trade credit, the exchange value of $1 per trade credit should be used in recording revenue and assets acquired in trade credit transactions.

The conceptual framework goes on to describe perhaps a higher threshold for recognition where revenue and gains are involved. This is to be contrasted with, for example, recording an asset at the amount paid. Here, the sort of transaction contemplated is the recording of a receivable equal to sales price in exchange for inventory at a lower cost, resulting in a gain.

(R)ecognition involves consideration of two factors, (a) being realized or realizable and (b) being earned, with sometimes one and sometimes the other being the more important consideration.

> a. Realized or realizable. Revenues and gains generally are not recognized until realized or realizable. Revenues and gains are realized when products (goods or services), merchandise, or other assets are exchanged for cash or claims to cash. Revenues and gains are realizable when related assets received or held are readily convertible to known amounts of cash or claims to cash...
>
> b. Earned. Revenues are not recognized until earned. An entity's revenue earning activities involve delivering or producing goods, rendering services, or other activities that constitute its ongoing major or central operations, and revenues are considered to have been earned when the entity has substantially accomplished what it must do to be entitled to the benefits represented by the revenues. Gains commonly result from transactions and other events that involve no "earning process", and for recognized gains, being earned is generally less significant than being realized or realizable (FASB Concepts Statement No. 5 paragraph 83).
>
> In recognizing revenues and gains:
>
> a. The two conditions (being realized or realizable and being earned) are usually met by the time product or merchandise is delivered or services are rendered to customers, and revenues from manufacturing and selling activities and gains and losses from sales of other assets are commonly recognized at the time of sale (usually meaning delivery) (FASB Concepts Statement No. 5, paragraph 84).

The foregoing passages contain several ideas that are relevant to accounting for tarde credit transactions. Trade credit transactions should be recognized on a $1 per trade credit basis when they are realizable. In normal transactions, trade credits are realizable because they may be exchanged for fulfillment goods and services that would otherwise have to be acquired by outlay of cash. The criterion for realizability (convertible to cash or claims to cash) is satisfied by acquisition of goods or services for which cash outlay would be required, because a principle purpose of cash is to acquire goods or services needed by an entity. It is IRTA's experience that intelligent companies participating in a barter exchange or engaging in large trade credit transactions with corporate barter companies to not do so without the belief that the trade credits are realizable by the expected acquisition of goods and services that would otherwise require outlay of cash. Firms can demonstrate realizability by (a) a past track record of utilizing trade credits, (b) evident capacity to utilize the trade credits in a reasonable time, indicated by the quantity of trade credits relative to the size of the firm's procurement budget for items the trade credits may be used for, and (c) by the preparation of a trade plan for timely utilization of the trade credits on a $1 per trade credit basis for needed goods and services that will be available in the particular trade environment. Such trade plans are customarily prepared as part of due diligence before entering into a significant trade credit transaction with a corporate barter company. Because the transactions are ordinarily much smaller, this sort of corroboration of realizability readily exists for clients of barter exchanges.

The revenues represented by trade credits received are earned because the firm has conveyed to the barter company or to another client of the barter company the goods or services exchanged for the trade credits. Therefore, the firm has substantially accomplished all that it must do to be entitled to the benefits represented by the trade credits. Likewise, the above passages indicate that gains would be recognized when other assets are exchanged for trade credits.

### *Considerations in an Exchange for Media*

Media (advertising services) is the bread and butter of the barter business and is exchanged extensively. There are various types of media a company may require for its advertising program. The following covers the most common forms and the method of determining fair value.

### *Publications*

Publications are sold on the basis of rates printed in the Standard Rate and Data Services ("SRDS") and indicate the rates and earned discounts that all advertisers pay when purchasing space in each specific publication. Most of the better publications offer no additional discounts to any potential advertiser. Therefore, if a company is charged those rates and offered the opportunity to pay all or part of the cost with trade credits, then the net result is that the value of the trade credits is a dollar when purchasing print advertising.

### *Electronic Media (or publications that offer additional discounts beyond the SRDS)*

With respect to electronic media (i.e., radio/television), all company advertisers and their advertising agencies possess media plans containing planned media costs (or efficiencies) laying out the parameters of the media required including the proper costs based on historical data. This would also apply to publications that discount their space. Again, if the company is charged its planning rates and the media delivered is based on the parameters indicated in its media plan, then the trade credits are replacing cash payments at 100% of their issued value.

The summation of the above process is that it is consistent with the following logic...Since the company is charged the same price they would have paid if they paid with cash, then the trade credits used are worth full dollar value. Since i) a good portion of the media plan for the ensuing year has probably been determined and is available for review, and ii) the cost of this identifiable media could be priced for cash outside of a barter deal, and iii) prior experience of the company with similar transactions may exist, it is not difficult to establish the real value to be received as denoted by the amount of trade credits possessed by the company.

***Nonmonetary Aspect of Trade Credits Related Accounting Considerations***

Discussions about accounting for trade credit transactions typically jump immediately to Accounting Principles Board Opinion No. 29, *Accounting for Nonmonetary Transactions.* IRTA believes that the notions of the FASB's conceptual framework discussed above must first be considered to develop a sound foundation. Furthermore, IRTA believes that the trade credit is privately-created currency and may not even be a nonmonetary asset and that therefore Opinion 29 may not even be relevant to accounting for trade credit transactions. However, IRTA believes that whether one goes through Opinion 29 or through other accounting guidance, one must arrive at the same conclusion—trade credit transactions should be accounted for on the basis of $1 per trade credit.

Opinion 29 defines monetary assets and nonmonetary assets as follows:

> Monetary assets ... are assets ... whose amounts are fixed in terms of units of currency by contract or otherwise. Examples are cash, and short or long term accounts and notes receivable in cash (APB Opinion No. 29, paragraph 3a).

> Nonmonetary assets ... are assets ... other than monetary ones. Examples are inventories; investments in common stock; property, plant, and equipment (APB Opinion No. 29, paragraph 3a).

The definitions of monetary and nonmonetary assets contained in Opinion 29 support that a trade credit is a monetary asset. Its amounts are fixed in units of currency. If a receivable is a monetary asset, then a trade credit must also be a monetary asset—something in between a receivable and cash. For example, say that a firm wishes to purchase goods or services. It may either collect a receivable and then spend it on the goods or services, or alternatively, it may simple spend trade credits on the goods or services. Trade credits are closer to cash than receivables—therefore, since receivables are monetary assets, trade credits must be monetary assets.

However, the more common argument up to now has been that trade credit transactions are nonmonetary transactions. The FASB's conceptual framework comments on nonmonetary exchanges as follows:

> If product, services, or other assets are exchanged for nonmonetary assets that are not readily convertible into cash, revenues or gains or losses may be recognized on the basis that they have been earned and the transaction is completed. Gains or losses may also be recognized if nonmonetary assets are received or distributed in nonreciprocal transactions. Recognition in both kinds of transactions depends on the provision that the fair values involved can be determined within reasonable limits (FASB Concepts Statement No. 5, paragraph 84).

Opinion 29 follows the same direction.

> The Board concludes that in general accounting for nonmonetary transactions should be based on the fair values of the assets (or services) involved which is the same basis as that used in monetary transactions. Thus, the cost of a nonmonetary asset acquired in exchange for another nonmonetary asset is the fair value of the asset surrendered to obtain it, and a gain or loss should be used to measure the cost if it is more clearly evident than the fair value of the asset surrendered (APB Opinion No. 29, paragraph 18)

The view of IRTA is that whether the accounting for trade credit transactions is considered by monetary or nonmonetary accounting rules, the result is the same. For the reasons discussed in the preceding sections, the value of $1 per trade credit is the most readily determinable value.

If say, trade credit transactions are viewed as nonmonetary transactions and a lower value than $1 per trade credit is recorded for trade credits received, then another nonmonetary transaction occurs when the trade credits are redeemed, resulting in gain, assuming that the goods or services purchased were worth $1 per trade credit—and it will be, because that is the way the barter industry functions—$1 per trade credit.

### *Accounting if There Are Uncertainties About the Value of Trade Credits or About the Realization of Trade Credits*

Only after considering all the above is it appropriate to even begin to consider the matters raised in Emerging Issues Task Force (EITF) Issue No. 93-11. The issue reads:

> (H)ow do the principles of APB Opinion 29, Accounting for Nonmonetary Transactions, apply to a barter trans action when there are uncertainties surrounding the value of barter and other exchange credits or the realization of these credits(?)

The EITF issue taken together with the two views expressed (View A and View B) presume that APB Opinion 29 applies. As discussed about IRTA believes that there are strong arguments supporting that trade credits are monetary assets—not nonmonetary assets. The answer to the question as framed may be as simple as that Opinion 29 does not apply.

IRTA senses a danger that a consensus with respect to the issue as framed could establish rules for accounting for all transactions in trade credits as a result of considering only a subset of such transactions, possibly even in the wrong arena (nonmonetary transactions) altogether. *A "quick fix" to a $6 billion industry, with all of its possibly inappropriate ramifications, would be unconscionable and beyond the proper scope of the EITF.*

In the barter industry, most trade credit transactions involve exchange of assets for trade credits, denominated at $1 per trade credit, and then spending of the trade credits for goods or services worth $1 per trade credit. For recurring isolated transactions, the trader will generally perform extensive due diligence as to the value of the goods and services that can be obtained, verifying the $1 per trade credit value. Detailed spending plans are often prepared prior to entering into the large trade credit transactions.

However, in some circumstances, there may be uncertainty about the realizability of the trade credits. These circumstances are somewhat similar to those present when there is question about a firm's ability to collect a receivable—the barter company is akin to the creditor and as we know, not all creditors pay. If this were the case for the preponderance of trade credit transactions, there would not be a commercial barter industry.

IRTA believes that for a standard-setting body to undertake to set practice for accounting for trade credit transactions, it should not begin with the question that has been asked if EITF Issue 93-11. Many issues worthy of further review and discussion, along with IRTA's current views, are discussed in the preceding sections of this paper. If the EITF Issue 93-11 question must be asked, it should be clearly pointed out that the question relates to only a subset of transactions in which the circumstances raise uncertainties or doubt about a trader's ability to complete the entire cycle of the trade credit transaction in the fashion that most trade credit transactions are successfully completed.

IRTA's view with regard to the subset of trade credit transactions alluded to in EITF Issue 93-11 is that if a firm cannot determine or demonstrate the customary due diligence that provides evidence of the probability that the trade credit transaction will be successfully completed, the trade credits should be recorded at $1 and a reserve should be established for the trade credits based on the estimated recoverable value. It would be appropriate to record the reserve as part of the exchange in which the trade credits are acquired. Thereafter, cost-recovery accounting should be used.

### *Impairment of Assets Prior to Trade Credit Transactions*

IRTA does not see the idea expressed in paragraph 13 of View B of EITF Issue No. 93-11 as uniquely relevant to trade credit transactions. This would apply to all situations of impairment of assets to be sold. However, IRTA does not believe that trade credit transactions should be necessarily preceded by an overzealous write-down of the asset to a hypothetical impaired value that could be realized based on a "fire-sale" liquidation. Values can be realized from assets with patience, work, and strategy. If a firm decides to exchange an asset for trade credits, it does not mean that the asset should be written down to the worst possible value that could be realized after "giving up" on the asset and dumping it into a liquidation.

IRTA believes that to do so could also result in convoluted financial reporting. If a significant write-down is recorded followed by a trade credit transaction, if IRTA's approach using $1 per trade credit is used in accounting for the trade credit transaction (as IRTA believes it should be), a significant gain would result. IRTA does not see the sense of recording a loss based on a hypothetical liquidation value followed by a gain on a trade credit transaction.

### *Conclusion*

IRTA's conviction is that no changes are needed to existing accounting rules elating to barter transactions. The concepts of recognizing trade credits as an asset to be valued as a currency or medium of exchange, the fact that trade credit receipts and expenditures are each separate and distinct completed cash-to-cash cycles, and the need to recognize gain or loss at the time of the transaction whenever trade credits are exchanged, may require reinforcement.

FASB Concepts Statements and APB 29 currently provide maximum flexibility for the accounting profession to determine the proper accounting, that is, whether a transaction represents the normal case where trade credits can be valued at a dollar and gain or loss recognized at the time of the transaction, or the atypical case where circumstances create doubt about the ability to fulfill the trade credits. This flexibility has proven to be of value in an admittedly complex arena of accounting, and should be retained.

## International Reciprocal Trade Exchange

# 12. Statement of Condition Trade Exchange System

This is not a Balance Sheet of (The Company), but of the client/member system

______________(Date)

**Assets:**

**Current:**

Total negative member balances or revolving accounts xxx
Less estimated allowance for doubtful accounts
(not provided for in Loan Loss account) . . . . . . <xxx>
XXX

Trade dollar loans, current portion . . . . . . . . . . . . . . .xxx
Inventory owned by system . . . . . . . . . . . . . . . . . . . . .xxx

Total Current Assets . . . . . . . . . . . . . . . . . . . . . . . . .XXX

**Non-current:**

Trade dollar loans, less current portion . . . . . . . . . . . .xxx
Less estimated allowance for doubtful accounts
(not provided for in Loan Loss Accounts) . . . . .<xxx>
XXX

House accounts with negative balances . . . . . . . . . . .XXX

**Total Assets** . . . . . . .XXX

**Liabilities:**

**Current:**

Total positive member balances . . . . . . . . . . . . . . . . . .xxx
Total positive house accounts . . . . . . . . . . . . . . . . . . .xxx
Other system liabilities . . . . . . . . . . . . . . . . . . . . . . . .xxx

Total Current Liabilities . . . . . . . . . . . . . . . . . . . . . . .XXX

**Non-current:**

Loan Loss Reserve Account . . . . . . . . . . . . . . . . . . . . .xxx

**Total Liabilities** . . . .XXX

**System Deficit (surplus)** . . . . . . . . . . . . . . . . . . . . . . . . . . . . . .XXX

**Total Liabilities & System Deficit** . . . . . . . . . . . . . . . . . . . . . .XXX

### *IRTA Regulation 1*

SUBJECT: Deficit Spending by Trade Exchanges and Trade Exchange Owners, Officers and Other Principles.

SECTION I. General

A. **Purpose.** The purpose of this regulation is to establish controls on unsecured deficit spending by IRTA member trade exchanges, their owners, stockholders, directors, managers, and other principals who are in a position to influence exchange policy. Other requirements concerning deficit spending may be found in the IRTA Code of Ethics.
B. **Applicability.** This regulation is binding upon all members of IRTA, and will be considered as the standard in judging situations, involving non-member exchanges.
C. **Effective Date.** This regulation is effective immediately.
D. **Definitions.**
   1. **Deficit Spending**. Spending of trade dollars in excess of earnings by an exchange, exchange owner, stockholder, or other principle.
   2. **System Deficit.** The algebraic sum of members' total positive accounts plus 90% of the members' total accounts, not including any "House Accounts" such as Client Assets' Accounts, Inventory Accounts, Service Fee Accounts, Renewal Accounts' and Defunct Members' Accounts. The shall deficit be computed in accordance with the format developed by the Barter Accounting Standards Board, Appendix A.

   ***Example***

   An exchange with 6 members having the following members balances:

| | |
|---|---|
| Hardware Store | 2,000 TD |
| Restaurant | 1,000 TD |
| Shoe Store | 500 TD |
| Chiropractor | 0 TD |
| Advertising Agency | –500 TD |
| Account | –1,000 TD |

The positive accounts total is 3,500 TD (2,000 TD + 1,000 TD + 500 TD).
The negative account total is –1500 TD (–500 TD + –1,000 TD).
The deficit is 2,150 TD (3,500 TD – .9 x 1,500 TD).
This exchange has a 2,150 trade credit deficit, regardless of what the exchange may show as its house accounts balance.

3. **Member's Deficit.** The amount by a member of a trade exchange in excess of earnings from sales.
4. **Exchange Deficit.** The system deficit, minus the exchange's positive trade dollars (see, deficit calculation chart, Appendix B.)

***Example***

| | |
|---|---|
| System Deficit | 2,150 TD |
| Inventory Account | 500 TD |
| Service Fee Account | 500 TD |

The system deficit is 2,150 TD. The exchange's positive trade credits are 1,000 (500 + 500) TD. The exchange's deficit is 1,150 TD (2,150 TD –1,000 TD).

Note: The exchange's house accounts should total –1,000 TD, which is the amount of the exchange deficit when the system deficit is figured using 100% of members' negative accounts.

**Principle: Member's Account Balances – House Accounts Balance = 0.**

5. **Acceptable Collateral.**
   a. Merchandise (inventory, travel/media credits, scrip, and other owed assets), valued at the lower of cost (purchase price) or fair market value, not at asking price.
   b. Furniture and fixtures at cost (less any depreciation taken).
   c. cash receivables, assets pledged to the Exchange (stocks, bonds, marketable securities; real-estate; gold, diamonds and other gemstones; ect.) at fair market value. A maximum of 5% of total assets may be gemstones or diamonds.
   d. Promissory notes, secured with pledged assets described in the preceding paragraph (5c).
   e. To qualify as acceptable collateral, none of the assets listed in paragraph 5a - 5d above may be pledged as security for any current or long-term liabilities of the exchange, such as mortgages or notes payable.
   f. Valuation of collateral is to be preformed in accordance with generally accepted accounting principles.
6. **Principle**
   a. Any owner, franchisor, franchisee, stockholder, director, manager, partner, or other person who, by virtue of their relationship of the exchange, are in a position to influence policy relative to unsecured borrowing (deficit spending) in the exchange's own accounts or the accounts controlled by these persons is a principle.
   b. Any principle, as defined in paragraph 6a, who acquires, merges with, or exercises managerial control over, an existing exchange shall, within the

limits of his abilities and resources, honor outstanding trade credit balances of the exchange being acquired or controlled in the newly formed or reorganized exchange. See also the requirements of IRTA Regulation No. 3.

SECTION II. **Actions Required**

A. The standard for IRTA members is to adequately secure an exchange deficit, and accounts controlled by principles, with acceptable collateral

B. Members with an exchange deficit which does not meet the foregoing standard may be required by the association's Chief Executive to submit a plan to achieve compliance within a specified period, and to render periodic reports on progress towards attaining the goals of the plan. In the interim, the public may be informed that the member is in probationary status.

C. Exchanges in a deficit positions may not convert trade merchandise to cash for the purposes other than purchase of inventory or collateral or resale to the membership.

D. Members of IRTA will, when called upon by the association's Chief Executive pursuant to a duly authorized investigation, submit a report together with supporting documentation, including a listing of all accounts and their balances, showing the statement and condition and computation of Exchange Deficit, as defined in Appendix A and B, with the assets pledged as collateral (as defined in paragraph D5 of section I) listed separately. The Chief Executive will be notified in writing of any change in collateral used to secure an exchange deficit.

E. Excessive liquidity resulting from an exchange deficit may pose a threat to the system through price inflation and cessation of trading. Members of IRTA, when called upon by the Association's Chief Executive pursuant to a duly authorized investigation, may be required to submit supplemental reports and documentation, during a period a formal monitoring by IRTA, until any condition of excess liquidity is brought under control.

F. 1. Member franchisors, licensors. And other companies doing business through affiliates shall establish polices and maintain controls over franchisees, licensees or affiliates to ensure the protection of their clients' trading privileges and they shall reserve in their contractual agreements with their franchisees, licensees, and affiliates such power as is necessary to effectively implement this article.

2. In the event it becomes apparent that the business practice of a franchisee, licensee or affiliate are inconsistent with prudent standards and the protection of the clients' trading privileges is in doubt, it shall be the duty of the franchisor, licensor, or parent company to promptly undertake remedial action.

3. If necessary, where a franchisee, licensee, or affiliate fails to operate its business accordance with the appropriate standards set forth in its contract and this article regarding the protection of the Clients' trading privileges, the franchisor, licensor, or parent company shall recognize their responsibility to honor outstanding trade credit balances and assume management control over such franchisee, licensee, or affiliate office until such time as that office is properly disposed of in accordance with pertinent federal, state, and local laws and IRTA regulations, or is resold or reassigned to another party deemed capable of operating the business in a proper manner.

G. Information submitted to the Chief Executive will be treated as confidential except as required to permit the Board of Directors or governmental body to preform their official duties. The Board of Directors may review the reports and compliance plans of exchanges who have a compliance problem, and may provide advice and guidance to the exchange concerned.

SECTION III. **Enforcement**

A. The basic policy on enforcement actions is to educate assist exchanges to comply with this regulation in their own interest, as well as the public's. Since members of the public believe that IRTA membership signifies an exchange that they may deal with in confidence, IRTA has a responsibility to initiate an inquiry when material allegations are made against an exchange or a principle. Such allegations may not initially involve deficit spending, for example, they may deal with the honesty or prudence of principles; however, since excessive deficit spending is prime danger to the solvency of an exchange, a deficit spending inquiry may be appropriate in many cases, and may benefit the exchange by dispelling mistrust or rumor concerning its integrity or condition. In executing such an investigation, IRTA will seek an exchange's voluntary cooperation and endeavor to educate and assist it to comply. Proceeding and findings may be kept confidential so long as these goals are being met, provided the public is not harmed by the withholding of information in IRTA's possession. With consent of the exchange, peer review comites combing the powers of inspection and examination with those of education and assistance may be formed by the Chief Executive to carry out the investigation and report to him and the Board of Directors.

B. Industry members who fail to submit the report required by Section II D pursuant to an authorized investigation may be asked by the Chief Executive to show cause why they should not be disciplined, expelled, or barred from membership in the Association by the Board of Directors.

C. IRTA members who do not submit the required report within 30 days of notification of noncompliance will be suspended and not permitted to vote or participate actively in the affairs of the Association.

D. Suspended members will be given 30 days to cure their suspension by submission of the required report. If they still fail to comply, their case will be reviewed by the Board of Directors, who may take such action as it deems warranted, including explusion from the Association in accordance with the by-laws. A member may appeal suspension to the Board of Directors and exclusion to the General Meeting of Members.

E. The Chief Executive may reject any report submitted under the provisions of Section II if it is found to be incomplete or inconsistent. The Chief Executive may also require the submission of supplemental information or answers to questions, in order to gain a clear understanding of the report submitted.

F. The Chief Executive is authorized to take any reasonable measures deemed necessary and proper to carry out the mandate of this regulation. These measures may include, but are not limited to, inspection of the exchange's premises and assets, examination of books and records, appointment of a peer review committee to both inspect and examine, as well as educate and assist, the exchange to comply, and calling upon an independent Certified Public Accountant to conduct additional review. The Board of Directors will be notified of all actions taken by the Chief Executive under the authority of this section.

# D. Other Documents

## 1. Paper Addressed to ITEX Corporation

November 20, 1992

Michael T. Baer, President
ITEX Corporation
P.O. Box 2309
Portland, OR 97208

Dear Mike:
This letter is in response to your request for a statement of IRTA's position on the character, uses, and valuation of trade dollars in our market economy. Your interest is in the principles applicable to recognition and treatment of trade dollars in a public corporation's financial statements. i will address the principle issues that we see in considering a subject as fundamental to the barter business as the exact nature of trade dollars and their proper valuation and accounting. In doing so, let me state at the outset that what I am about to recount is based upon the practice of the commercial barter industry in the U.S. for approximately a decade, that is, since passage of the Tax Equity and Fiscal Responsibility Act of 1982.

### *Character and Use of Trade Dollars*

Trade dollars arise in the course of barter trade between buyers and sellers who are organized into a network of trading partners by means of written agreement with a company know as a barter exchange. Section 6045 of the Internal Revenue Code defines the term "barter exchange" as follows: "The term 'barter exchange' means any person with members or clients that contract either with each other or with such person to trade or barter property or services either directly or through such person."

The contract that organizes the barter network and establishes the terms and conditions of trade is executed by each client with the barter exchange. Under the terms of a typical contract, the client agrees to make available a certain dollar amount of goods or services for barter trade with other clients and with the exchange. In so doing, they agree to accept a specified minimum amount of barter business by selling goods or services in return for payment received in the form of trade dollars.

As defined by the International Reciprocal Trade Association, a trade dollar is a unit of account that denotes the right to received, or the obligation to pay, one U.S. dollar's worth of goods or services available within a barter system. (The terms "barter network" and "barter system" are identical). The Treasury Department has recognized the existence of trade dollars in Treasury Regulations T.D. 7873 (26 CFR Part 1) issued March 11, 1983: "Property or services are exchanged through a barter exchange if payment for property or services is made by means of a credit on the books of the barter exchange or scrip issued by the barter exchange or if the barter exchange arranges a direct exchange of property or services among its members or clients or exchanges property or services with a member or client." The fact that a credit on the books of the exchange is linked in the same sentence with a direct exchange of property or services indicates the essential equivalence of the two transactions in the eyes of IRS. Where credit is given on the books of the exchange, payment is to be make by delivery of goods or services in the future, rather than in the present as occurs in a direct exchange.

In the cash economy, when a sale is made and payment is deferred, there is an extension of credit from seller to buyer. In a barter network, when a sale is mae and payment (in goods and services) is deferred, there is likewise an extension of credit by the seller.

Under the exchange agreement, sellers accept trade dollars as payment and look to the other participants in the barter network to fulfill their trade dollars.

At any point in time within a barter network, some participants will be net creditors, that is, holders of trade dollars. They have given up greater value than they have received in goods and services, and so they hold the balance as an asset or claim on goods or services available from the system. They are said to be in a positive or surplus position in their account. Other participants will be net debtors, that is, they will have spent more than their earnings and will owe trade dollars. They are said to be in a negative or deficit position.

Trade dollar assets are collectively the liabilities of those members who owe the system. It is an axiom that barter assets and liabilities should always balance, that is, for every trade dollar outstanding there is a contractual obligation imposed on the debtor members of the network to make available a U.S. dollar's worth of fulfillment goods and services.

The Internal Revenue Service has analyzed barter exchanges to determine whether trade dollars received in payment constitute income. In Revenue Ruling 80-52, IRS promulgated the "valuable right" doctrine. Under this doctrine, trade dollars are a "valuable right" and receipt of trade dollars as payment constitutes receipt of income. Promulgation of the "valuable right" doctrine validates IRTA's view that trade dollars constitute real claims upon valuable goods and services available from the members of the barter system. This capability is underpinned by the exchange agreement and by the debtor-creditor relationship established in the normal course of business. Trade dollar assets are offset by an equal number of trade dollar liabilities, that is, an unqualified obligation of debtors within the exchange network to pay in goods and services an amount certain by a date certain.

Writing in *Minnesota Law Review*, Vol. 67:441, 1982, Professor Robert I. Keller states in "The Taxation of Barter Transactions":

> Trade units, however, represent more than the mere promise of the individual member for whom the taxpayer performed services or to whom he or she sold goods. Rather, each trade unit represents the promise of the entire exchange membership, as a group, to allow the receipt of the unit to use it to acquire the goods and services offered by the membership. Moreover, at least in the case of the established exchanges, these promises represented by trade units, are readily assignable or transferable to other members of the trade exchange (p.494).

Concerning the exchange's own use of trade dollars, Professor Keller writes:

> It is in its capacity as broker that the Exchange receives commission from members. Any commissions the Exchange receives in trade units it can use in the same manner as any member to acquire goods and services within the system. The Exchange may use the goods and services it acquires from its members for its own business purposes or may transfer them to the individual shareholders, proprietors, or partners of Exchange to be used by them for personal purposes. Frequently, however, Exchanges use their trade units to acquire merchandise which is maintained in the showrooms and warehouses of the Exchange for retrade to members. This results in the Exchange's second role as a trader of goods.
>
> To the extent the Exchange sells the acquired merchandise for the same number of trade units it paid for them, it simply acts as a clearing house for members' goods. Nevertheless, the Exchange clearly benefits from this activity. Most importantly, by acquiring members' goods for trade units, the Exchange keeps units circulating and thereby maintains an active barter economy. Also, to the

extent the Exchange succeeds in retrading the acquired goods to members, the Exchange earns additional commissions.

As a participant in the barter system, the exchange earns trade dollars through commissions and profits on sale of goods and services to the other participants. Clearly, the trade dollars earned by the exchange represent a valuable claim on the goods and services of other members of the barter system. These members may be those seeking to earn trade dollars to repay their debt, or those seeking additional sales to increase their stock of trade dollars. In preparing the exchange's financial statements, it would be inappropriate, even irresponsible, to fail to account for the exchange's trade dollar assets, liabilities, receipts, and expenditures.

### *Valuation and Accounting for Trade Dollars*

The U.S. Government, in Treasury Regulation T.D. 7873 cited above, addresses the question of trade dollar valuation as follows: "The amount received by a member or client in an exchange includes cash received, the fair market value of any property or services received, and the fair market value of nay credits to the account of the member or client on the books of the barter exchange or scrip issued to the member or client by the barter exchange, but does not include any amount received by the member or client in a subsequent exchange of credits or scrip. For purposes of this section, the fair market value of a credit or scrip is the value assigned to such credit or scrip by the issuing barter exchange for the purpose of exchanges unless the Commissioner requires the use of a different value that the Commissioner determines more accurately reflects fair market value."

In requiring trade exchanges to set the value of their trade dollar for all participants in the barter system, and to set that value at the amount (in dollars) used "for purpose of exchanges," Treasury was following an approach recommended by Professor Keller. Professor Keller called his method of valuation the "medium of exchange" approach and describes it as follows:

> The value of a trade unit should be determined by what it can buy within the exchange, and not the cash price for which it can be purchased or sold. By analogy, if a U.S. taxpayer receives foreign currency, usable within the foreign country to acquire goods and services, but not readily convertible into U.S. dollars, an informal market often develops, in which the taxpayer can sell the foreign currency to U.S. citizens wishing to invest or spend the currency in the foreign country. In such circumstances, it would be clearly improper to value the currency at the dollar amount realizable in the United States, since "the dollar amount realizable in the United States might be but a fraction of the dollar value of the property ... which the foreign income would buy in the foreign country." Since trade units are the equivalent of a foreign currency, they too should be valued by their "purchasing power" within the trade exchange, and not by what they would bring in a cash sale....
>
> The more appropriate approach, both as a matter of substantive law and from the viewpoint of administrative convenience, would be one that treats trade units, when used to acquire goods and services, as a medium of exchange. Under this approach, the goods and services acquired would be conclusively assumed to be equal in value to that of the trade units used to acquire them. Good deals and bad deals would simply be ignored. The taxpayer would, in effect, be treated as receiving the average value of the goods and services a trade unit could buy, which, absent exchange fluctuation, would be the same amount the taxpayer took into income on receipt of the unit. Assuming that there is indeed no change in the value of the trade unit itself from the time of acquisition to the time of disposition, this approach would result in no gain or less to

> the taxpayer on the disposition of trade units, and produce tax deductions, if deductible business goods and services were acquired, equal to the value of the units used.

The basic accounting doctrine for barter exchanges is set forth in Accounting Principles Board Opinion Number 29, "Accounting for Non-Monetary Transaction." This document was issued in 1972 by the predecessor to the current Financial Accounting Standards Board. It is an authoritative pronouncement of the accounting profession.

Bost and Yeakel (*Management Accounting*, November 1992) summarize the basic tenets of APB 29 as follows:

> APB Opinion No. 29. Accounting for Nonmonetary Transactions," defines nonmonetary assets and liabilities as those which are not fixed in terms of units of currency by contract or otherwise. With these transactions, questions may arise due to the subjectivity in valuation of an asset received or resulting liability, or the recognition of any gain or loss on the transaction. The Opinion states that the cost of a nonmonetary asset should be recorded at the fair value and book value given is recognized as a gain or loss. If fair value of the asset received is clearer than that of the asset given, the former should be used in valuation. Fair value should equal estimated realizable value for cash transactions involving same or similar assets, quoted market prices, independent appraisal, estimated fair value of merchandise or service received in exchange, or other available evidence. No gains should be recognized if fair value is not determinable within reasonable limits or if an exchange is not the culmination of an earnings process, such as exchanges of similar productive assets. Disclosures are required on the nature of the transaction, the basis of accounting, and any gains or losses recognized.

> It should be stressed that *"Fair value should equal estimated realizable value for cash transactions involving same or similar assets, quoted market prices, independent appraisal, estimated fair value of merchandise or services received in exchange, or other available evidence."*

In light of the foregoing authorities, the sole issue is the validity of the International Reciprocal Trade Association's position, which expresses the view of the leading members of the commercial barter industry, that the value of a trade dollar in an operating commercial barter exchange (one that executes above 1,000 transactions per year) is, on average, equal to one U.S. dollar. IRTA's position asserts that one trade dollar equals one U.S. dollar not because the barter industry has arbitrarily assigned this value, set it for administrative convenience or simplicity, or established it for tax compliance purposes, but that the value of a trade dollar is in fact one U.S. dollar, on average over a broad range of transactions executed through a commercial barter exchange.

The key to this proposition is that, while trade dollars are indeed a unit of account and a medium of exchange within a barter system, the prices of goods and services bought and sold are denominated entirely in U.S. dollars. This means the trade dollar is a unit of account, but not a standard of value. A trade dollar has meaning in value terms only by reference to the U.S. dollar prices of the goods and services it can purchase. U.S. dollar prices are the same for the barter system as for the cash system.

The trade dollar is a unit that has no intrinsic value, because prices set in trade dollars would be meaningless and, in fact, are non-existent. Prices are set only in U.S. dollars, and the number of trade dollars given or received is determined entirely by U.S. dollar prices and quantity. Put another way, a trade dollar is a financial unit of identical value to a cash dollar, except that a trade dollar is redeemable only by a dollar's worth of goods and services and not by cash.

The crucial role of U.S. dollar prices as the standard of value in the barter economy means that, on average, across thousands of transactions, the value of trade dollars spent within the barter system is one U.S. dollar. While in particular cases there can be a variance between cash and trade dollar prices, in the vast majority of transactions these prices are the same.

### *Trade Dollars Are Money*

The medium of exchange for barter transactions is no more nor less in value than the U.S. dollar. But this is not to say that the two currencies are of equal utility for commerce. The supply of one is controlled by government, the other is privately-created and capable of expanding with trade. The value of one erodes steadily with inflation, but the trade dollar can realize constant-purchasing power by means of an annual price level adjustment applied to each deposit. The trade dollars required to pay for this adjustment can be obtained by transfer from debtors, or by a small levy on the gains from trade.

Trade dollars are a form of privately-created money based upon contract. They are not lawful currency of the United States, but this does not mean that their financial consequences can be ignored in the preparation of financial statements. Under APB 29, the financial consequences of any contract for non-monetary exchange can and should be valued. The IRS holds that only in rare and exceptional cases can a non-monetary transaction not be valued for tax purposes.

Trade dollars are a medium of exchange or currency within the barter system, not within the U.S. economy. They represent a claim on an ascertainable stock of assets held by participants in the barter system, who are obligated by contract to make a specified portion of that stock available for trade upon demand, and who willingly accept trade dollars and seek to acquire them to finance their purchases.

True, unlike lawful currency, trade dollars are not claims on the gross national product. But a trade dollar nonetheless represents a legal claim for a U.S. dollar's worth of real goods and services. The fact that the claim is on a specific subset of firms in the economy, and not on the economy at large, has little relevance. All that matters is that the owners of trade dollars hold legally binding claims against others—not just a single firm but the entire group of firms who comprise the barter network. This lends solidity to the contractual promise to provide goods and services to the holders of trade dollars on demand.

In sum, trade dollars originate in real economic transactions and have real economic implications. The proper presentation of a firm's financial statements should incorporate treatment of trade dollar transactions based on generally accepted accounting principles. Were a public corporation to fail to do this, it could run afoul of the law. It is especially important for a company whose principle business is to facilitate barter transactions to ensure proper accounting treatment of its trade dollar assets and liabilities, receipts and expenditures.

I hope this information has been of assistance to you. Should you have any questions, please feel free to contact me.

Sincerely,

Paul E. Suplizio
Chief Executive Officer

# 2. Paper Addressed to Coopers & Lybrand

July 1, 1994

Dale Teague
Coopers & Lybrand
Austin, TX By Fax: 512-477-8681

Dear Mr. Teague:

Barter Exchange, Inc. is a member of the International Reciprocal Trade Association and has informed this body of your intention to send a letter to the Securities and Exchange Commission requesting approval of the accounting treatment you propose to adopt for barter transactions as BEI's auditor. Because of IRTA's knowledge of the barter industry's business practices and our participation in the Financial Accounting Standards Board Emerging Issues Task Force deliberations that led to the issuance of EITF 93-11, Barter Exchange has requested our assistance in commenting on the draft of your proposed letter to the SEC.

Your letter and the SEC's reply will be highly significant, and perhaps even precedential, for the barter industry as a whole. Therefore, IRTA appreciates the opportunity you are affording us to comment upon your proposed letter.

We have no comment at the present time on the section of your letter dealing with corporate barter transactions. I assume that the accounting treatment of corporate barter transactions was included for the sake of completeness, as I am aware of no accounting issues to be decided in this area. *If there are accounting issues in corporate barter that you expect the SEC to resolve, it would open up a wholly new area for SEC involvement in the barter industry, so I would appreciate being informed of any issues leading you to include this section in your letter to SEC.*

A little over a year ago, a delegation of IRTA members, myself included, met in Washington with the chief accountants of the Corporation Finance and Enforcement Divisions of SEC and were able to educate them about the barter business and get a pretty good idea of their thinking. I have personally spoken to the Commission's Chief Accountant, Walter Schuetze, and his views are well-known because he represented the SEC in EITF's consideration of barter credit transactions. Basically, the SEC got what it wanted in EITF 93-11, so any approach to the Commission staff should rest itself on a straightforward application of the statement's principles.

Essentially, what does EITF 93-11 say? The statement is a clarification of Accounting Principles Board Statement Number 29, "Accounting for Non-Monetary Transactions." APB 29 remains the basic doctrine and is in no way repealed by EITF 93-11. Especially important is APB 29's acceptance that, when there is an exchange of assets, the exchange should be accounted for *when it occurs.*

To this EITF adds that, when one of the assets is barter credits, the presumption is that the barter credits should be valued at the *fair market value of the asset they have been exchanged for.* However, "that presumption may be overcome if an entity can covert the barter credits into cash, as evidenced by a historical practice of converting barter credits into cash, or if independent quoted market prices exist for items to be received upon exchange of the barter credits."

In the accounting sense, barter credits are converted into cash when an entity uses them to acquire an asset or pay expenses for which it would otherwise have to expend cash. Such transactions are commonplace, in that they routinely and frequently occur in the barter business, therefore evidence of a historical practice of converting barter credits into cash is readily available.

As a general rule, independent quoted market prices can be shown to exist for the vast majority of goods or services for which barter credits are exchanged. Indeed, the invoices that record the exchange of barter credits to acquire an asset or pay expenses document that price involved, and because these are arms-length transactions they are market prices. When necessary, price quotes can readily be obtained from independent sources for almost all the products and services exchanged in barter trade.

The financial statements of a barter company, which may enter into thousands of transactions each year involving barter credits, are presented exclusively in U.S. dollars. They are not a mix of U.S. dollars and trade dollars because for financial statements purposes the trade dollars are valued in U.S. dollar terms using the principles of EITF 93-11.

### *Specific Comments*

Para 1, change last sentence to read, "We request your reply as to whether or not these policies, *which are based on APB 29 and EITF 93-11,* are acceptable as a basis for preparing BEI financial statements..."

### *Specific Comments on Section "Transactions With the Retail Exchange":*

Para 2, accounting for receipt of service fees in trade dollars, change the name of the account from "Trade dollars receivable/payable" to "Due from or owed to members in goods and services." *Reason:* This account will appear in the financial statements, and when it does it will lead to the confusion that the statements are a mix of trade dollars and U.S. dollars. The trade dollars will be assigned a value in U.S. dollar terms under EITF 93-11 in any event. Changing the name reflects the basic character of the account as either an asset or liability that reflects a claim or on an amount owed to members of the exchange.

Para 5, delete 2nd and 3rd sentences and substitute the following. Reason: the para as written gives the impression that a trade dollar is valued as one U.S. dollar as an arbitrary convention and not as a matter of accounting valuation.

> In the valuation of trade dollars, the principles APB 29 and EITF 93-11 apply. When the trade dollars are paid by BEI to acquire an asset or to pay an expense, they have a value equal to the fair value of the product or service received from members of the exchange. When trade dollars are earned by BEI, they have a value equal to the fair value of the product or service surrendered to members of the exchange. As these transactions are arms-length and are made and recorded in U.S. dollar prices, so that the number of trade dollars exchanged is exactly equal to the total value in U.S. dollar terms, the invariable result is that for transactions on the exchange the trade dollar has a value of one U.S. dollar.

Para 8, add at the end, "In cases of distressed sales of trade dollars for cash, the value of the trade dollars is not accurately determined by the amount of cash given up, but by the value of the trade dollars in commanding goods and services on the exchange. BEI enters into such transactions because they are "good deals" for itself, and the reason for this is that the trade dollars have the value of a full U.S. dollar when spent on the exchange. Accordingly, we believe this is a case where the presumption of EITF 93-11 is properly overcome because of BEI's ability to convert the barter credits into cash, and because independent quoted market prices exist for items to be received upon exchange of the trade dollars."

Para 13, include in the quotation from EITF 93-11 the section that the presumption may be overcome "if independent quoted market prices exist for items to be received upon exchange of the barter credits." *Reason:* This strengthens the case for valuing trade dollars at one U.S. dollar. Somehow, the accounting profession is hearing that this section was included to cover the case of oil swaps. Neither EITF 93-11 nor the minutes of the meeting mention oil swaps or anything else to limit the applicability of this section. We believe EITF 93-11 should be taken literally and not applied based on heresay.

Para 14, delete third sentence and substitute: "In all such cases where BEI exchanged trade dollars for goods and services, the number of trade dollars given was equal to the U.S. dollar value of the asset received or expense paid, and this is documented by actual invoices of the transactions. Hence, the trade dollar had a value of one U.S. dollar in the transactions, and any remaining unspent trade dollars held by BEI at the close of the accounting period are properly valued at one U.S. dollar based on:

1. the fact that when BEI earned the trade dollars, it gave up an asset or rendered a service valued at an equivalent number of U.S. dollars, so the trade dollars are properly valued at one U.S. dollar by applying the basic rule of EITF 93-11 that barter credits should be recorded at the fair value of the asset surrendered; and
2. in cases of an exchange of trade dollars for cash, where the amount of cash given is less than the number of trade dollars, EITF 93-11 allows the presumption to be overcome that the trade dollars should be valued at the amount of cash given, and it is both reasonable and appropriate to do so because the conditions established by EITF 93-11 for overcoming the presumption are fulfilled and it can be demonstrated that a trade dollar has a value of one U.S. dollar in a vast preponderance of cases when used on the exchange."

Paul E. Suplizio
Chief Executive Officer

# 3. ITEX Trading Rules

## A. AGREEMENT

1. **Contract.** The following Trading Rules constitute the contract between Client and ITEX Corporation (ITEX) and the ITEX Retail Trade Exchange (EXCHANGE) and are a part of the ITEX Client Application. Any trade purchase or sale by an Exchange member, (which is a client of ITEX), constitutes acceptance of all terms and conditions of the ITEX Trading Rules as most recently furnished by ITEX Corporation. Trading Rules apply to all ITEX Clients.
2. **Change in Rules.** At its sole discretion, ITEX may change, delete, or add to Trading Rules by giving client thirty (30) days written notice. Notice must be authorized and issued from the ITEX Corporate Office in Portland, Oregon. Any trade purchase or sale after the thirty (30) day notice period constitutes acceptance of the changes to the Trading Rules.

## B. PARTICIPATION IN THE ITEX BARTER SYSTEM

1. **Nature of the Parties.**
   a. The ITEX Barter System, commonly referred to the "Exchange," is an association of businesses and professional organization members who have joined together to barter their goods and services among themselves through an organized system which is regulated by the recordkeeping and administrative services of ITEX. The Exchange functions as a clearinghouse for the barter transactions of its membership.
   b. ITEX is a trading company that manages the Exchange. ITEX also acts as a third party recordkeeper and administers the clearinghouse function of the Exchange of barter transactions among members of the association who subscribe to ITEX' recordkeeping and related barter services.
   c. Client is a legitimate business that wants to exchange its goods and/or services with other members of the Exchange and subscribes to ITEX recordkeeping and barter services. (The term "Trade Dollar" is defined in Paragraph D.1 herein.)

2. **Sales: Surcharge.** Client will sell merchandise and/or services for Trade Dollars at its prevailing or normally advertised prices and on the same priority given cash customers, but may exclude 'sale' items. Client may charge part cash, or go on reserve status, ONLY during the period Client maintains a trade balance which exceeds $15,000.00. In the case of a single transaction exceeding $5,000.00, buyer and seller MAY negotiate for a portion of the excess of the price over $5,000.00 to be paid in cash. ITEX may authorize surcharges in Trade Dollars to be added to a client's price in certain categories such as food, gasoline, appliances, electronics and others where the gross margin of profit is extremely low. Surcharges may only be authorized by ITEX Corporation and must be clearly indicated to purchaser prior to making the sale.
3. **Continuing Services Fees.** Client will pay ITEX continuing service fees for recordkeeping and administrative services. These fees are:
   a. Association Fees: $15.00 cash and $15.00 Trade Dollars are charged each four week accounting cycle. Trade Dollars are automatically deducted from Client's account.
   b. Purchase Fee/Sales Fee: Five percent (5%) cash on purchases and five percent (5%) cash on sales when Client pays with an approved major credit card or through Electronic Funds Transfer (EFT) on a continuing basis. Clients who remit fees on open billing pay six percent (6%) cash on purchases and six percent (6%) cash on sales.
   c. Purchase Fee Out of Area: An additional cash service fee of two percent (2%) shall be assessed on Client purchases made outside assigned areas when the first three digits of buyer's account number are different than the first three digits of the seller's account number.
   d. Interest: If purchases and trade fees exceed sales, (negative trade balance), an interest charge of one and one-half percent (1.5 %) in Trade Dollars will be charged per accounting cycle on the amount by which purchases and trade fees exceed sales.
   e. Finance Charge: A charge of one and one-half percent (1.5 %) cash per accounting cycle will be charged on cash fees due and not received by ITEX by the close of the next accounting cycle.
   f. Conversion Service Fees: If Client is converting to ITEX from another trade exchange, additional service fees may be assessed according to the ITEX Conversion Rules which are in addition to the terms in Paragraphs 3(a) through (e) above.
   g. Remittance: Cash fees are due and payable upon receipt of statement. Cash fees are to be sent to the ITEX Corporate office in Portland, Oregon, not to a broker's office.
4. **Payment of Fees: Interest.** All fees and charges that Client pays ITEX are for services rendered in processing Clients into the Exchange, maintaining records, operating the clearinghouse, administering the Trading Rules, and facilitating Client's use of the Exchange. If cash fees are past due beyond four (4) weeks, Client waives all rights to the use of any positive Trade dollar balance in Client's account and grants ITEX the right to freeze the balance until paid.
5. **Trading Assistance.** ITEX will assist Clients to trade among themselves with: a) periodic distribution of client directories, b) maintenance of current member information on computer files at the Corporate Office, c) appointment at ITEX' discretion of independent agents as local brokers who provide information on participating Clients' goods and services, d) periodicals and other publications to advertise Clients' goods and services available through the Exchange, and e) BarterWire, a computer based barter information network. Client may specifically promote or limit an item or service by notifying ITEX.

Client acknowledges that the sole principals in any trade are the buying and selling Clients involved, that trades are entered into voluntarily, and that ITEX or the Exchange is not the guarantor of any transaction or trade dollar.

ITEX will use its best efforts to record trades accurately, to administer the Trading Rules in accordance with their terms, and to assist in the sale of Client's goods and services to other ITEX clients. However, the initiative for using ITEX' services for economic benefit is exclusively that of the Client.

6. **Availability of Customer's Products and Services.** ITEX shall use its best efforts to enroll new businesses with products and services to meet the needs of Clients. Neither ITEX nor the Exchange is responsible if a Client cannot find specific products or services or customers for their products and services within the Exchange.
7. **Definition of Clients in Good Standing.** A Client who complies with the current Trading Rules and any other agreements in effect with ITEX, who is current in any monies or Trade Dollars owing to ITEX and who has a valid Client account, is a "Client in Good Standing". Only Clients in good standing are entitled to the services of ITEX.
8. **Advertising Authorization.** Unless otherwise notified in writing, Client authorizes ITEX to inform other clients of the availability of Client's products or services. This includes listings in local, regional or national directories. ITEX is neither a party to these sales listings nor responsible for their accuracy.

**C. BARTER TRANSACTIONS**

1. Trade Procedure. ITEX will guarantee the crediting of ITEX Trade Dollars only when the procedures outlined below are followed:
   a. Trade Drafts must be properly completed with account numbers and names, signature, and date. Trade Drafts received without the buyer's signature may be returned to the seller or seller's broker.
   b. An authorization number must be secured from ITEX Credit Clearance. Authorizations are not required if the purchase amount is less than the amount automatically guaranteed by the "Letter Identifier." Letter identifiers are located to the right of the name imprinted on the buyer's personalized trade draft and represent the following:

      "E" All drafts require an authorization
      "D" ITEX guarantees drafts up to $25.00
      "C" ITEX guarantees drafts up to $50.00
      "B" ITEX guarantees drafts up to $100.00
      "A" ITEX guarantees drafts up to $250.00

   c. ITEX has no obligation to post a transaction unless authorization is obtained at time of sale or purchase amount is within letter identifier limit and the trade draft is received by the Corporate office within seven (7) days from the date authorized. ITEX reserves the right to refuse to issue an authorization number under any of the following conditions:
      i. Buyer does not have sufficient Trade Dollars to cover purchases.
      ii. Either party is not a Client in good standing.
2. **Transaction Materials.** The following may be used in ITEX trade transactions:
   a. ITEX counter-style trade drafts
   b. ITEX computer-printed trade drafts
   c. ITEX EXPRESS debit card-either through point of sale terminal or 3-part voucher
   d. Broker Posting Ledger or Group Buyer Record

3. **Recordkeeping.** ITEX will issue periodic statements to Clients reflecting account activity and amounts due and owing to ITEX. Statements are deemed accurate as printed unless Client notifies the ITEX Corporate office in writing of any discrepancy within thirty (30) days of statement date. Interim account activity summaries may be requested at any time at no charge. Clients requesting copies of processed trade drafts will be charged $3.00 cash per copy, unless the examination reveals an accounting error. NSF cash check returns will be charged $20.00 cash per incident, or the maximum allowed by law, against the originating account. NSF trade drafts will be charged $20.00 Trade Dollars against the originating account.

   ITEX operates on a four (4) week accounting cycle which may or may not conform to any given calendar month.

   Transactions entered through an ITEX EXPRESS point-of-sale (POS) terminal are posted automatically. Maintaining any written documentation of the transaction, including an authorizing signature from the buyer, in case of dispute, is the sole responsibility of the seller. If no signed authorization from the buyer is kept, the transaction may be reversed at the buyer's request. ITEX EXPRESS three-part vouchers may be used to record the buyer's transaction and signature, but MUST NOT be submitted to ITEX if the transaction has been posted by POS terminal, unless specifically requested by ITEX.

   ITEX has the right but not the obligation to reverse transactions due to non-compliance with these Rules or failure to provide goods or services as represented, in which event it will be the seller's responsibility to collect from the buyer. Transactions are subject to final audit and verification by ITEX and, in case of inaccuracies, or non-compliance, ITEX may debit or credit Client's account without notice.
4. **Special Trade Procedure.** The following applies to transactions involving special or long distance orders, construction jobs, service work, long term leases and other work-in-progress transactions. Barter transactions should be conducted in the same manner as cash transactions. Buyer should obtain a written estimate or description of product and price before authorizing work to begin or shipments to be made. Before starting, Seller should obtain a deposit or down-payment in trade dollars in the same manner as a cash transaction.

   The Funds-in-Transfer (FIT) Program has been designed to assist clients with transactions, in excess of $1,500.00 Trade Dollars or those transactions that require more time than the ITEX authorization process allows. This Program will assure the seller that funds have been set aside for the specific transaction.

   A trade draft and FIT Initiation Form must be submitted to the Corporate Office before funds may be deposited into a FIT account. Before funds can be released from a FIT account a completed and signed FIT Release Form must be submitted to the Corporate Office. The buyer will be assessed a 2% out-of-area fee for processing and handling.

   Any cash payments, e.g. shipping or postage, are the sole responsibility of the buyer and seller. ITEX' only responsibility is to record transactions according to the guidelines outlined above and ITEX is not responsible for the interpretation or fulfillment of any of the obligations of the buyer and seller.
5. **Tips and Gratuities.** Client shall pay gratuities in cash at point of purchase unless seller agrees to accept Trade Dollars for this purpose.
6. **Products Sold by ITEX.** On all products and scrip for services owned and sold

by ITEX, the only warranty ITEX makes is that it has title free and clear from any lien or encumbrance. Products are sold "As is, where is". ITEX makes no warranty either express or implied, by operation of law or otherwise as to the merchantability or fitness for a particular purpose of such products or services, and Buyer shall look solely to the manufacturer, distributor or retailer of such merchandise for any warranty.

7. **Client Transactions With Brokers.** ITEX brokers are independent contractors who sell ITEX services and assist Clients in trading. Brokers are free to buy and sell on trade, but do so on their own behalf. Every provision of the ITEX Trading Rules applies equally to Brokers and Clients. ITEX is not a party to, and is not responsible for, transactions between Brokers and Clients.
8. **Disclaimer of Warranty and Liability.** ITEX makes no representation or warranty either express or implied, and disclaims all liability as to the fitness, quality, delivery date, merchantability, prices or any term of any trade transaction. Client does hereby indemnify and hold ITEX harmless with respect to any claim, debt, or liability whatsoever, arising out of any transaction wherein Client is a buyer or seller. Client acknowledges that any trade transaction in which it participates will be on a voluntary basis.
9. **Taxes.** Seller shall charge the appropriate sales and excise taxes and collect and record these as required by law. Under no circumstances is ITEX responsible to pay any sales, excise, use or other taxes on behalf of any Client. Transactions involving trade dollars are generally treated as taxable events for Federal, State, and local tax purposes. The declaration and reporting of applicable local, State, and Federal taxes resulting from trade transactions rests solely with the Client. Further, ITEX is required by Federal law to obtain the Client's taxpayer identification number and corresponding name. Client's failure to provide this information will result in termination of the client's account. Client agrees to hold ITEX harmless for any actions ITEX takes to comply with Federal, State or local laws.
10. **Disputes.** Transaction disputes are ONLY between the buyer and seller, and ITEX has no responsibility other than recording transactions. ITEX is not responsible for use of Trade Dollars by unauthorized persons nor for transactions that do not comply with the ITEX Trading Rules. ITEX is not a buyer or seller unless it so states in writing.

    Disputes arising from barter transactions between clients within the same broker code may be settled by an Arbitration Panel as set out in the ITEX Retail Trade Exchange Arbitration Rules and Procedures. The ITEX Corporate Executive Committee may resolve disputes between clients from different broker codes or within the same broker code where an Arbitration Panel has not been established. Buyer and seller must BOTH authorize the Arbitration Panel or Executive Committee to arbitrate the dispute. The decision of the ITEX Corporate Executive Committee is final.

**D. ADMINISTRATION OF THE EXCHANGE AND ITS TRADE DOLLARS**

1. **Nature of Trade Dollars.** A "trade" is a barter purchase or sale of goods or services. Payment is made by posting the debits and credits to the buying and selling Clients' accounts, pursuant to these Rules.

    A Trade Dollar is an accounting unit used to record the value of trades determined by the selling Client. Trade Dollars denote the right to receive goods or services available from other Exchange Clients, or the obligation to provide goods or services to other Exchange Clients. Trade Dollars may not be redeemed for cash. Trade Dollars may be used only in the manner and for the purpose set forth in these Rules. Neither ITEX nor Client shall consider Trade Dollars as legal tender, securities, or commodities. ITEX disclaims responsibility for the negotiability of trade dollars or for the availability of goods or services from any source.

2. **Liability for Trade Dollars.** Client acknowledges that Trade Dollars in the barter system (positive balances) are the liabilities of persons who have spent more than their earnings (negative balances); that there is a creditor/debtor relationship between such persons, and that trade transactions incur the normal business risks associated with any credit transaction. Trade Dollars are solely the liability of Clients who owe the Exchange.
3. **Bad Debt Reserve.** An Exchange Operations and Bad Debt Reserve fund shall be maintained to cover (1) expenses of administering Exchange operations and (2) bad debts for which clients are collectively liable. Funds shall accrue from charges to clients accounts for this purpose, from fees and interest on trade loans, from any positive balances abandoned or surrendered by former clients in accordance with this agreement, from collections of charged-off accounts, and from any unspent positive balances left in the Traveler's Check Fund at the end of each fiscal year. All funds in this account shall be the property of the clients of the Exchange collectively.

   Client grants to ITEX the right and power to assess a reasonable service fee for its administration of Exchange operations, which assessment if made shall be paid from the Exchange Operations and Bad Debt Reserve on a schedule determined by ITEX. Client further grants to ITEX the right and power to determine whether the funds in the Exchange Operations and Bad Debt Reserve are in excess of anticipated need, and if so, at its sole discretion to distribute any surplus to clients in good standing in accordance with such definitions and formula that ITEX may determine.
4. **Trade Dollar Loans.**
   a. All Trade Dollar loans are made by the members of the Exchange and administered by ITEX. Client grants to ITEX the right to make Trade Dollar loans on behalf of the Exchange to any Client on terms and conditions consistent with Client's credit worthiness and ability to repay. Client understands and acknowledges that all aspects of Trade Dollar Loans are at the sole discretion of ITEX Management. Clients wishing to apply for a loan may be required to submit a loan application, financial statement, credit agreement, promissory note or equivalent collateral or to prepay cash service fees prior to approval. ITEX and the Exchange are under no obligation to extend credit at any time. ITEX will use its best efforts to ensure timely repayment of principal and interest, appropriate security and perfection of security interest.
   b. Client grants to ITEX the right to extend loans in Trade Dollars on behalf of the Exchange to trade exchange owner/operators whose exchange systems have become "deficit spent" and who wish to endorse the conversion of their member's trade credits into ITEX Trade Dollars. Client acknowledges that such conversions are designed to improve membership growth and to increase available Trade Dollars in order to benefit the Exchange. Conversion loans are made, predicated on pay back analysis only, and not on specific collateralization.
   c. Client acknowledges that all fees, charges, and other proceeds, (except interest) from such loans will be the sole and exclusive property of ITEX. The interest earned on the loans made by the Exchange is the property of the Exchange and will be added to the bad debt reserves, as set forth in Paragraph 3.0 herein.

5. **Allocation of Goods and Services.** Client acknowledges that regulation of purchases, control of credit extension, and allocation of goods or services in short supply are inherent in ITEX' responsibilities. Decisions regarding exercise of this responsibility are at ITEX' sole discretion. Every effort will be made to do so in an equitable manner. Client acknowledges that some accounts are primarily or solely for the use of ITEX, its principals or employees.
6. **Right to Regulate and Borrow.**
   a. Client acknowledges and grants to ITEX the right and power to regulate and control the number of Trade Dollars within the Exchange.
   b. Client recognizes and grants to ITEX, its shareholders and officers the right and power to borrow from the Exchange and to spend an aggregate amount not to exceed three (3) years' earnings of Trade Dollars.

**E. BREACH OF TRADING RULES; PROHIBITIONS**

1. **Trading Rule Violations.** ITEX has the right, but not he obligation, to inquire into complaints of Trading Rule violations by a Client. Client grants to ITEX the right to take the actions which, in ITEX' sole discretion, are deemed necessary. Violations of these Rules may result in termination of Client's account and/or immediate adjustment to the transactions involved. If Client fails to buy from and sell to other Clients in good standing in accordance with these Rules, Client will be in material breach of these Rules.

   If Client violates any term of the currently effective Trading Rules, ITEX may immediately terminate Client's account or may freeze all activity in the account without notice. At its sole discretion, ITEX may reinstate the Client or unfreeze Client's account.
2. **Suspension of Trading Privileges.** ITEX reserves the right, at its sole discretion, to suspend the trading privileges of any client who is in violation of any local, State, or Federal law, who engages in overpricing, direct trades, or otherwise violates these Rules, or when cash fees are due for more than four (4) weeks. In this case, trading privileges shall be reinstated immediately upon payment of cash fees due.
3. **Past-Due Fees.** At its discretion, ITEX may terminate client accounts with cash fees owing beyond twelve (12) weeks and may assess a $25.00 cash collection fee.
4. **Termination.** Either party may terminate this Agreement upon five (5) days written notice to the other party. Upon termination:
   a. All cash and Trade Dollar service fees outstanding become due and payable.
   b. Any Client with a negative trade balance (where purchases exceed sales) must balance their account with Trade Dollars within four (4) weeks of termination date. After the four (4) week period, Client must immediately pay ITEX any remaining negative balance in cash.
   c. Any Client with a positive trade balance (where sales exceed purchases) may spend the positive balance after paying ITEX the cash service fees on the positive balance. After payment of fees, ITEX Trade Exchange Traveler's Checks will be issued to Client with a ninety (90) day expiration.
   d. ITEX EXPRESS cards and unused trade drafts must be returned immediately upon termination. No service fees will be refunded.
5. **Liquidated Damages if Terminated for Cause.** A violation of these Trading Rules damages ITEX and the Exchange in a number of ways that are difficult to quantify. These may include, but are not limited to, administrative costs in dealing with the violation, financial injury due to loss of cash service fees and/or expenditure of funds, such as in collection actions, loss of Client goodwill towards the Exchange and ITEX, and loss of trading volume and clients. Client and ITEX agree that Client shall pay ITEX the sum of $500.00 cash, as

liquidated damages to ITEX, if Client is terminated for cause, i.e., for violation of the Trading Rules for other than overdue cash fees. Damages must be paid within four (4) weeks of the date of notice of termination of Client's ITEX account. If Client has a positive trade balance, the liquidated damages must be paid in addition to the requirements of Paragraph E.4 above before the trade balance will be converted to Traveler's Checks.

6. **Direct Trades and Draft Passing.** Client shall not give or receive an ITEX trade draft with the seller's name left blank or receive a third-party trade draft. Direct trades between Clients for the purpose of avoiding service fees are prohibited, and if consummated, are subject to a fifteen percent (15%) cash transaction fee payable upon demand. Such trades may also result in suspension or termination.
7. **Spend Out/Cancellation.** If ITEX reasonably believes that a Client is spending out their trade balance in anticipation of canceling future participation in ITEX, or if Client has requested termination, then ITEX shall require the prepayment of cash service fees on the remaining trade balance held in Client's account.
8. **Security Interest, Insolvency.** Client grants ITEX a security interest in all Trade Dollars to be credited to Client's account for the amount of all unpaid cash fees. If Client becomes insolvent or bankrupt, all cash fees shall be due and payable in full. Upon filing of Petition under Chapters 7, 11, or 13 of the Bankruptcy Code, or an Assignment for the Benefit of Creditors, no trading shall be allowed until all cash fees due ITEX have been paid in full. If the petition under Chapter 7 of the Bankruptcy Code is filed by or against Client, or if the plan filed pursuant to either Chapters 11 or 13 does not provide for the full payment of all cash fees due ITEX, ITEX shall have the option in lieu of filing as a creditor of treating the Trade Dollar balance as equal in value to the amount of cash fees owing, and terminating the account; provided, however, that if ITEX does receive all of its cash fees in full, ITEX shall reinstate the Trade Dollars to the Client's account.
9. **Joint and Separate Liability.** If this Application is accepted and an ITEX Trade Account is opened, the company, and the individual signing for the company, hereby assume joint and individual responsibility for all purchases and fees as outlined in this Agreement.
10. **Preferential Treatment.** ITEX warrants that it will not engage in preferential treatment of owner, employees, their families and associates, in discharging its responsibilities.

F. **MISCELLANEOUS**

1. **Fax Signatures.** ITEX will accept a faxed signature as an original, legal signature.
2. **Rules for Clients Converting From Another Exchange.** If Client is converting from another trade exchange, additional rules may apply as set forth in the ITEX Conversion Rules for the exchange membership being converted.
3. **Legal Requirements.** Client shall abide by applicable Federal, State or local laws or regulations pertaining to Exchange transactions. ITEX shall not be responsible for any failures on the part of Client to comply. Client agrees not to hold ITEX liable for any action ITEX takes to comply with applicable laws or regulations.
4. **No Waiver of Right.** ITEX's failure or delay in exercising any right, will not operate as a waiver of that right, or shall the partial exercise of a right not preclude any other or further exercise of any right. ITEX's remedies are cumulative and are not exclusive of any remedies provided by law.
5. **Severability; Attorney's Fees.** Every term contained in these Trading Rules is severable from every other term herein. If any term should be judged unenforce-

able, it shall not affect the enforceability of other terms outlined in these Trading Rules.

If legal action must be taken by ITEX against a Client to enforce any provision of these Trading Rules, Client shall pay ITEX reasonable attorney's fees, costs, plus simple interest at the rate of eighteen percent (18%) per year from the date of default until payment in addition to any other proceeds as granted by a court of law or an acceptable arbitration.

6. **Dissolution.** If the ITEX Exchange terminates or otherwise ceases to do business, all Clients in a negative Trade Dollar position will pay amounts they owe in cash (one Trade Dollar being equal to one dollar in cash in U.S. currency) into a fund. The fund, less expenses, will be distributed pro rata to all Clients who are in a positive Trade Dollar position. ITEX is not liable to any Clients for cash or Trade Dollars beyond the distribution of such funds, except as provided in these Rules.
7. **Statement of Conditions.** ITEX may make available a report on the status of the Exchange to members in good standing on a periodic, "unaudited" basis. This report sets forth totals of the negative and positive member balances, reserves, inventories and other assets and liabilities of the Exchange. ITEX is a public company and its financial reports are filed regularly with the Securities Exchange Commission in Washington D.C.
8. **Warranty of Information.** Client warrants that it provides all information to ITEX in good faith and that such information is accurate to the best of its knowledge.
9. **Applicable Law.** All interpretation of these Trading Rules shall be governed by the laws of the State of Oregon.
10. **Venue.** Any action brought by any party to this agreement shall be filed, and venues shall lie, in the courts of the State of Oregon.

Effective October 15, 1993

# About the Authors

Terry Neal has served, for more than 11 years, on the board of directors of the International Reciprocal Trade Association (IRTA), the barter industry's oldest and largest trade association. He is the founder and chairman of IRTA's Barter Accounting Standards Board, the past chairman of the IRTA Government Relations Committee, and is the current IRTA chairman of the board of governors for the development of a universal currency.

ITEX, a public corporation with 150 offices worldwide that is traded on the NASDAQ stock exchange, is but one of a number of companies Neal has founded. He has owned or served as partner in three equipment-leasing companies, a radio syndication production company, a music production company and a data-processing service bureau. For 12 years, he served as president of Pacific Mountain Corporation, a company with 37 corporate subsidiaries in 23 U.S. states. His creative approach to various business problems has been the topic of numerous radio and television reviews.

The widely traveled Neal, in addition, is the former publisher of the *Travel Agent's Hotel Guide* and *Barter Age* magazine, currently serves as the advisory board chairman of Nostalgia Broadcasting Corporation and is active on a number of civic and corporate boards. A yachtsman, sailor, pilot and enthusiast of ancient history and archeology, Neal is married, has eight children and 13 grandchildren.

Gary K. Eisler is coauthor of four books besides *Barter and the Future of Money* and is a former newspaper reporter, editor and publisher/owner. Publications he has managed have received awards for General Excellence and Best Investigative Reporting, among others. *Forbes,* the *Wall Street Journal,* the *New York Times, USA Today, Barter Age* magazine and a variety of other national publications have carried his work. His feature stories, editorials and photography have garnered personal recognition.

In addition to his writing projects, Eisler developed Eisler Spring, the largest source of natural spring water in the metropolitan Portland area of Oregon. He also raises timber on the same forestland. A member of Rotary for almost 25 years, Eisler is the past president of the Rotary Club of La Grande, Oregon, and initiated the Internet Website for his Rotary district while managing its newsletter. He has three children and a grandson.

# Other MasterMedia Business Books

To order additional copies of any MasterMedia book, send a check for the price of the book plus $3.00 postage and handling for the first book, $1.00 for each additional book to:

MasterMedia Limited
17 East 89th Street
New York, NY 10128
(212) 260-5600
(800) 334-8232 please use MasterCard or VISA on 1-800 orders
(212) 546-7638 (fax)

*BEYOND SUCCESS: How Volunteer Service Can Help You Begin Making a Life Instead of Just a Living*, by John F. Raynolds III and Eleanor Raynolds, C.B.E., is a unique how-to book targeted at business and professional people considering volunteer work, senior citizens who wish to fill leisure time meaningfully, and students trying out various career options. The book is filled with interviews with celebrities, CEOs, and average citizens who talk about the benefits of service work. ($19.95 cloth)

*DARE TO CHANGE YOUR JOB—AND YOUR LIFE,* by Carole Kanchier, Ph.D., provides a look at career growth and development throughout the life cycle. ($9.95 paper)

*HOW TO GET WHAT YOU WANT FROM ALMOST ANYBODY,* by T. Scott Gross, shows how to get great service, negotiate better prices, and always get what you pay for. ($9.95 paper)

*LIFETIME EMPLOYABILITY: How to Become Indispensable,* by Carole Hyatt, is both a guide through the mysteries of the business universe brought down to earth and a handbook to help you evaluate your attitudes, your skills, and your goals. Through expert advice and interviews of nearly 200 men and women whose lives have changed because their jobs or goals shifted, Lifetime Employability is designed to increase your staying power in today's down-sized economy. ($12.95 paper)

*LEADING YOUR POSITIVELY OUTRAGEOUS SERVICE TEAM,* by T. Scott Gross, provides a step-by-step formula for developing self-managing, excited service teams that put the customer first. T. Scott Gross tackles the question businesses everywhere are asking: "How do I get ordinary people to give world-class service?" A must-have for creating tomorrow's corporation today! ($12.95 paper)

*THE LOYALTY FACTOR: Building Trust in Today's Workplace,* by Carol Kinsey Goman, Ph.D., offers techniques for restoring commitment and loyalty in the workplace. ($9.95 paper)

*MANAGING IT ALL: Time-Saving Ideas for Career, Family, Relationships, and Self,* by Beverly Benz Treuille and Susan Schiffer Stautberg, is written for women who are juggling careers and families. Over two hundred career women (ranging from a TV anchorwoman to an investment banker) were interviewed. The book contains many humorous anecdotes on saving time and improving the quality of life for self and family. ($9.95 paper)

*OUT THE ORGANIZATION: New Career Opportunities for the 1990's,* by Robert and Madeleine Swain, is written for the millions of Americans whose jobs are no longer safe, whose companies are not loyal, and who face futures of uncertainty. It gives advice on finding a new job or starting your own business. ($12.95 paper)

*POSITIVELY OUTRAGEOUS SERVICE: New and Easy Ways to Win Customers for Life,* by T. Scott Gross, identifies what the consumers of the nineties really want and how businesses can develop effective marketing strategies to answer those needs. ($14.95 paper)

*POSITIVELY OUTRAGEOUS SERVICE AND SHOWMANSHIP: Industrial Strength Fun Makes Sales Sizzle!!!!,* by T. Scott Gross, reveals the secrets of adding personality to any product or service. ($12.95 paper)

*A SEAT AT THE TABLE: An Insider's Guide for America's New Women Leaders,* by Patricia Harrison, provides practical and insightful advice for women who are interested in serving on a board of directors, playing a key role in politics and becoming a policy- or opinion-maker in public or private sectors. This is one book every woman needs to own. ($19.95 hardbound)

*SIDE-BY-SIDE STRATEGIES: How Two-Career Couples Can Thrive in the Nineties,* by Jane Hershey Cuozzo and S. Diane Graham, describes how two-career couples can learn the difference between competing with a spouse and becoming a supportive power partner. Published in hardcover as Power Partners. ($10.95 paper, $19.95 cloth)

*STEP FORWARD: Sexual Harassment in the Workplace, What You Need to Know,* by Susan L. Webb, presents the facts for identifying the tell-tale signs of sexual harassment on the job, and how to deal with it. ($9.95 paper)

*TAKING CONTROL OF YOUR LIFE: The Secrets of Successful Enterprising Women,* by Gail Blanke and Kathleen Walas, is based on the authors' professional experience with Avon Products' Women of Enterprise Awards, given each year to outstanding women entrepreneurs. The authors offer a specific plan to help women gain control over their lives, and include business tips and quizzes as well as beauty and lifestyle information. ($17.95 cloth)

*A TEEN'S GUIDE TO BUSINESS: The Secrets to a Successful Enterprise,* by Linda Menzies, Oren S. Jenkins, and Rickell R. Fisher, provides solid information about starting your own business or working for one. ($7.95 paper)

*TWENTYSOMETHING: Managing and Motivating Today's New Work Force,* by Lawrence J. Bradford, Ph.D., and Claire Raines, M.A., examines the work orientation of the younger generation, offering managers in businesses of all kinds a practical guide to better understand and supervise their young employees. ($22.95 cloth)

IRTA

Barter Corp

Barter Wire

ITEX.net

~~Globart~~

Global Mktng Rcsrcs